Real
Cop

Real Cop

A Memoir of a Career Street Officer

David Leonard

FIRST EDITION, NOVEMBER 2019

Library of Congress Control Number: 2019916943

ISBN 9781734041408

Interior Design: Bree Byle
Cover Design: Ed Kettle

Dedicated to my guardian angel,
who for 27 years protected me from every danger I faced
while working as a career first responder.

Contents

Introduction   ix

1. Josiah Ward   1
2. Humble Beginnings   7
3. Slick-sleeved Recruit   25
4. "Stinky"   43
5. Prime Time   61
6. "Union Boss"   79
7. Death, Lies, and Videotape   97
8. Sixty-two Miles to Nowhere   117
9. No Experience Necessary   135
10. The Street Cop, Race, and Politics:
    Observations from a Blue-eyed Devil and
    Overpaid Government Employee   155
11. Better to Burn Out Than Fade Away   177
12. Josiah Ward: Part Two   193
13. Aftermath   207

Afterward   221
About the Author   225

Introduction

Perusal of the True Crime section of almost any bookstore reveals a good selection of books depicting undercover law enforcement agents daringly outwitting the bad guys to bring down drug cartels and mob bosses through elaborate stings and covert operations. Plainclothes detectives get their fair share of titles devoted to exploits investigating high profile murder cases or serial killers. The glorification of police investigators is further solidified through numerous TV shows and movies.

On the academic side, journals and textbooks give police chiefs and administrators the opportunity to describe police work and its dynamics from a managerial perspective. Still other police specialists provide instructional guides to such things as tactical operations, crime scene investigations, and responses to special incidents.

Glaringly missing in the wide array of police resources is the perspective of the everyday first responder: the career patrol officer. As underrepresented as the patrol officer is, he is the real backbone of any police department. He or she is the first to respond to *everything*. It's not the SWAT team, not the brilliant gumshoe detective, and almost never the chief of police who arrives first at every incident. It is the patrol officer—no matter how large or small the incident is, and no matter what time of day. Whether it's something as big as the attacks on the World Trade Center or as small as a fender bender, the patrol officer is the first responder.

The patrol officer can go from assisting school children at a crossing guard assignment to, minutes later, rushing to a call about an armed gunman. The dichotomy of constantly straddling both kinds of assignments and incidents, often in rapid succession, coupled with the internal and external politics of modern policing, can take a major toll on the men and women providing society's first line of defense. The end result is that the career patrol officer usually pays a heavier price emotionally, physically, socially, and sometimes spiritually than their counterparts in other forms of investigation or administration.

The career patrol officer is becoming a thing of the past, yet it was in this class of officer—career patrolman—that I spent over 27 years in law enforcement. I wasn't a bureaucrat pretending to be a cop by donning command rank brass on my collar. I never wore plain clothes as a detective. I wasn't a SWAT guy. No, I was a street cop. Except for a three-week stint of light duty while recovering from surgery, I never sat behind a desk.

For 26 straight years in Grand Rapids, Michigan, I put on a Class A patrol uniform and responded to thousands of citizens' calls for service. Some are vividly etched in my mind to this day. Others I forgot minutes after responding. I was the proverbial jack of all trades. I was a peacekeeper, problem solver, improvisor. At times, I was a marriage counselor and even a spiritual guide. I often use a sports analogy to describe career patrol officers like me. We are like the offensive lineman on a football team—doing most of the heavy lifting, but rarely receiving any of the glory.

My hope with this book is to use my story to give readers an inside look at the life of a career patrol officer. I don't claim to have lived a typical life, but I certainly experienced all the highs and lows, personal struggles, insecurities, big hopes, and quiet desperation that only those who have been in the trenches of a career in law enforcement can fully understand. This book is intended to remove the Teflon armor shrouding the street cop's persona and allow a glimpse into the officer's human side at this critical juncture in America's police-community relations.

What is it like having to decide whether to shoot or not? What is a typical day like in the life of a street cop? What is the most difficult part of being a police officer in America today? The answers to these questions may surprise you.

Those looking for the police equivalent of Navy Seal sniper Chris Kyle may be disappointed, but those hoping to discern the thoughts, feelings, and experiences of the past quarter century in police work from a hands-on street cop should read on. I experienced it all. I felt fulfillment and despair, fear and boredom. There was glory and burnout. I know of few careers that can so profoundly touch the extremes of the emotional spectrum.

In addition to personal accounts of life on the street, this memoir includes my perspective on where law enforcement stands today. I provide a common cop's view on everything from the Black Lives Matter movement to what some refer to as the militarization of policing in America. I give social analysis on a variety of topics involving the culture we work in and from which we come.

Readers will have the opportunity to learn a former union president's opinion on police management, the assault on public employee (including police) benefits, and the effect these trends have on the ability of front-line police officers to effectively protect and serve. I also provide glimpses into my personal life and struggles that serve as the backstory for a career of public service.

You will meet a host of characters. War stories abound. In the end, I believe my story offers broad appeal not only to the law enforcement community, but to citizens from many other walks of life as well. I hope non-police readers will get a taste of the personal side of what those who serve their communities endure, and that those in political or police leadership will better empathize with the struggles of the common street cop.

I don't disparage line officers who chose other career paths. I know some fine officers who spent the bulk of their careers in investigative or other units and served the community well. My purpose is to provide a unique viewpoint that only a career patrolman can give.

I have tried to recall incidents as accurately as possible. However, precise dates and times were not readily available in many cases; they are filed away in patrol logs or reports now unavailable to me as a retired officer. I also tried to respect victim privacy by omitting full names and addresses, unless they were already in the public domain thanks to media coverage.

My type is a dying breed. I am an anomaly. It is rare in this era for a police officer to spend his or her entire career on the street. Today's formula for career success in law enforcement calls for a brief stint on patrol followed by constant angling to get into high-profile or politically correct specialized units, followed by promotion as soon as eligible. The formula works for hordes of police chiefs and command personnel nationwide. But guys like me know that most of these guys are pretend cops. They might as well be Hollywood actors wearing a police uniform. I was a real cop. This is my story—the story of a common man often thrust into extraordinary circumstances.

1

Josiah Ward

Down these mean streets a man must go who is not himself mean, and who is neither tarnished nor afraid.

—Raymond Chandler

I have always had the ability to put tragic events I witnessed on the job into perspective. Some police officers take these things home at night and have a hard time getting them out of their minds. I honestly can't tell you how many homicides, shootings, or dead body calls I responded to in almost three decades on patrol. It's not because I'm apathetic; I think my psyche always had a way of processing events in such a way that I never dwelled on gruesome deaths or human tragedy. I had a healthy way of viewing such incidents as a part of the job and, unless I felt I handled something improperly, I could usually move on to the next call without dwelling too much on the negative. I'm sure there was (and is) a long-term psychological effect after viewing so much death and despair, but while on the job I was good at compartmentalizing in a way that allowed me to keep pushing on.

The 1998 homicide involving Josiah Ward was different. Josiah Ward was a white kid in his late teens who was raised primarily in the inner city. He was one of those white kids who identified with black

1

culture, likely due to his time living in predominately African-American neighborhoods. Of slight build, Ward tried to gain "street cred" by wearing hip hop-style clothes, gaudy rapper "bling," and trying to speak with a ghetto accent.

Disfigured in an auto crash, Ward had received a large insurance settlement for the injuries he sustained in the accident. Consequently, Josiah had more money than a teenager from the inner city ever dreamt of. He didn't need to work. He had fancy vehicles, a house in a respectable northeast Grand Rapids neighborhood, and plenty of fair-weather friends and hangers on from the 'hood who were more than willing to spend this "gangsta" wannabe's money.

I'm not sure what confluence of events led to the tragedy that night, but in the early hours of that 1998 morning, my partner—and one of my best friends in the department—Chad Kooyer and I were dispatched to Ward's home after he called 9-1-1 claiming his girlfriend had shot herself. We found Ward's girlfriend lying on the kitchen floor in a pool of blood with a gunshot wound to her head. Ward was the only other person there, so there were no witnesses to shed light on what had occurred.

Ward gave us a story saying that the two had been arguing and his girlfriend suddenly produced a handgun and killed herself in an apparent response to the impossibility of resolving the domestic quarrel. This seemed highly unlikely. Chad and I could sense very early on that we had much more on our hands than a spontaneous suicide. This was a homicide.

To begin with, Ward's story obviously did not make sense. Domestic arguments rarely end in a suicide attempt. Intense anger is directed at the other person, not at one's self. The prospect of the death being a suicide was made even less likely because Ward's girlfriend was African-American. This is only relevant because it is extremely rare for black women to commit suicide. I do not recall ever responding to a suicide involving a black female in all my years on patrol. Just because it is rare doesn't mean it couldn't happen, of course, but Ward's demeanor and shaky story clearly made his claim suspect.

Chad and I quickly ushered Ward out of the house and away from the immediate scene, securing him in a police cruiser. It is proper procedure to remove a potential suspect from the immediate scene to prevent tampering with evidence. Ward was placed in a cruiser where he was guarded by Chad pending further interview by detectives. I then returned inside the house and did what I could to secure the scene.

Paramedics had by now arrived to render treatment to the victim. As is common practice in a deadly shooting, a sergeant was also dispatched to the scene. Sgt. Chris "Posty" Postma subsequently responded. Posty was a new sergeant at the time, but he clearly showed his considerable supervisory abilities in the events that followed.

With no witnesses to the incident, physical evidence was going to be critical in determining what had occurred. While it's always the first officer-on-scene's duty to secure the crime scene, this incident had the potential for being solved based on physical evidence alone. This made preservation of the scene paramount. All we had at this point was a dead body and Josiah Ward, who showed no sign of breaking from his unlikely version of events.

The entire scene was on the brink of being contaminated beyond repair, however, when paramedics wanted to transport the victim to the hospital. While the victim had no pulse, was not breathing, and had a gaping bullet hole in her head, paramedics found some indication of electric brain activity while running one of their tests. This is not uncommon in a deceased subject in which major lethal trauma has just occurred. The subject may be clinically dead, but electrical brain pulse may remain minimally present for some time, despite no chance of resuscitating the patient. Paramedics had contacted a local hospital emergency room doctor, who ordered transport of the victim based on these electrical brain pulses.

Sgt. Postma wisely overruled the paramedics intent on transporting the victim. It was a bold decision by a relatively new and young sergeant and it probably saved the case. It took a decisive leader to overrule paramedics and a hospital ER doctor and leave the body there. I gained immense respect for Posty while working this incident with him.

3

With Ward and the scene secured, forensic evidence technicians began the laborious task of processing evidence. In a fortuitous twist of fate, one of the crime scene techs on duty that night had recently attended a blood splatter training class. Blood splatter patterns can tell investigators volumes about what occurred. In an incident like this, blood splatter evidence was crucial. For example, far-flung blood splatter on a floor or wall can indicate the force of a blow or direction from which it came. Splatters can also determine the height from which an object fell and whether it was free-falling due to gravity or had centrifugal force behind it.

In this case, we had blood splatter evidence that contradicted the version of events given by Josiah Ward. A handgun found by the victim's body appeared to have been placed there, due to the blood splatter evidence (or lack thereof). Later, swabs of the hands of the victim and Ward revealed gunpowder residue. Gold traces found on the victim were from an expensive shirt Ward had been wearing and bolstered the theory of a physical altercation prior to the shooting.

Careful securing of the scene and outstanding processing of the blood splatter evidence by our crime scene technicians led to Josiah Ward being charged and convicted of second-degree murder. It was a clear-cut case in which the critical factors of solid crime scene protection, excellent supervisory decision making, and fantastic evidence processing led to a conviction in what otherwise would have been a difficult case to prove.

The Josiah Ward incident garnered a fair amount of local press coverage. Internally, there was a minor controversy because a current GRPD officer had close ties with Ward's family. This prompted concern from investigators that there could be the possibility of interference in the case by this officer. However, my role ended when I left the scene and completed my report.

The case was unique enough that, years later, a syndicated cable TV crime show produced an entire episode on it. The crux of the show emphasized the importance of crime scene preservation and the potential significance of blood splatter evidence. The lead detectives were interviewed for this nationally broadcast show. True to form, Chad and I as the patrol officers were never approached to appear on the show, and neither was Sgt. Postma. But such is life for the patrol officer. We are the unsung heroes—the grunts. A patrol officer can't be in it for the attaboys because they rarely come.

On a personal level, the Josiah Ward case marked a turning point in my career. I had started with the Grand Rapids Police Department in June 1991. At the time of my hire, the department was dominated by old-guard officers hired mostly in the late 1960s. Many of these veteran officers were retired or preparing to retire by 1998.

The Josiah Ward incident was the first big one I remember handling where the old heads, many of whom had ruled the northeast end of the city for over a quarter century, were not there. The onus of a big case was now squarely on the shoulders of a new generation of officers. The torch had been passed. From here on out, my deferring to the veterans of the old wars would no longer be possible. It was now my generation, those of us hired in the late '80s and early '90s, who would be assuming the role of veteran officer.

The competent way we handled the Josiah Ward incident was one of those seminal moments where I learned I was up to the challenge. The job of patrol officer had slowed down for me by then. Extreme youthful energy was tempered by experience gleaned from eight years of street work and the tutelage of the previous generation. I was heading into my career's prime. What a ride it would be.

A final note: Posty, the sergeant who supervised the scene that night, would suffer a debilitating eye injury in a hunting accident a few years later. Consequently, he spent most of his remaining career working plainclothes in the detective unit. This was the last major incident I would work with him on while he was a street sergeant. However, he always remained a standup guy in my eyes due to the outstanding supervision he demonstrated in the Josiah Ward incident.

2

Humble Beginnings

Wisdom is knowing the right path to take. Integrity is taking it.

—M.H. McKee

Grand Rapids is the city of my birth and boyhood, the city that led me to a career in law enforcement. A mid-sized city of 200,000 people, it is the second largest city in Michigan. Located on the west side of the lower peninsula, Grand Rapids is situated approximately 150 miles west of Detroit and about 30 miles east of Lake Michigan.

Grand Rapids' most famous son is former U.S. President Gerald R. Ford. His name is emblazoned on a freeway, the airport, his presidential museum, and a host of other public places.

Grand Rapids embodies everything in middle America. The city has been awarded the National Civic League's All-America City Award on three separate occasions. It is one of the most philanthropic cities in the United States.

Politically, Grand Rapids proper leans Democrat, but the suburbs and surrounding counties are among the most conservative and Republican-dominated in the country. Once known as The Furniture City, today Grand Rapids has a more diverse economy. It is still reliant on manufacturing—primarily of auto parts and products related to the auto industry—but has diversified into the medical field with top-notch research facilities, universities, and hospitals.

Today Grand Rapids offers a revitalized and vibrant downtown. It is constantly growing with new development and attractions opening regularly. For an urban area in a rustbelt state, Grand Rapids remains prosperous with unemployment rates below those of most other comparable cities. Unlike other Midwestern cities such as Flint or Youngstown, Ohio, Grand Rapids has avoided the burned-out factories and blocks of vacant, boarded-up houses. It also has not seen a significant population decline.

Grand Rapids is large enough to have big-city attractions and problems, but small enough to retain its Midwestern values.

It was in this city I was born at 6:30 AM on March 16, 1967. Weighing a diminutive 6 lbs. 6 ounces, I remained short my entire life (I'm 5'8"). What I lacked in height, I made up for in a stout build. Later I tried to enhance this solid build and minimize the detriments of my short stature through weight training and physical fitness.

My father, James Leonard, is also a Grand Rapids native. He is of Irish and Lithuanian stock, with his Irish father, James Sr., and his pure Lithuanian mother Margaret. He met my mother, Shirley Thompson, while both attended Western Michigan University.

My mother, Shirley, was born in Detroit in 1941 to Clifford and Dorothy Thompson. Mom's parents were of British origin, with her father born in England in 1907 before emigrating to Ontario, Canada, as a boy. Grandpa Thompson moved to the States as a young man when jobs became scarce in Canada around the mid-1920s. My Grandma Thompson was raised in Glennie, Michigan in rural Alcona County, to English-Irish parents. She also migrated to Detroit to find work as a seamstress in the late 1920s.

After marrying my dad in 1966, my mother relocated to Grand Rapids. Both of my parents were the first in either family to graduate from college. Each received a teaching degree from Western Michigan University and entered the field of education; Dad was an industrial arts teacher, while Mom taught elementary school. My dad left teaching after four years and spent most of his working years in product engineering jobs in several Grand Rapids-area furniture companies.

My mom remained in teaching her entire career. She began in Grand Rapids Public Schools, leaving teaching for several years to be a stay-at-home mom after my younger brother Jeff was born. Later she returned to teaching in Wyoming Public Schools, a suburb southwest of Grand Rapids. She worked challenging hours when she returned, mostly working in adult education, while at the same time going to graduate school to get her Master's degree in education.

When I was an infant, we lived on Grand Rapids' near westside on Quarry Avenue in a traditional, working-class Polish and Lithuanian neighborhood. We lived across the street from my great-grandfather Kashmires Martinaitis. Great-grandpa Martinaitis was Lithuanian, having immigrated to the U.S. directly from the Old Country shortly after the turn of the 20th century. While living on the westside, I was baptized at St. Peter and Paul Catholic Church. Decades later, a great friend and GRPD Police Chaplain Fr. Dennis Morrow would become the long-serving pastor of this church.

While I was still a toddler, my family moved to Northlawn Street on the city's northeast side. People often don't believe me, but I had my first memory there at just two years old. My brother, Jeffrey, was born two years and six days after I was on March 22, 1969. I clearly remember seeing him in his cradle the day he was brought home. I remember being fascinated by his tiny newborn hands and feet. I also have vague memories of the moon landing a few months later in July 1969, and my dad, a life-long science buff, being transfixed as he watched it on our black-and-white Zenith TV.

Just before I began grade school, my family moved to the city of Wyoming. Wyoming was also a blue-collar community comprised largely of workers at the huge Steelcase furniture plants or the General Motors Fisher Body factory.

Our neighborhood was safe with good neighbors and mostly well-kept homes. In the summer with the windows open at night, our street was typical quiet suburbia, with only the sound of crickets and the occasional tick-tick-tick of teenagers riding by on their ten-speed bikes.

9

Sometimes we could hear the distant wail of trains in the CSX rail yards several miles to the north. On many summer nights, I listened to the soothing play-by-play call of Detroit Tigers radio broadcaster Ernie Harwell and his sidekick Paul Carey on my handheld transistor radio—long after my parents had gone to bed whenever the Tigers were on a West Coast road trip. I had the radio hidden under my pillow and kept the volume low enough to avoid detection.

Unlike the houses we lived in before, our house in Wyoming had a large yard by city standards. It had the added benefit of having several acres of abandoned farm field directly behind it. This created a buffer between our yard and the backyards of the next street over and gave us kids ample room to play. Despite being a strictly residential neighborhood, it didn't feel like our neighbors were right on top of us.

At the south end of the abandoned farm field was a dilapidated, boarded-up hen house that hadn't been functional for decades. At the north end was an old pet cemetery, complete with headstones that marked graves of animals buried mostly in the 1940s and 1950s. The pet cemetery had also been abandoned, with many headstones overturned and the land overgrown with trees and brush. The combination of an idle farm field and forgotten pet cemetery directly behind our house made for great adventures and much fodder for a young boy's fertile imagination.

The early 1970s marked the end of TV's fascination with the Western genre. As kids, we often played cowboys and indians in the field or, as we called it, "playing guns." Our weapons of choice were usually our Daisy pop-guns as we mimicked the TV characters from *Bonanza*, *Gunsmoke*, or *Daniel Boone*.

The old farm field gave our street a slight taste of the country, with rabbits and even the occasional pheasant. The original farmhouse in what now made up our subdivision was just two doors down from ours and set back well off the road, which added to the country feel.

However, our street was far from being an upper-class neighborhood. Although demographically much more dominated by Dutch influence than the Polish-Lithuanian westside, Wyoming was a more modern extension of the same kind of working-class neighborhoods we had lived in before. While Wyoming was a good place to live, it was not the area for those who wanted to be movers and shakers. The upwardly mobile and the rich kids lived in East Grand Rapids, Forest Hills, Ada, or Cascade. As a boy, I remember most of the other neighborhood kids' dads worked factory jobs. My parents were two of the few parents on our street with college degrees.

I was raised Catholic, so after moving to Wyoming we attended St. Pius X Catholic Church in neighboring Grandville. The Calvinist, Dutch-dominated southwest side of suburban Grand Rapids included few Catholic churches at that time, making St. Pius a large parish. I attended catechism at St. Pius where I received First Communion, was later confirmed, and served as an altar boy. My Catholic faith remains an important part of my life today and became firmly ingrained in me while I attended St. Pius X.

My elementary school was on the next street over from where we lived so I walked to school. By my upper elementary years, I had devised a system whereby I waited until the last minute before making a mad dash to school and always still arrive on time. Our house was close enough to the school that I could hear the school's warning bell before classes started. I would wait to hear the bell, then sprint from home and make it to class before the final bell rang, utilizing a short-cut through our neighbor's yard across the street. This method allowed me to maximize my lunch period and sometimes go home for lunch. Of course, it only worked in the warm months when there was no deep snow to impede my travel.

Elementary years

My childhood years from kindergarten through sixth grade at Gladiola Elementary were among the happiest of my life. I excelled academically in these years and would typically be one of the smartest kids in class. School was very easy for me. My teachers always liked me, as I was well-behaved, followed the class rules, and had good attendance. On three occasions I won awards for creative writing and had my stories "published" in a school-produced book along with other kids from the

11

district who also had been selected for their writing skills. A couple of times I received certificates for perfect attendance.

I was a responsible kid. I was chosen as a captain of the school safety patrol when I was in fifth grade. This designation made me the student in charge of the crossing guard assignments before and after school. Many years later, while serving as a police officer, I would occasionally be required to fill in as a school crossing guard at key intersections of the city if the actual crossing guard called in sick. This led me to jokingly lament that I had not progressed very far in my career since those early days in fifth grade!

I was somewhat of an aloof kid, not a quick joiner. Even as a child I needed my alone time. It took me time to warm up to people I didn't know. I wasn't really shy, but I was unquestionably reserved. This characteristic has been present throughout my life.

By the time I reached fourth grade, I loved sports. My dad had little interest in sports, so I had to cultivate my enthusiasm on my own and through my Grandpa Thompson. However, I was far from being a gifted athlete. I rarely won any Field Day events and was not any better than average (and that may be a generous assessment) in team sports like baseball or basketball. I wasn't very coordinated, but my main handicap was my short stature which, at that time, also included a thin build.

Despite my lack of God-given talent, I loved playing and following sports. My favorite baseball team was, of course, the Detroit Tigers. As a young boy, I remember seeing the tail end of the career of Tigers legend Al Kaline. I can still recall the Tigers' batting order from 1977, and I even remember most of the players' batting averages. I was an avid collector of baseball cards and I studied all the player stats. Later as an adult, I sought to relive this simpler time by becoming a sports memorabilia collector.

In 1976, Tigers rookie sensation Mark "The Bird" Fidrych made an appearance at local Rogers Department Store. My mom took me to see him. After waiting hours in line with hundreds of other Grand Rapids kids, I met my first major league baseball player. The event made a big impression on a nine-year-old.

As a boy I dreamed of being a sports announcer when it became clear that my athletic ability would not lend itself to being a pro athlete. I used to imitate the Arkansas accent of Tigers TV play-by-play announcer George Kell while calling the neighborhood pick-up baseball games I was playing in.

My favorite sports figure of all, though, was Muhammed Ali. Boxing, and especially the heavyweight division, was at its zenith in the 1970s. Ali was bigger than life.

However, the 1980 U.S. Olympic Team's "Miracle on Ice" defeat of the Soviet Union, on its way to winning the Olympic gold medal, was far and away the greatest sports moment I had ever seen. I still find it inspiring.

While my talents weren't geared to athletics, I truly admired the tremendous dedication that went into training for sports like boxing and the Olympics. I remember as a ten-year-old boy seeing *Rocky* and finding myself for the first time inspired by a movie. My mom would yell at me for trying to drink raw eggs out of a glass as I tried to emulate Rocky's training.

The grit and discipline associated with great athletic champions always motivated me. Later in life it would provide me the inspiration to "gut it out" or "play hurt," whether physically or mentally, when met with challenges as a police officer. I concluded that virtually every one of life's lessons can be learned on a football field.

We remained a working-class family throughout my childhood. While my dad was fortunate enough to work in an office instead of on the factory floor, the non-unionized wood furniture industry traditionally had lower wages than other manufacturing jobs. This was especially true when compared to the auto industry jobs of those days.

With Mom staying home to care for us children, we lived on dad's relatively modest salary for many years while I was growing up. Money was often tight. We never went hungry, but we never had the extras that many kids had. We rarely went on vacations when I was young. Things became easier financially when my mom returned to teaching in the late 1970s, but that did not last for long. Any hope of the

Leonard family entering the middle class ended abruptly when my parents divorced in 1983.

Prior to that, however, what my parents lacked in money they made up for in dedication to their children. My parents were always involved in our education. My mom was often a "room mother" in my grade school classrooms. She was a PTA member. My dad regularly helped set up school carnivals and other school fundraisers. I always felt wanted and that my parents cared about me.

I was also blessed to have two of the greatest sets of grandparent role models anyone could hope for. My grandpa, James Leonard, Sr., was the quintessential model of the tough Irishman. He worked mostly hard labor jobs his entire life in Grand Rapids and in Prohibition-era Chicago. For many years, he and a friend owned their own contracting business where Grandpa Leonard specialized in painting. He earned a reputation as a sort of daredevil, often taking jobs as a steeplechase and painting the large Grand Rapids church steeples that other contractors did not want to touch.

He and my grandma, Margaret Leonard, often took me and my brother to their cottage 45 miles north of Grand Rapids in Newaygo County on the weekends. The cottage on Brooks Lake was built brick by brick by my grandfather and my dad in the mid-1950s, while Dad was still a boy. We usually were joined there by my aunt, Mary Leonard. We were regaled with stories of the Great Depression and the rationing that took place during World War II. Our family was small, but close knit. Grandma and Grandpa Leonard's cottage provided me with an idyllic Huck Finn/Tom Sawyer type of boyhood with swimming, fishing, mushroom hunting, and BB guns. These experiences inspired a love for nature that has been an important part of my life ever since.

I would often take my Crossman BB gun out in the forest surrounding the lake for hours at a time. I would shoot at everything from tin cans to grasshoppers. I became an excellent marksman with a rifle thanks to all the shooting I did back then with a simple Crossman 760 air rifle and iron sights. That skill naturally came in handy later when shooting grasshoppers evolved into small game and eventually deer hunting—not to mention the proficiency needed for a police duty weapon.

Mom's parents, Grandma and Grandpa Thompson, remained in the Detroit area but we visited them every four to six weeks while growing up. While there, I again heard stories of the olden days, including the early struggles of the labor movement in Detroit. Grandma used to talk about the times Grandpa would be out on violent picket lines at night while she slept with a hammer under her pillow for protection in case strike breakers showed up at the house. I still have one of Grandpa Thompson's old UAW union membership cards.

Grandpa Thompson worked his way up through the ranks at Champion Spark Plug in Hamtramck, eventually becoming a journeyman skilled tradesman plumber. Despite living difficult blue-collar lives, I always remember Grandpa and Grandpa Thompson as possessing dignified British refinement and manners. They embodied class and decency.

Grandpa Leonard taught me hunting skills and planted the idea in my mind of someday owning my own hunting land. I subsequently dreamed of being a mountain man or pioneer living off the land. He told stories of deer hunting in Michigan's rugged Upper Peninsula in a rustic cabin during the 1930s and '40s. When October and November came around, there was no greater anticipation for my brother and me than waiting for Grandpa and Dad to come home from weekend hunting trips; we wanted nothing more than to see a harvested deer and hear the exciting stories of the hunt.

Later I felt fortunate to have hunted with my Grandpa Leonard during my first bow season in 1979 when I was just 12 years old. I didn't know at the time that it would be his last deer season.

Meanwhile, Grandpa Thompson helped foster my love for sports with annual trips to Detroit Tigers and Lions games. Grandpa was active in the local Kiwanis club and one year his Kiwanis chapter was honored on the field at the old Tiger Stadium. He brought my brother and me onto the field with him. I couldn't believe I was actually standing on the same field that Ty Cobb and Babe Ruth had once played on! I have continued Grandpa Thompson's annual ritual of going to Detroit for a Tigers games long after his passing. Tiger Stadium may have been replaced by Comerica Park, but the tradition remains the same.

Grandpa Thompson also taught me about my family's rich British and Canadian ancestry. Some of my earliest memories are of my Grandpa Thompson and my Canadian relatives gathered around the TV watching hockey. I saw the spirited United States vs. Canada rivalry that ensued whenever the Detroit Red Wings played the Toronto Maple Leafs.

Holidays at my Grandma and Grandpa Thompson's house were special. There was always extended family present from both the Detroit area and Canada. Christmas seemed magical. I was unaware as a young boy that it was really Grandpa Thompson who had donned the Santa Claus suit on Christmas Eve and handed out presents to all of us children. Grandpa conveniently seemed to always have to step out briefly before Santa arrived and he would somehow miss Santa's visit.

None of my grandparents graduated from high school. Despite lacking in formal education, they were rich in wisdom from working hard and persevering through difficult times, trying jobs, the Great Depression, and World War II.

Both sets of grandparents had tremendous influence on me. From them I developed a strong work ethic and came to understand the need for a common man to be careful with his money. They genuinely wanted things to be better for their children and grandchildren than they were for them, and emphasized the need for higher education. My grandparents epitomized what has become known as "The Greatest Generation."

With loving parents and grandparents, I had a very happy childhood through junior high school. My family seemed to me like a typical, kind of nerdy, almost Brady Bunch-like 1970s family. There were everyday problems for sure, but my family always appeared to be a bedrock of stability.

Things changed dramatically in the early 1980s. In rapid succession, both of my grandfathers died in 1981 and 1982. My parents separated in 1982 and divorced in 1983. All this completely shattered what previously had been a sheltered, happy childhood.

I took my parents' divorce hard. Looking back, though, it probably helped me in the long run. The divorce and deaths of grandfathers I was so close to jarred me loose from the naïve, comfortable cocoon I had lived in up to this point. While it caused me great anguish at the time, it helped me forge the mental toughness I would need throughout life. It was my first real experience with the truism, "That which does not kill me only makes me stronger."

I was old enough that the courts allowed me to choose which parent I wished to live with. I chose my dad because he remained in our childhood home and at the time provided me with the only semblance of stability in my no-longer-tranquil life.

My parents' divorce occurred during what were the already difficult adolescent years. While I learned in my mid-teens how quickly life's stability can be shattered, I did not act out. I filed it away and learned from the mental scars. I think some of the tumult of the time affected me socially, along with my grades, but I did not let it make me become a rebellious teen.

As an adult, several women I dated tried to assert that I avoided serious relationships and marriage because of what happened to my parents. I have never agreed with this, but I do think it solidified a pre-existing independent streak. It led me to believe that I can only count on and trust myself. I had already shown signs of being an introvert and had loner tendencies established even as a small child. My parents' divorce solidified that bent, if it did anything.

Lessons from the football field

I entered Wyoming Park High School, a perennial football powerhouse, in 1981. Led by legendary coach Jack Verduin, Wyoming Park was one of the most respected Class B football programs in the state. Obviously, football was very important in this blue-collar community. I could relate to the football hysteria depicted in the movies *Friday Night Lights* and *All the Right Moves*, where adolescents find football—and their respective towns' fanaticism over it—to be the central themes of their high school years.

I played my freshman and junior years. I was a 150-pound fullback on offense and a cornerback on defense. My athletic ability never improved much even with a modest teenage growth spurt. I remained a backup to the backups, but did have moderate success carrying the ball in the games I got into.

Despite never being more than a scrub, playing high school football for a great program was a tremendous character builder. Beyond the cliché lessons on teamwork, football teaches you to dig deep. It teaches you to persevere and to push yourself. Being limited in ability showed me how to deal with failure, harsh criticism, humbling disappointment, and how to win on heart alone when skill won't do it. Again, I applied all these lessons to similar adversities I experienced in law enforcement.

A few years after starting at the Grand Rapids Police Department, I worked crowd control for a high school football game at Houseman Field. Wyoming Park wasn't playing, but I saw Coach Verduin at the game, apparently scouting one of the teams. I was in full police uniform and had duties to fulfill, so I did not talk to him. However, I always regretted not telling him that night what a profoundly positive impact Wyoming Park football had on me. I never saw him again. Many years later, I was pleased to see Coach Verduin inducted into the Grand Rapids Sports Hall of Fame. It was a fitting tribute for a man who made a great impression on a lot of young men's lives across West Michigan.

My high school years were difficult for me and I do not have a lot of happy memories. In addition to having my formerly safe little world rocked by my parents' divorce and the deaths of my beloved grandfathers, I began to show signs of conditions that would impact me the rest of my life: anxiety and depression.

Anxiety and depressive conditions are often hereditary. My family has a long history with these issues on my father's side so I have no doubt that I have a strong genetic link to these disorders. Treatment for anxiety and depression was primitive in the 1980s when compared to today. There was also a greater social stigma back then toward any mental health-related condition. For a teenager in the early '80's, being told you suffer from a mental condition of any kind was synonymous with being crazy or insane—at least that's what I thought. I remained in denial and did nothing.

Consequently, my conditions went undiagnosed and untreated until I was 30 years old. This is significant, because both illnesses affected me greatly. I remember times in high school when I was so anxious I would almost tremble. This kind of nervousness affected my ability to concentrate scholastically and to relate to others socially. The typical insecurities already prevalent during the teenage years were amplified exponentially in me.

I went from being the smartest kid in the class in grade school to a B and C student in high school. There were some semesters where I made the honor roll, but despite having far greater abilities I remained about a B- student. Reflecting on this later in life, I have viewed my grades metaphorically because I often viewed myself as a B- human being.

I have often wondered how different my life would have been had I been diagnosed and treated for anxiety and depression when I first experienced the symptoms as a teenager. I have never been one to use an impediment as an excuse for failure. I firmly believe we all have trials we have to bear; it's how we handle these trials that defines our character. However, it is still food for thought when I consider how different my grades, athletic performance, and social interaction could have been had I not had those feelings of self-doubt, an inability to focus, and social impairment that anxiety breeds.

Despite these conditions, I remained relatively grounded. I may have been anxious and sad, but I remained on the fringes of the popular crowd if not part of the inner circle. I had fast 1960s and '70s muscle cars that I worked on with my brother, dad, and friends. My crowd of friends loved heavy metal music, with Def Leppard, Van Halen, and Motley Crue our favorite bands. I stayed out of trouble.

In high school, I found the one physical trait at which I excelled. I learned through weight training for football that I was very strong for my size. As a junior, I once bench pressed 305 pounds, while barely weighing 150 pounds soaking wet. This was considerable for the early 1980s, which was well before the era of supplements and today's sports science. Strength was another quality I later used as a police officer to make up for a lack of height.

In the summer of 1982, after my freshman year, I also had my only successful foray into the realm of team sports. During summer baseball, I developed into a good contact hitter. I earned a starting job in center field and was the team's lead-off hitter. Summer jobs prevented me from playing baseball after that summer, however, so my skills never developed beyond that.

By the time my senior year rolled around and with little hope of starting, I made the fateful decision not to go out for football. I needed to work and save money for college. With my parents now divorced and maintaining separate homes, money was tight again. In addition to going to school full time, I worked two jobs. I was a night custodian cleaning my former grade school, Gladiola Elementary, every day after school, and on weekends I worked at Studio 28 movie theater.

While my intention to work and save for college may have been honorable, it caused me to miss playing on a state championship football team. In 1984, Wyoming Park won its only state championship in its storied history, capturing the Michigan Class B title. It broke my heart to not be on that team and not to be out there when my friends played for the championship in the Pontiac Silverdome.

I graduated from Wyoming Park in 1985 with little fanfare. Frankly, I was just glad to be done with this phase of life. I even passed on having a graduation open house. Instead, I started working as many hours as I could at the theater and prepared for my freshman year at Grand Rapids Junior College.

When I entered college, I was still unsure of what I wanted to study. I began seeking the usual ho-hum, generic business administration degree but business classes did not inspire me. I was not an '80s yuppie type. I didn't come from that kind of neighborhood or that type of upbringing. I've always been a hard worker and a driven person, but hawking some meaningless widget in some management position to make some millionaire even richer never appealed to me. Business simply bored me.

By happenstance, I took a criminal justice course as an elective and loved everything about it, especially the law enforcement part of the curriculum. I had finally found my calling. Academic apathy was replaced by inspiration and motivation. By the end of the semester, I decided I wanted to be a police officer. There was no longer any question as to what my profession would be.

People often ask me how I got into police work. They assume that someone in my family was a cop, as both my brother and I became police officers. In reality, none of my relatives were police officers. I think my career selection was the result of my upbringing, socioeconomic class, and personality type. Maybe it was due in part to the struggles I faced as a depressed teenager from a broken home. For whatever reason, I developed an intense desire to serve. I wanted to right societal wrongs. To me, this call to public service was almost like the calling of those who are inspired to take up a religious vocation.

In the Cold War 1980s, military service did not look like it would fulfill that yearning. I did not have the family name or social connections to pursue politics. Social work paid too little and was too dominated by what I perceived at the time to be wimpy liberals (I have since changed my perception of social workers!). Police work fit the bill perfectly.

I became consumed with being a police officer. I read everything I could about law enforcement. I listened to a police scanner while doing my homework and even while watching TV. A long-time family friend, Hank Gorkowski of the GRPD, arranged for me to do a ride-along with him on patrol. I absolutely loved it. I was hooked!

There are so many misconceptions about what motivates people to go into law enforcement. Critics like to stereotype police recruits as jack-booted thugs with a deep-rooted authoritarian streak hellbent on thumping underprivileged citizens, primarily minorities. Nothing could be farther from the truth. Most of us enter the profession as the result of a true calling like mine.

I switched my major to Criminal Justice and enrolled at Grand Valley State University in 1988 for my junior and senior years. Grand Valley was (and still is) one of the premier Criminal Justice programs in Michigan. It even had its own police academy.

I had a great time during these years and had a fantastic core group of friends. Grand Valley was just west of Grand Rapids, with its main campus in Allendale. This allowed me to retain my old friends from Wyoming Park and from working at the theater, as well as make new college friends. There was hardly a night when there wasn't something going on socially.

While at Grand Valley, I played hard but also worked hard. In addition to a large credit hour load, I worked two jobs that I hoped would help me break into a police career. I secured a job as a cadet for the Kent County Sheriff's Department working in the jail. One of the fringe benefits was that I could go on ride-alongs with road patrol deputies on my own time. I did this on several occasions and found the experiences to be an invaluable learning tool.

I also worked for the Salvation Army Starting Point Detoxification Center in Grand Rapids. This job prepared me for police work more than I originally imagined it would. The Salvation Army created the center as a three-day detoxification facility for all forms of substance abuse. I became familiar with the various aspects of drug addiction and its culture. I also had my first real exposure to homeless people and chronic alcoholics. People from all walks of life passed through those doors. I was exposed to everyone from prostitutes to a former NFL player.

The things I learned at the detox center helped me immensely when dealing with drug addicts and homeless people when I hit the street as a cop. Unfortunately, I often saw the same people I had met at Salvation Army Starting Point later on while working as a street cop.

I graduated from GVSU in 1989 with a Bachelor of Science degree in Criminal Justice and attended the police academy there. Completely inspired and motivated, I returned to good student status after my lackluster high school and junior college years. I was a Dean's List student at Grand Valley, and now it was time to pursue my chosen field. There was nothing in the world I wanted to do more. I was a 22-year-old college and police academy graduate. I was ready and couldn't wait to get started.

I sent out resumes to every police department within driving distance of Grand Rapids. With relatives still living in the Detroit area, I even went down to Detroit PD's headquarters with my Uncle Cliff to inquire about applying for Detroit PD—even though Detroit was at that time known as "the murder capital of the world." It didn't really matter where I got hired. I just wanted a department to give me a chance. I didn't have to wait long.

3

Slick-sleeved Recruit

Rejoice, O young man, in thy youth . . .

—Ecclesiastes 11:9

Making the transition from college kid to uniformed police officer involves a major culture shock. Nothing, not even the police academy, prepares a police recruit for the disparate types of human existence and depravity that all rookie officers are exposed to. It truly is a baptism by fire. I was a 22-year-old kid from suburbia when I became a police officer and my life underwent dramatic change. I went from attending college keg parties to policing heated domestic marital conflicts—often involving people twice my age—within a matter of weeks after graduation.

Many things go through a rookie officer's mind. Will I make it in this job? How will I respond to tragedy? How will I react under fire? Will I fit into the police subculture? Cutting one's teeth in police work is intense and a time of real insecurity. Some of an officer's most vivid memories come from his or her first few years on the street because everything is a new experience and leaves a lasting imprint on the newbie's memory.

My first police job was as a deputy sheriff assigned to road patrol in Montcalm County, a poor rural county northeast of Grand Rapids. In addition to having never been a police officer, I was not used to rural communities. I was a city boy and this added to an already steep learning curve. However, the Montcalm County Sheriff's Department was a wonderful place to work. I was thrilled they gave me a chance. It was a professionally-run department and I learned things from my training officer, Bob Surdam, that stayed with me for the rest of my career.

Shortly after completing my field training, I was dispatched to a fatal pickup/motorcycle crash. The motorcycle driver had his leg amputated by the force of the crash as he slid under the frame of the truck. He was eventually flown to a Grand Rapids hospital by Aeromed, a Grand Rapids-based helicopter with advanced life support capabilities. He was barely clinging to life. As Aeromed paramedics tended to the injured man, I was charged with trying to pull out the victim's leg from the wreckage in hopes it could be reattached at the hospital.

The leg was severed just below the knee and was still inside the victim's boot. I remember what a surreal moment it was pulling out an unattached human leg from a tangle of twisted steel and handing it to paramedics. I had never done anything like that. Sure, we'd had first aid practicals in the police academy, but they were unable to simulate anything close to this.

Sadly, the motorcycle driver later died at the hospital and the recovery of the leg was all for naught. The incident proved to me, though, that I could handle tense situations and keep a calm and level head. I found I could take the sight of blood and not fall to pieces.

I enjoyed my time working for the Montcalm County Sheriff's Department. For a while I contemplated making a career there but, as with many rural communities, pay is considerably lower than in urban departments. There also aren't as many opportunities within a small department. Then there was the lure of the city for a young man craving excitement.

Grand Rapids was my hometown, so when the Grand Rapids Police Department in 1990 announced they were hiring, I immediately applied. In the late '80s and early '90s, police jobs were at a premium. Approximately 1,200 applicants took the civil service test to be considered for only nine officer positions. The number was so big that the city had to administer the test at Devos Hall, at that time Grand Rapids' largest entertainment venue.

The Grand Rapids Police Department was at a crossroads in 1990. Most people are familiar with the deadly race riots in Detroit that occurred in 1967. While not as widespread as those in Detroit, Grand Rapids was also struck by rioting during that summer of unrest. In response, Grand Rapids PD engaged in mass hiring throughout the late '60s and early '70s to bolster its ranks in case such an incident were to happen again. By 1990, the department was preparing for a mass turnover in personnel as the first retirements from this generation of officers were set to begin.

I took the civil service test very seriously. I studied hard because Grand Rapids PD was by far my first choice to work as a police officer. I would've settled for one of the suburbs, but GRPD, with its potential big-city action, wide array of different jobs, and high profile in West Michigan, made it my first choice as a career. I was thrilled when I scored 98% on the civil service test. This score tied me with eight other applicants for the top overall score of the 1,200 people who took the test. After an extensive process, my dream came true and I was hired by GRPD. Only nine of us made the final cut and were hired. I was 24 years old.

I officially started on June 10, 1991. Though I had already completed a college police academy and served as a deputy sheriff for the past year and a half, I was required to attend three weeks of in-house training at Grand Rapids PD. This was followed by six weeks of working patrol with a field training officer. By August 1991, my class had completed our training assignments and we were out on our own as patrol officers. I would never leave that first assignment, only changing shifts and service areas over the next 26 years.

The police skills I gleaned from my time in Montcalm County served me well, but there was still a lot for me to learn once I struck out on my own. Understandably, call volume was much greater in Grand Rapids and things moved at a much faster pace. I also noticed people in the city were quicker to confront or flee the police. Street violence was much more prevalent. Grand Rapids was located only an hour north of the infamous I-94 Detroit to Chicago drug corridor. In the early 1990s, rival Detroit and Chicago gangs battled our own homegrown dopers for control of the emerging crack cocaine drug trade. It produced a large upswing in drug-related shootings and robberies.

Seniority is very important in the police culture. I found that this was even more evident at GRPD. Obviously, as a rookie I was at the bottom of the seniority totem pole. There is an old term in policing that refers to rookie officers as "slick-sleeved recruits." The less-than-flattering term is little used today, but originated from the practice in law enforcement of earning service stripes, which are worn on the lower sleeve of the uniform.

Service stripes are a source of pride among officers. They are an indication that you have arrived; that you are a veteran officer. One stripe is earned for every five years of service. For example, an officer with one stripe on his sleeve has five years of service. An officer with two stripes has achieved ten years, and so on. Each stripe earned is another sign of having paid one's dues—almost like battle scars. They are a subtle reminder of the pecking order. By virtue of being new, a recruit has no stripes at all. He or she is therefore called "a slick sleeve."

Slick-sleeve mistake

I remember making a huge, and nearly tragic, slick-sleeve mistake on one of the first weekends on my own in Grand Rapids. At that time in 1991, hundreds of inner-city youth gathered on Friday and Saturday nights at the corner of Franklin Street and Eastern Avenue and occupied Franklin east to Neland Avenue. I was armed with too much youthful courage and handicapped by an equal amount of naivety; I wasn't about to let the huge mass of people intimidate me.

Stupidly, I thought it was okay to make a traffic stop for a minor, expired plate violation amid that sea of mostly unfriendly anti-police miscreants, many of whom were looking for a reason to confront the police. Veteran officers knew better. They stayed on the periphery of this mess, recognizing that we were seriously outnumbered and the best we could do was monitor the crowd from afar. But not this rookie.

As I walked up to the violator's vehicle, I saw a juvenile open the door of my marked police cruiser, take the keys out of the ignition, and run away with them! He ran into the vast sea of disorderly humanity, which by now had been drawn to the flashing strobe lights of my cruiser's lightbar like insects to a bug light. I gave chase and waded into the crowd. Somehow, I caught the kid. I retrieved my car keys and tried to lead the juvenile back to my surrounded police car, which still had the expired plate violator stopped in front of it.

I called over the radio for assistance, just hoping to get out of the area with my tail between my legs. The first officer to respond was a fellow rookie classmate, Officer Tim Orent. Tim watched my back as I hurriedly sent the expired plate driver on his way. I even kicked the smart-assed kid loose who had stolen my car keys after first giving him a stern tongue lashing that I'm sure had no effect on him. As Tim and I tried to drive out of the area, parting the crowd with our cruisers, we heard several gunshots ring out from the massive group. We both felt fortunate to have escaped unscathed.

However, the next night Tim and I reported for our shift only to find the cruiser Tim had been driving the previous night cordoned off with crime scene tape. Evidently, the shots we heard as we retreated from Franklin and Neland the night before had been directed at us. Tim Orent's cruiser had been struck by the bullets, with ricochet damage done to the roof of the cruiser and full-force impact from another bullet striking the lightbar. In the chaos of the moment, Tim never realized his car had been hit. It was not until a day shifter, who was preparing to use Tim's cruiser, noticed the damage in the brighter light of morning. By now, of course, any suspect was long gone and any crime scene long since contaminated. No one was ever arrested.

The incident was a huge lesson for me. I'd had a successful stint as a deputy sheriff in Montcalm County, but now I learned I wasn't as street smart or tough as I thought I was. I had the point driven home that discretion is usually the better part of valor. It was the last time I tried playing Dirty Harry and I never did something that stupid again. By the grace of God, neither Tim nor I were hit by any of the shots. However, forensics estimated that another few inches lower and one of the bullets would have struck the back window directly behind Tim's head.

Tim and I remain great friends to this day. These kinds of brushes with death create a bond between officers who live through them, not unlike bonds between soldiers in war time. Two years later, I was honored to serve as best man at Tim's wedding. Tim Orent also remained a career street cop and is another of the unheralded officers who make the GRPD work.

Tim has often ribbed me about being the one who always got stuck with all the worst calls when we were young officers. While it is true I've had more than my share of gruesome scenes and trying incidents, Tim has been like a magnet for almost every kind of projectile known to man. One time, an unknown suspect shot a cross bow at him while he was taking an unrelated routine report. Fortunately, the perpetrator missed.

Another time, he took off his uniform shirt at the end of his shift and found a flattened piece of lead embedded in his bulletproof vest. It appeared that someone had shot him and struck his vest with some type of lower-velocity projectile and Tim never realized it. Tim just went on with his business and the command staff was never informed.

In March 2017, the last call that I was ever on with Tim, he and Officer Glenn Brower were attacked by a fleeing kidnapping suspect after he was cornered in the basement of a building. Tim had to shoot the suspect to prevent further assault on Glenn, potentially saving Glenn's life.

We typically worked one-man patrol units in Grand Rapids. A few days into an early solo patrol, I was again working the inner city when a suspect fled a traffic stop on foot. I gave chase and caught the suspect in a nearby alley. However, the fight was now on. I had called in the foot pursuit while chasing the perpetrator, but once I caught him he knocked the portable radio out of my hand before I could give my current location. The radio went flying and was no longer within reach. My choice was to either let go of the suspect and let him flee again, or ignore the radio. I chose to continue battling the suspect. I was unable to handcuff him due to his resistance, but I was starting to get the upper hand in the fight.

I was no longer responding to attempts to contact me, so a 10-39 (officer needs assistance) broadcast was put out by dispatch. I struggled to get one handcuff on the suspect. I couldn't get his other arm behind his back. I improvised and took the one arm I had cuffed and latched the other handcuff to a chain link fence that was right next to us. It wasn't a conventional collar, but handcuffing the perpetrator to the fence secured the guy long enough to allow for the cavalry to arrive and help me fully take him into custody.

Once the dust had settled, I identified the subject as Ray Pena. I had dealt with Pena a few months earlier as a deputy in Montcalm County! Who would have thought that a guy I had arrested 75 miles away would pop up again during one of my first nights on patrol in inner city Grand Rapids? This was one of those "it's a small world" moments that I could've done without.

That first summer was exciting and demanding, but in a good way. There were myriad aspects of the job to learn and it was also the only time to make a good first impression. Police departments have a distinct pecking order, and so much of how you are perceived and eventually labeled by the brass and fellow workers comes down to those first couple of years. Very rarely does anyone redefine a career after that, as sad and unfair as that may be. Consequently, young officers are often overly concerned and quite insecure about how others view them within the department.

The new recruit also gets acquainted in that first year with an affliction that will plague him or her for the remainder their careers: sleep deprivation. A new officer with no seniority gets assigned to afternoons or nights. This alone is a big adjustment from the normal sleep cycle. In addition, as part of trying to make a good impression the new recruit usually makes a ton of arrests and traffic stops. In his youthful enthusiasm, he shows up on calls he is not dispatched to. This translates into endless court appearances weeks and months down

31

the road when these activities get adjudicated—except that court is conducted during the day and the rookie officer works nights. It is not uncommon for a new patrol officer to work all night long and then spend a good portion of his day in court.

There was no doubt I would end up working afternoons when Fall 1991 rolled around. The department was so old then that it took something like 22 years to have enough seniority to secure a position on day shift patrol. An officer was required to have 12 years of seniority just to make third shift. This meant that I would be assigned to Patrol Unit 2 (afternoons) with the rest of my classmates.

There was still a good smattering of veteran officers on afternoons. I was both intimidated and somewhat in awe of the older officers. Many of them appeared crusty and cold. One older officer told me, "GRPD is the only place you'll ever work where you can't wait to get old so that you can get out of here." I could see the burnout and cynicism in the lines on their faces. However, I always showed them the deference and respect their years of service deserved and got along with the older guys just fine.

As they got to know me, I developed many friendships among the veteran officers, especially on second and third shifts. Maybe it was because I had similar interests as a lot of the older guys, like hunting and fishing, or maybe it was because I had genuine respect for the battles they had fought both on and off the job. Regardless, I fared a lot better than many rookies when it came to developing a good working relationship with the old heads. I always felt fortunate to have started at GRPD at a time when the department was so rich in experience. I took to heart what the old guys told me and I learned volumes about the job and life in general from them.

During the first year of service, a police officer in Grand Rapids is a probationary employee. While on probation, the employer may terminate an officer without cause. This puts a lot of pressure on a rookie to abide by the rules and make every effort to perform mistake free, both on and off duty. I think every recruit class is warned about the two biggest pitfalls for young officers: punch and Judy (better known as booze and women). I kept a very low profile socially at the department that first year to avoid any chance of trouble. I socialized mainly with my non-cop friends and didn't participate in a lot of the police social scene until I was off probation. During that first year, I was quickly able to size up who were the golden boys, the slackers, the suck-ups, and the screw-ups. There are career ramifications associated with how the new officer mingles with each.

Once on Patrol Unit 2, I was quickly assigned to "Baker Sector," the phonetic radio call sign for the city's northeast quadrant. I enjoyed the northeast side with its diverse neighborhoods and variety of call types. My family had lived there before moving to Wyoming and my Grandma Leonard and Aunt Mary still lived on the northeast side. It was the sector of the city I most identified with.

One evening shortly after starting on PU-2, I responded to a simple domestic call at a relatively new apartment complex in a nice, low-crime section of the northeast side. The woman involved had fled to another apartment to call police. She indicated that she'd had an argument with her husband. He was supposed to leave and she waited in the neighbor's apartment for him to gather his belongings and go. The woman requested that I check her apartment to make sure her husband had, in fact, left.

I proceeded to her apartment. I had her permission to go inside, so I entered through the unlocked door when no one answered my knocks. Once inside, I found the apartment completely dark. It appeared no one was there. I cleared the various rooms by the light of my Maglight and didn't find the husband. It looked like he had left. I was about to tell the complainant that it was clear to return home when I decided to check one remaining portion of the apartment—the outside balcony. It had caught my attention because lights were on there. With the premises otherwise dark, I thought it strange that this one location was lit. The balcony was accessed by a sliding door. Drapes were drawn so that I could not see the balcony from inside the apartment. I pulled away the drapes to find the husband seated in a chair—without a head!

The husband had not left as he had promised. Instead, he got out a 12-gauge shotgun and put it in his mouth. He apparently wrapped his mouth around the barrel as he pulled the trigger and the force of the gases being released, along with the shotgun charge, literally exploded the man's head.

It was a cold evening and all that remained of where his head had been was the steam rising from his brain stem.

The balcony was located on the second floor of the apartment building. The force of the blast had actually embedded some of the victim's teeth in the ceiling above him. Blood and cerebral fluid seeped downward to the balcony below and brain and skull fragments were found on the children's playground many feet away from the actual scene. I remember assisting the medical examiner with picking up pieces of brain matter off the kids' teeter totter. I'm not sure a rookie officer needs any more than that to end any semblance of youthful innocence.

While the incident was a tragic loss of life, it served as a good reminder to me about how differently calls can turn out from the way they sound upon initial dispatch. This simple domestic/property removal quickly turned into a death investigation without any warning. It was another lesson learned. At this stage of an officer's career, nearly every day leads to new experience gained and the hard-earned seasoning that eventually turns a rookie into a veteran.

Suicides are never easy to deal with. I seemed to get more than my share of extremely grisly ones—as a rookie and throughout my career. A couple years into the job, I was again exposed to suicide by shotgun blast. However, this time the suicide occurred right in front of me. I, with three other officers, responded to a subject threatening suicide. Upon arrival, we could see through a window that the subject lay in bed in a downstairs bedroom with a shotgun in his hands. He was laying on his back with the muzzle of the shotgun under his chin.

Attempts to get him to put the shotgun down and come to the door were unsuccessful. We tried for several minutes to talk this guy into letting us in so we could get him some help. As if almost sneering at us, he instead put the shotgun to his head and pulled the trigger. We kicked the door in a desperate attempt to render aid, but to no avail. He was clearly dead. Seeing someone take his life right in front of you is a shocking and sobering experience.

The next day, the department called me and the other officers who had been at the scene to see if we wanted counseling to deal with what we saw. I declined. I did a lot of reflecting on the call. I went over in my mind all the events leading up to the act to assess if I could have done anything differently to prevent the suicide. When I concluded that there wasn't anything else I could've done, I was quickly able to put it out of my mind. I know this may sound insensitive, but it really didn't bother me in the days and weeks that followed after I got over the initial shock. However, I'm sure the cumulative effect of seeing something so graphic, combined with numerous other horrible events I witnessed, did take its toll psychologically over 27 years. But I don't recall it bothering me at that time.

The hits kept coming. Around this same time, GRPD responded to a call from the west side for one of the cruelest suicides we ever encountered. I didn't personally respond, but heard about all the grisly details from others. It was Christmas Day. Holidays often are hard on depressed people. This subject took things well beyond just crying in his beer, though. Estranged from his wife and hoping to get back at her, the guy waited for his wife to pull out of the garage on her way to a Christmas Day church service.

Once he was confident that she was gone, he broke into the garage. He lowered the overhead garage door and placed a chair in the empty stall where his wife parked her car. Before shooting himself with a .30-06 rifle, the man sat in the chair and hung a sign around his neck that read, "Merry Christmas."

I can hardly fathom the mental trauma and anguish that must have overcome his wife when she returned home from church and saw her dead ex-husband, as the garage door lifted, sitting in a chair with a placard offering the world's most sinister Christmas greeting.

Street cops are constantly thrust into these kinds of disturbing situations. The slick-sleeve learns early on whether he has the mental disposition to handle it. He learns from not only the calls he responds to, but also the major incidents investigated by co-workers who describe in vivid detail the harrowing incidents. The young officer's mind sucks it all up like a dry sponge.

Not everything at this stage of my career was so dark, however. I had a lot of good times on the job while I was a rookie. This is the time when a young officer forges a lasting kinship with his coworkers, and I was no exception. Several life-long friendships began during this early stage of my career.

Like most young officers, I was energetic and a good producer. I went through the normal young guy's phase of making lots of traffic stops and arrests. I was sometimes complimented by supervisors for my report writing skills and my pro-active production. I was never a glory hound, though. I just did my job with enthusiasm. I wasn't trying to impress anyone. I simply wanted to be viewed as a competent street cop that my co-workers knew they could count on.

On a personal level, I made what was probably my best financial investment while still a probationary employee in 1991. Ever since hunting the forests of Michigan's Lower Peninsula with my dad and Grandpa Leonard, I'd wanted my own hunting land. No one in our family ever had that luxury. As working-class city people, we had no family farm, nor did we have any relatives with access to private land. We were always forced to hunt overcrowded public land within an hour or so drive from Grand Rapids. We still enjoyed ourselves and I got my first deer on public land, but it was far from the experience of hunting on private land under your control.

Growing up, the open spaces and ranches depicted in the old westerns I watched always appealed to me. I enjoyed reading about mountain men like Jim Bridger and Jeremiah Johnson. I liked reading histories of the fur traders and the early pioneers. Owning a little chunk of wilderness would give me a glimpse into that world.

While on a weekend getaway in northern Michigan with an old high school friend in August 1991, we decided to stop to talk with a few realtors and see what land was available. We located a 120-acre parcel adjacent to hundreds of acres of Manistee National Forest. The land was priced to sell and was only an hour and a half north of Grand Rapids. My new job provided me with a salary that allowed me to afford hunting land. I went in on it with my brother and bought it on a land contract. At age 24, I had my career job and had fulfilled my dream of owning my own hunting land. Things were going well.

My grandparents' cottage in Newaygo County may have served as the focal point of my boyhood years, but my hunting land became the passion of my adulthood. I immersed myself in land management, doing whatever I could to enhance the property for wildlife. We planted tree seedlings every year from 1992 to 2017; I figure we've planted upwards of 50,000 trees over the last 25 years. We had a pond built. We clear cut stands of aspen to enhance new growth for deer and grouse. Eventually my brother bought an old tractor that we still use for planting 10 to 12 acres in food plots each year for the deer and wildlife.

The pleasure I get from giving back to nature is difficult to fully describe. It's a spiritual experience for me. Today, seeing acres of pine forests full of bustling wildlife where there was previously only barren pasture land brings me great pride. There is nothing more rewarding than harvesting a nice buck on my own land, especially because there were no deer there when I bought it all those years ago.

The first several years we owned the property, we stayed in an old travel trailer when we were there. There was no electricity, no running water, and an unreliable propane furnace as a heat source. Nonetheless, there was no place I would rather have been. Eventually we "upgraded" to a beat up mobile home. Power was eventually put in, and a well for running water.

Finally, in 2001, I had saved enough money to have a modest A-frame cabin built. My dad and I finished off the interior, spending most of my days off for the next several years completing one room at a time whenever I had saved up enough money.

The 40 acres adjacent to my property came up for sale in 2002 so I purchased it to give me 160 contiguous acres, or a quarter section.

Salvation in the woods

The cabin and property saved me. Maybe not in the first few years, but as time went on it kept me focused and goal-oriented. It provided me with a much-needed respite from the stress of front-line urban policing. The peace and serenity nursed me back to health mentally and spiritually from bad break-ups, union conflicts, and bouts with depression. It gave me and my buddies a place to hoot and holler without disturbing anyone or getting into trouble.

It's important for a young officer to establish a similar hobby or activity away from the job. If he doesn't, the officer runs the risk of becoming over-invested in the job. He will find it more difficult to turn off the job when not at work, dwelling on police work even while off duty. A healthy passion is needed for a balanced life away from the department.

I was still growing as a police officer well beyond my first year. In 1994, I saw for the first time the aftermath of an officer-involved shooting. Two of the best street cops I ever met were John Klomparens and Craig Miller. Both were career patrol officers who had worked Grand Rapids' west side for a generation. On this fateful occasion, they responded to a call where an assault suspect was observed leaving the residence as they arrived on scene. A brief vehicle pursuit ensued, with the chase ending in a used car lot at the corner of Leonard Street and Hamilton Avenue.

The perpetrator opened fire on both officers with a semi-automatic pistol. Like the cool, steady veterans they were, John and Craig demonstrated tremendous courage under fire and returned rounds, killing the suspect.

I arrived on scene seconds after the last shots were fired. I can still remember the smell of gunpowder in the air as I exited my cruiser. I assisted in any way I could, mainly securing the scene. I remember afterward thinking that I'd never been involved in anything so intense up to that point in my career.

Years later I sat on the department's Board of Awards and had the opportunity to read Officer Klomparens' police report. Both John and Craig were being considered for a much-deserved medal for their courageous actions demonstrated while under fire. In the report, John mentioned exiting his cruiser at the end of the pursuit. He wrote that something caused him to drop his flashlight. John reached down to pick up the flashlight when bullets from the suspect whizzed over his head. Had he not bent over to grab the light, he almost certainly would have been shot. I remember that in his written account of the incident, John credited a divine force for knocking the flashlight out of his hand and essentially saving his life. I have no doubt John was right. There is an old saying in the army that "God loves the infantry." I also believe this applies to the street police officer.

Despite having a lot of positive things going on in my life, I was still plagued by the inner demons that had haunted me since adolescence. While I was doing well at GRPD and seemed to be accepted by my peers, I had a nagging feeling that has persisted my entire life. I was beginning to realize that I was different from most people. In some ways, my differences were positive. In other ways, I felt like a misfit.

Good and questionable qualities

I was in many ways very mature. I could stay focused on goals or responsibilities and delay gratification. I was financially responsible, avoiding the youthful pitfalls of credit card debt and frivolous toys. I began investing for retirement from my very first paycheck at GRPD. I had a very strong will and wisdom that people often told me was beyond my age. Those were my good qualities.

There were other sides of my life and personality, however, where I felt like an oddball. While other people my age and from my socio-economic background were buying their first houses, I was buying hunting land. While my friends were getting married, I could never seem to find the right girl. When I did date women who had their acts together, I usually became bored. Other times I felt trapped and ran away from the feeling of being suffocated.

I remember going to a pool party at another young officer's house. The other guys were frolicking around in the pool playing some dodge ball game, while I stayed poolside trying to figure out how I could politely excuse myself to go up north and hang the tree stand I had in the back of my truck.

I had always shown some of the personality traits of an introvert. There was that definite, ever-present loner in me. Still, I never fully

39

accepted that I was an introvert until later in life. At this age, though, I assumed introverts were shy people who were often meek and anti-social. It almost had a negative connotation to me. I certainly was not meek. I quickly developed a reputation at a young age of being vocal about my opinions and was quick to assert myself at work. And I loved the party scene in my youth. I was very social. How could I be an introvert? These contradictions exacerbated my feelings of not really fitting in anywhere.

It was not until the science fiction film *Divergent* was released some 20 years later that I found the perfect tongue-in-cheek characterization for me. In the movie, a future civilization forces each person to accept a distinct categorization as to their role in society. Those who didn't fit any of the categories were labeled "divergent." That was me. I was divergent! That explains it! I really didn't fit any stereotype. I was the quintessential purveyor of "the path less traveled." However, I must admit in all seriousness that I still have some insecurities related to it even now.

I also had not yet dealt with my depression while I was a young officer. I remained completely in denial. I knew I often experienced sadness, but I always attributed it as situational and still could not bring myself to admit I had an actual mental condition. When I was depressed in college, I could always rationalize that it was because I was sick of school. When I was depressed while working in Montcalm County, I knew everything would be just fine if only I could get into GRPD. When the feelings persisted at GRPD, I could always find an excuse other than that I had chronic depression. If only I had the right girlfriend. If only I had my own place. If only I could get off nights. On and on it went for several more years.

By now my mental condition had manifested itself primarily as depression more than anxiety, but the depression was regularly present and not properly dealt with. I often medicated my symptoms on my own. In college, it was socially acceptable to party and binge drink. After all, I was young, sowing my wild oats, and you only live once. I had fully embraced the college party scene. I know now that part of this was true—I was being a typical college kid—but there was more to it. I was also medicating my depression.

Once out of college, the party lifestyle became less and less acceptable. However, throughout my twenties there was still a large enough contingent of partiers and bar hoppers, even within the police culture, that I could partake of binge drinking and still appear to be just a single guy doing what single guys do. This allowed me to remain in denial. But I was becoming more and more disenchanted with the bar and party crowd.

Things in my personal life would eventually need to change, but they didn't do so while I was a slick-sleeved recruit. My time as a new guy was quickly coming to an end because I was no longer low man on the totem pole. GRPD had initiated mass hiring shortly after I arrived to fill the many vacancies created by retirements of the old guys.

I was learning my craft well and growing in confidence as a street cop. Within just a few years, I would already have considerable seniority. I became a field training officer only a couple of years after starting at GRPD and I got along well with my bosses and coworkers. There were some rough patches at times and some things in my personal life that eventually needed to come to a head, but for the most part I was doing quite well as I ended my status as a slick-sleeved recruit.

4

"Stinky"

Good people sleep peaceably in their beds at night only because
rough men stand ready to do violence on their behalf.

—George Orwell

Friends sometimes ask me if cop movies or TV shows are an accurate
depiction of what it's like to be a police officer. My answer is always
a resounding, "No!" There are two exceptions, however, that I think
come close. They are the older films *Colors* and *The New Centurions*.

Colors (1988) does a credible job depicting the inner workings of
LAPD's CRASH unit and its response to gang wars at the inception of
the crack cocaine epidemic in the late 1980s.

The New Centurions (1972) was based on the book by former LAPD
officer Joseph Wambaugh. It portrays the trials and tribulations of
patrol officers better than any other Hollywood production I have seen.
While somewhat dated now and using police tactics that are terrible
by modern standards, the film still shows realistic patrol scenarios and
does a great job depicting the personal struggles of the common cop.

It focuses primarily on two officers. Roy Fehler, played by Stacey
Keach, is a young officer partnered with veteran Andy Kilvinski (George
C. Scott), who is nearing the end of his career. The two form a close

43

bond while working night shift patrol in Los Angeles. Kilvinski has his own set of rules he has developed to apply to almost any situation, known as "Kilvinski's Law." He is charismatic and tough and has tremendous influence on the younger Roy Fehler. The latter part of the movie delves into the struggles each encounter after Kilvinski retires and Fehler is left without his mentor.

From 1991 through 1997, the Andy Kilvinski on night shift at GRPD was Mike "Stinky" Venroy. Mike Venroy began his career at Grand Rapids PD in January 1967, or as he liked to put it to me, "Two months before you were even born!" From a Dutch blueberry farming family in neighboring Ottawa County, Mike did a four-year stint in the Navy before becoming a police officer with GRPD.

He was quickly nicknamed "Stinky" for his ability to fart on demand. Yes, that is correct. Mike prided himself in being shamelessly crude. While not as dedicated to police work as *The New Centurions'* Andy Kilvinski, Mike shared that character's wisdom for the intricacies of the job. Stinky was a great storyteller with a raw comedic wit that was often disarming, even to suspects. He had a loud baritone voice that got peoples' attention. First and foremost, Mike "Stinky" Venroy was a character.

Stinky had a portly build and stood about 5'7", although when asked his height he always barked, "I'm 6 foot." Although not very tall, the combination of his heft, booming voice, crudeness, and gruff demeanor made him an intimidating guy. It was nothing for him to greet you in the locker room at HQ by dropping his drawers and demonstrating his talent for loud, impromptu flatulence while he assumed a squatting position similar to a dog defecating. He would then bellow loudly, "that one was unfiltered!" as he gleefully chuckled like a naughty child.

Another famous and oft-repeated outburst heard throughout the locker room after a long shift was Mike proclaiming in tired frustration, "The human being: the worst animal God ever placed on the face of the Earth—and I have to deal with the worst of them every day!" Of course, as fate would have it, I was assigned a locker right next to his.

Mike was from the last generation of officers whose education was limited to high school. In the years that followed, there was a nationwide push toward professionalizing law enforcement by putting a greater emphasis on recruiting officers with college degrees. While Stinky and those of his time lacked formal college instruction, they were filled with wisdom from life's most difficult teacher of all: the streets themselves. Most had military experience, with many having served in Vietnam.

These guys were strictly old school. When they began their careers, a street cop was equipped only with his service revolver, a night stick, and a pair of handcuffs. They didn't carry portable radios at the beginning of their careers and many remembered the use of police call boxes as the primary mode of communication with headquarters. Consequently, modern technology was typically not their forte. Bridging the gap between the simpler days of the 1960s and evolving technology of the 1990s was often the job's biggest challenge for guys like Stinky.

This was evident shortly after I met Stinky. After I started at GRPD, the Michigan Council on Law Enforcement Standards (MCOLES) implemented a mandate requiring all Michigan police officers to be trained as breathalyzer operators. The state provided the training and all officers were eventually certified in using the new Datamaster breathalyzer machine. This new technology was far more than Stinky could handle this late in his career, however. He would proclaim to any supervisor who would listen, "If I've gotta use that new machine, they don't get run for drunk!"

Drunk driving arrests are a chore to begin with. The process of arresting someone for what amounts to a simple misdemeanor is lengthy and cumbersome. There are chemical test rights, preliminary breath test rights, vehicle impounds, and detailed reporting. A typical DUI will take at least two hours if everything goes well. It is not uncommon for the process to take four hours if there are mitigating factors like the need to get a blood search warrant. Anyone who has been around an obnoxious, uncooperative drunk for four hours can attest to what a miserable experience it is.

Contrary to public belief, most bigger city police officers aren't creeping along the streets at night looking for drunk drivers. That's not to say we condone drunk driving, but the process is so lengthy and the call volume so great in urban areas that DUI arrests are not something we typically seek out. We'll do our job when we come across a drunk driver, but we don't sit across from bars just waiting for a drunk to leave the parking lot.

One night shortly after we switched over to the new breathalyzer, Stinky's nightmare came to fruition. He was sent to a report of a drunk driver who had wrapped his car around a tree. The driver and a passenger were now frantically trying to dislodge the vehicle. Mike would not only have to "run him for drunk" on the dreaded new machine, but also deal with an accident scene.

Hopping mad, Stinky located the vehicle involved. However, the driver and passenger had fled the scene. No one was around. Mike breathed a deep sigh of relief. This wasn't going to be so bad after all. With no driver, there could be no DUI arrest. Mike would merely tow the car, do a crash report, and let the traffic unit follow up with the registered owner for leaving the scene of the accident. Simple.

In the middle of this process, however, the driver returned to the scene. He was drunk as a skunk. Now Stinky was back to square one with a drunk he would have to process on that new breathalyzer. Angry now, Mike asked the driver, "Why did you come back?" The drunk responded, "I had to. My friend is hurt." Mike retorted in the loudest, most perturbed voice he could muster, "I don't care. RUN, YOU SON OF A BITCH! RUN!" The quote is legendary around GRPD to this day. Eventually one of the younger officers responded and processed the drunk. I don't think Mike ever did use that new breathalyzer.

Stinky was brilliant at off-the-cuff comments. Another time, several of us officers were converging on a suspect who had been breaking into cars. As Stinky tried to catch up to the suspect on foot, another cruiser rolled up and came to a screeching halt in front of him. Mike ran full tilt into the fender of the responding police cruiser. He flipped over the hood, end over end, and hit the pavement in front so hard he almost bounced off it—as if on a tightly-strung trampoline. We all ran over to Mike to ask him if he was okay because the impact with the cruiser and the ground was significant. Mike immediately bounced back up and yelled, "Of course I'm okay! I've jumped out of second story whorehouse windows that were higher than that and hit the ground running!" Yep. That was vintage Stinky.

Stinky enjoyed both food and drink. In addition to contributing to his rotund midsection, it also raised eyebrows at work. One time a captain noticed Mike had been taking a lot of time off. Concerned about the increased absenteeism, the captain called him into his office. He sternly asked, "Venroy, do you have a drinking problem?" Unfazed by the inquiry into his personal life, Stinky calmly responded, "No, I don't have any problem getting drunk at all." The enraged captain screamed, "Get the hell out of my office!" The brass never inquired again.

Andy Kilvinski may have had "Kilvinski's Law" to rely on; at GRPD we had "Venroyisms." One of my favorites came while he and I were responding to a violent domestic call. Once on scene, I became alarmed. The front windows of the house had been smashed out and there was glass everywhere. Clearly there had been a major, knock-down-drag-out fight.

I began to reach for my portable radio to call for a precautionary extra officer in anticipation of what we were about to walk into. Mike stopped me. "We won't need another car here," he said in a relaxed voice. I asked, "How do you know? Have you been here before?" "No," Mike said. "But he broke glass. Breaking glass calms the savage beast. You'll find he's calm now and you'll be able to slap the cuffs right on him."

Sure enough, once inside the house the male was sitting there calmly and he had completely collected himself. We established that an assault had occurred and we effected an arrest for domestic assault. The arrest was made without incident, just as Stinky had predicted. Stinky's theory that breaking glass "calms the savage beast" held up for the remainder of my career. I cannot recall ever going to a domestic assault where the perpetrator fought with us if he had broken glass prior to our arrival.

As an older officer, Mike was well beyond the gung-ho youthful stage of proactive police work. The brass understood this, but every now and then they would give him a half-hearted prodding to get him to increase his traffic stops. Mike's favorite were equipment violations. He loved stopping vehicles with no mirrors or no functioning taillights. These violations are simple "repair and report" tickets in Michigan, meaning if the driver makes the necessary repairs to the vehicle, there is no fine. Equipment violations rarely are contested in court, making them the perfect pro-active stat for a veteran officer looking to pacify management when they bitch about numbers.

In the wee hours of one morning, Mike spotted the perfect daily log filler pulling out of the old Miller Zylstra lumber yard on Michigan Street: an old pickup truck with no taillights! Stinky quickly stopped it, hoping to get his personal monthly quota filled in one fell swoop.

Once Stinky got up to the driver's window, the occupant of the vehicle said in a resigned way, "Well, it looks like you've got me." Mike, not sure what the driver was referring to, played along by saying, "It looks that way." The driver then showed Mike the contents of the bed of his pickup, which contained scores of stolen items that he had just lifted from the lumber yard.

Mike's plan to make a simple traffic stop ended up netting a suspect involved in numerous larcenies of building materials in the area. The suspect was sure that Stinky had seen him steal the items and felt hopeless to do anything other than come clean. Had the driver not made the incriminating comment when first approached by Mike, he probably would've gotten off with a simple equipment violation ticket! But that is how things often go on patrol. A simple violation leads to something much bigger.

Communication system

Over the years, Stinky and the other guys on third shift had devised their own system of codes to stay under the radar of the brass and dispatch. When working nights, it's common to stop and park one's cruiser in areas that are usually out of the public's eye. It is unrealistic to drive for ten or twelve straight hours, especially when there is often little vehicular traffic in the early morning hours. Commonly, patrol officers will congregate in these spots. It is a time to decompress, get caught up on paperwork, or just chat with co-workers in between calls. These spots are usually no-man's land, meaning supervisors are not welcome.

In the days before in-car computers and cell phones, all communication was done via patrol car radio. Mike and the other north-end officers used a numbering system to designate which spot they were to meet. If one guy wanted to "car-up" with another officer, he would call that officer's car number and then simply give the location number of say, "12." The officer would then meet at that location, usually followed shortly by anyone else not on a call. This kept any management do-gooder from knowing where the guys were meeting.

When I began working the northeast end, Mike filled me in on the old code system. Whenever he called me and said "17," I knew what was up. That number was code for Northeast Junior High. When Stinky wanted to meet there, the first words out of his mouth usually were, "You got any new bow books?" He was referring to hunting magazines. An avid bow hunter, Mike would spend a good portion of his shift in between calls reading hunting magazines at 17. On a slow night, Mike and I would tell hunting stories and talk tactics for hours.

Then it was time for him to "rest his eyes." Shortly before his retirement, I was car to car next to Stinky at 17 as he was snoozing. With about a half hour left in our shift, I received a late call. Stinky briefly awoke from his slumber when I told him I was leaving to respond. I finished the nothing call and proceeded to headquarters at the end of my shift, known as "10-42 time" in police vernacular. At 10-42, all patrol units are called out of service by dispatch. This is the way dispatch can account for all units and ensure everyone has returned safely to headquarters at the end of the shift.

As I was heading down the motor pool ramp at HQ, I heard dispatch repeatedly calling Stinky's car number to call him out of service. Each time there was no response. Dispatch interpreted this as serious; other units could be sent to look for the unresponsive officer—the assumption being that the officer was in peril. I knew exactly where Stinky was.

Now off duty, I quickly jumped into my personal vehicle and sped up to Northeast Junior High. There was Mike, still in his cruiser sound

49

asleep with dispatch still frantically calling him over the radio. I rousted him out of his deep REM sleep. He looked up at me. For a split second, in his half-conscious state, he looked puzzled as to why I was sitting next to him in my own vehicle instead of my police cruiser. Then reality hit him like a ton of bricks. His eyes opened wide in a combination of surprise and panic. Stinky put his cruiser into drive and hurried out of the parking lot like a man possessed without even saying a word to me as he high-tailed it back to headquarters.

What I enjoyed most about Mike was his bluntness with the derelict element of society. While not as entrenched as it is today, political correctness had already made its way into police work in the 1990s. Internal Affairs was quick to investigate even the most piddling complaints of misconduct or discourtesy.

What career bureaucrats and police critics don't understand is that there is a small portion of the population that just needs to be told off now and then. Unfortunately, there is an element out there that only responds when you go down to their level. I never saw Mike give anyone a public shaming that was unprovoked. But when someone did provoke him, look out!

This was on full display at a domestic call we responded to on the west side of the city. Some of the most frustrating calls for patrol officers are domestic situations where people want us to essentially evict a significant other. So many people let a boyfriend, girlfriend, or wayward relative move into the home without understanding the consequences. Once that person establishes residency, they have just as much right to be there as the person named on the lease or the deed.

It takes a court-ordered eviction to get them out of the house. So many citizens are of the opinion that they can put out their shack-up boyfriend or girlfriend anytime they please because that person is "not on the lease" or "doesn't pay any of the bills." This simply isn't true, but don't tell that to the person wanting the former love of his or her life put out of the house upon demand. The combination of ignorance of the law and hostility toward the domestic partner often leads these people to misdirect their anger at the police. We are the agents who have the misfortune of telling them what they don't want to hear.

On this domestic call, the obese 300-pound welfare recipient caller demanded that we put out her 98-pound weakling boyfriend who had lived there for several years. I explained calmly that the law did not permit this amid the profane shouts of dismay from the complainant. The only thing bigger than this woman's physique was her foul-mouthed, piercing voice. She continued to berate us as we walked outside toward our cruisers. She ended her profane tirade with, "You fucking cops never do jack shit!" Mike, undaunted, turned around and yelled back at her, "That's right, fat hog!" That was all it took. Now shamed by the type of language she could understand, she returned inside and slammed the door. There was no return call.

There was another trend that began in the 1990s that made the street cop's job more frustrating. Chief William Hegarty essentially issued the decree that if a citizen calls and wants a cop, that citizen gets a cop. This was management kicking the can down the road. Rather than being honest with the public and informing them that not everything can be—nor should be—dealt with by the police, the chief put it on the backs of the patrolmen and women to deal with every nonsensical complaint.

His policy took away almost all of the call takers' discretion when screening out calls that should not merit a police response. It caused an inordinate number of calls that were silly for an officer to attend and that were certainly a waste of time. It created a lot more work for patrol officers and was a huge morale killer—especially for old guys like Stinky who remembered a time when common sense was applied.

On one such call, Mike was sent to a report that a church van was parked in a different space in the church parking lot located down the street from the caller. For some reason, the complainant thought this was somehow suspicious and required a police response. This caller wasn't reporting that the church van had been vandalized and wasn't reporting anyone breaking into it. He didn't mention anything other than that the van was parked at a different location in the lot than he was used to seeing. But he wanted to see a cop, so a cop was sent. Unfortunately for Mr. OCD complainant, he got Stinky.

51

Mike tried his best to be patient as the complainant explained his reason for calling. Finally, however, Stinky was overcome by the stupidity of the call. His lecture to the caller was swift and firm: "That's the church's van! That van and where it's parked is no concern of yours! Your job is to keep your eyes on the road when you drive by that church and to care for *your* family and *your* property. From now on that van is not your business! Don't ever call about something this stupid again!" If management wasn't going to inject common sense into call taking, a career street cop surely would.

I developed a close friendship with Mike. Off duty, I would sometimes go up to what he referred to as his "shack" in the woods in Luther, Michigan. We would drive the back roads shooting the breeze and looking for deer or bear sign. Other times he would come over to my cabin. We would shoot bows, share hunting stories, and drink beer sitting around bonfires well into the early morning hours. Mike made me a cooking tripod out of old bed frame rails. We would sometimes use it to cook over an open fire.

One time we were watching an old John Wayne western set in the 1800s. "We should've lived in those times," Mike said with a distant gaze. We both loved the independence and ruggedness that the wilderness provided. Mike's shack and my cabin were as close as we could come to that rugged lifestyle in our modern age.

Stinky was a lot older than me, so he had experienced a lot more outdoor adventure. He had hunted mule deer in Montana and had regularly gone walleye fishing in Canada. He is one of the few people I know who fell through the ice while ice fishing and lived to tell about it. It was clear from listening to his stories of the great outdoors that his antics weren't limited to the GRPD.

In Canada while on a fishing trip, his group had a scavenging black bear that regularly wandered into the campground and ravaged the trash barrels looking for food. As the week went on, the bear became more daring and Mike and his fishing party more intoxicated. One day when the bear made his appearance, he stuck his entire head into the trash barrel near Stinky's camp site. This prompted Stinky's uncle to offer the challenge, "Mike, go kick that bear in the nuts." He wanted to have Mike provide a little extra excitement for the now camp-side fishermen.

Mike was lubricated with enough booze to accept his uncle's challenge. He snuck up behind the bear, who still had his head completely immersed in the trash barrel, and kicked the bear in the backside. The bear removed his head from the trash barrel with breakneck speed, letting out a savage, primal growl as Mike ran away. The bear immediately gave chase. The only thing that saved Mike was his head start. Stinky made it to a nearby porta-potty and slammed the door with the bear right on his heels.

The large boar slammed his body repeatedly at the door of the outhouse. The porta-potty rocked back and forth, over and over again. Stinky had to keep his back against the rear wall and his legs outstretched against the door to keep the bear from getting at him. This went on for about two hours before Mike's uncle and the rest of the guys from his party sheepishly summoned the Ontario Conservation Department. Conservation officers used a tranquilizer dart to incapacitate the bear and allow a shaken Stinky to escape from a harrowing—and legendary--outhouse ordeal.

After that incident, bears were the only animal that made Mike squeamish. Shortly before retiring, he bought a .45 caliber derringer that he carried whenever he was even a short distance away from his shack in Luther, "just in case a bear was around."

The mid-1990s were the most enjoyable of my career. I was now on third shift at an age when I enjoyed the culture and comradery the night shift offered. We had a great mix of veteran officers and some of us younger guys. Together we formed what affectionately became known as "Jager PD."

Captain Phil Jager led the GRPD third shift for a generation. He was far and away the best unit commander I ever worked for. He had the rare ability to buck the chief and run his unit with a pragmatism that the challenging hours and low staffing levels required. He was a street cop's captain. He took the time to get to know his guys and he knew their strengths and weaknesses. He looked out for the men in his charge. Captain Jager would often go out on the street and respond to calls with us. PU-3 (night shift) in those days was like a family. On most nights I enjoyed coming into work. It never was the same after Captain Jager left.

I had some good arrests back then, too. One night I spotted a car driving around Little Caesar's Pizza near closing time with its lights out. I had been heading to 17 to meet up with Stinky, but this deserved a closer look. I stopped the vehicle as it left the parking lot traveling southbound on Fuller Avenue. As I lit up the back window of the car with my cruiser's spotlight, I noticed a rear passenger frantically shoving something under the seat in front of him. It turned out that he was trying to hide a sawed-off, 20-gauge shotgun. We speculated that he had been casing the Little Caesar's before robbing it because a similar robbery had occurred at a Little Caesar's in the neighboring city of Kentwood the week prior, during which employees were tied up and forced into the cooler. I'm not sure if detectives ever linked the two crimes, but the robberies stopped once this guy was locked up.

Put to the test

Jager PD was put to the test in 1993 when Grand Rapids had its most violent year ever, with 34 homicides. Something like 31 of them occurred in the summer months when we were the most short-handed due to officer vacations. I remember a couple of different nights during that summer when I would start my shift on a shooting and end my shift on a shooting. Our tight-knit third shift stuck together, though, and we weathered the storm despite being under-staffed.

I also had an atypical, potentially life-threatening experience during this time. The incident began when a young woman was abducted at a Meijer store just outside the city limits. The kidnapper forced the woman to drive him to her apartment inside the city. Once there, the suspect raped her. The perpetrator was high on drugs, and when he passed out in the apartment the victim escaped and called police.

Numerous officers converged on the scene, myself included. The perpetrator was now fully awake, paranoid, and going berserk. He attempted to flee by jumping off a second story balcony, only to be tackled by us when he hit the snow-covered ground. This guy was in a total drug-induced rage and seemed to have super-human strength. It took something like six or eight of us to handcuff him.

It was the dead of winter and I had small cuts on my hands due to my skin cracking in the low humidity. These cuts were opened as I and other officers fought with the suspect. The perpetrator was also bleeding from self-inflicted cuts he made after he came unhinged. I got some of the perpetrator's blood on my hands and possibly into my open cuts. Shortly after the arrest, I was informed that the suspect was believed to be HIV-positive.

Back in the mid-1990s, tests for HIV were not instant as they are now. It took a few days before we learned definitively that the suspect did not have HIV. However, I still went for testing for several months to ensure that I did not contract HIV or hepatitis from this guy. Shortly after his arrest, the individual hung himself in jail.

I always knew that I could die while being a police officer. However, the prospect of dying from AIDS due to blood contact with a suspect was not exactly going out in a blaze of glory. Communicable diseases remain something that street cops face every day thanks to the type of citizenry we have contact with.

I relished my time working with Stinky and all of the veteran officers on night shift in the early to mid-1990s. I was often the youngest guy in "Baker Sector" by twenty years or more. The experience and steady hands they brought to the job were invaluable to a still-young officer trying establish himself in the trade. On most nights, the four guys I worked with on the northeast side brought a hundred years or more of combined experience to the shift.

To be accepted by the older guys I admired was a tremendous confidence builder. During this time, I began to come into my own as a police officer. I honed my craft and achieved sure footing in my career by learning from these veteran officers.

Things were beginning to change, however. As the summer of 1997 rolled around, Stinky informed us that he was retiring in July. He had put in 30 years at GRPD—all of them on patrol and all of them on nights. Mike's pending retirement created mixed emotions in me. I was certainly happy for a guy who had unquestionably put in his time. However, I also knew that GRPD would be much different without him.

I was sullen during Stinky's last shift. I remember nearly tearing up when the captain afforded him the honor of reading off the patrol assignments at his last line-up. Unfortunately, I was training a recruit so I didn't get to spend much time with Stinky on his final night.

He didn't disappoint when it came to providing us with one last legendary Venroyism. In classic Mike Venroy fashion, he got to tell off a deserving jerk on his final drive into headquarters on this final shift. Mike had been sent to provide traffic control on a crash on East Beltline Avenue. It was his final call. When the crash had been cleared, Mike turned his cruiser around to head into the motor pool. It was the end of a long career.

However, some crusading citizen with an axe to grind with the police didn't like the way Stinky had veered across the lanes of traffic to enter I-96 to go back to HQ. The upset citizen followed Mike all the way downtown, eventually pulling next to Mike and rolling down his window. He told Mike he thought he had made an illegal lane change and that he was going to report him to Internal Affairs. Now within sight of headquarters, Mike pointed in that direction and replied, "Go ahead. The building is right over there, ASSHOLE!!" It was the ultimate "take this job and shove it" coup de grace. Mike couldn't have cared less if the guy reported him. In thirty more seconds he would be retired and beyond the reach of Internal Affairs or anyone else.

Big changes, new leadership

The flood gates opened at GRPD shortly after Stinky left, with numerous retirements and officers shuffling from nights to days. By now Chief Hegarty had put an end to Jager PD and relegated Captain Jager to working the Special Services Unit for the remainder of his career. It was the end of a golden era. It was also the beginning of the end of GRPD being a fun place to work. It lost its feeling of being a tight-knit family. Soon after, we would get a new chief, Harry Dolan, who had a completely different philosophy on how things should be done.

For me, Mike Venroy is emblematic of this era at GRPD. However, it could've been a host of other officers I had the privilege of working with during this time. There was James "Zippy" Zaidel, Stinky's best friend at the department and every bit the character Mike was. There was Pete Woodfield, the steady ghetto cop who had a nose for being Johnny-on-the-spot when it came to knowing where bad guy would be. There was the classy Bruce Weaver. I've already mentioned the grace and heroism of John Klomparens and Craig Miller. I will always appreciate the wise leadership of sergeants Bob "Buffy" Price, Jerry Rauwerda, Larry Tuttle, and Bob Mesman.

There are too many great officers who had a positive effect on me to name them all. To the casual reader unfamiliar with these guys, their names will mean nothing. But to me, I owe them all a debt of gratitude and it's only fitting I acknowledge their profound impact.

I stayed in touch with Stinky after he retired. He moved permanently to his beloved Luther, soon buying a five-acre parcel to put up a more deluxe "shack." He continued to hunt and remained interested in bows and guns. He later worked for the Lake County Sheriff's Department as a correctional officer in a juvenile correctional facility. A new generation of cops were exposed to his stories and Venroyisms.

In one such instance, deputies were instructed to report to defensive tactics training wearing sweatpants instead of their usual duty uniform. Mike didn't comply with the directive, prompting a co-worker to comment, "Mike, you're not wearing your sweats." Stinky responded with his usual, no-holds-barred wit delivered in his distinctive baritone voice, "That's because I don't plan on sweatin'!"

Typical of friends who move away and are in different stages of life, my contact with Stinky became less frequent as the years went by. In winter 2013, I received a call from Mike while up at my cabin. The call was mostly small talk but, in retrospect, he seemed preoccupied and trying to tell me something. He wanted to come over to my cabin for a visit. But I was about to head back to Grand Rapids for a family obligation and I had to take a rain check. Before hanging up, I was surprised when the normally non-spiritual Stinky asked if I still had contact with GRPD Police Chaplain Fr. Dennis Morrow. Fr. Morrow had on occasion come up to the cabin for visits and Stinky was aware of this.

Mike went on to say that he had not been baptized and wished to speak to Fr. Morrow about doing so. I was busy and didn't give the call much thought at the time, other than thinking it was good to hear from Mike again. I later was struck by how hauntingly similar the call was to Andy Kilvinksi's final call to Roy Fehler in *The New Centurions*. Mike was calling to say good-bye.

A couple of weeks later, word trickled down to me that Mike Venroy had died. He had suffered a massive heart attack that morning while at home and eventually passed away after being flown to a Grand Rapids hospital in a desperate attempt to save him. He was 72 years old.

I felt a shadow cross my heart when I heard he had passed. I did not cry, but in addition to sadness I felt like the last vestiges of my youth were now dead with him. I finished out the work week in a reflective and somber mood. I knew a big part of my past was now gone.

As usual, I headed to my cabin after completion of my work week. To my astonishment, on my answering machine was a message from none other than Stinky! He called to ask me a question about broadheads for his hunting arrows. He apparently left the message the evening before he died and I had not been to the cabin to check my messages since he had passed. It very well could have been his last phone call.

While it was a shock to hear a dead man's voice on my answering machine, I took considerable comfort in the message. It brought a smile to my face knowing that, even in the last hours of his life, Mike was dreaming of hunting and finding the right combination of gear to get that next big buck. He went out on his terms and with all his faculties. While it would have been nice had he lived longer, it would have been devastating to Mike if he suffered the fate of "the long good-bye" as so many people do. Stinky wasn't the kind of guy to go out wearing diapers, ravaged by dementia, and not knowing who he was. With the possible exception of dying while dragging a trophy buck out of the woods, Stinky went out the way I think he would've liked.

Right after Stinky's message on my answering machine was one from his wife, Mary, informing me of the fateful news. Mike had a long history of heart problems starting after he retired from GRPD. His wife told me that his doctor told him a few weeks prior to his death that his heart was deteriorating further and they didn't know how much time he had left. Mike, however, did not tell Mary or anyone else. She found this out from the doctor after he passed. In one of the most touching gestures I have ever experienced, Mary gave me Mike's old derringer as a keepsake—the one he always carried while in bear country. I cherish it very much.

There will be people familiar with GRPD who read this book and question why I chose an often crude, intemperate man—one who was far from a go-getter—as the subject of an entire chapter. They will contend that there were certainly "better" police officers than Mike Venroy from that period. They will have missed the point. Stinky, along with the other guys I mentioned, was the face and voice of a now-extinct brand of officer from the old school policing of the 1960s that we admired. That style eventually led into the modern policing rooted in the 1990s that we came out of. He represents a time gone by.

For me and many of the patrol officers who started around the time I did, Mike and his kind remind us of an age of wonder and innocence in our own lives and the embodiment of all the goodness, flaws, and complexities of the career patrolman. We look at him and his shenanigans with a nostalgic fondness, like hearing an old song on the radio. Even in the final days of my own career, certain Venroyisms would come to mind nearly daily and I relied on many of them to get me to the finish line. Godspeed, Michael J. Venroy, GRPD Badge #174.

5

Prime Time

Bravery is not the absence of fear, but action in the face of fear.
—Attributed to 18th century writer John Berridge

The length of a career for a patrol officer is dramatically different from that of workers in the private sector. In the corporate world, it is commonplace for workers to come into their own after the age of fifty and to sometimes achieve their greatest accolades and best earning power even later than that. However, a 50-year-old street officer is an old man in the police profession. In fact, a street cop usually enters the prime of his career six to eight years into the job. This can vary, of course, but that prime lasts from around year six through year fourteen at the latest. The job's stress, physical demands, and politics ensures a relatively short-lived career.

I define a police officer's career prime as that period when he or she has experienced enough to handle most situations, yet is still young enough to enjoy the job and adapt. Confidence replaces insecurity. Young-officer overreaction is replaced by tempered judgement. Youthful apprehension yields to a feeling of being in tune with one's patrol beat.

In an officer's prime, the game slows down. Impulsive gung-ho enthusiasm of youth is exchanged for a more balanced approach to policing. The street cop in his prime knows all the major players in his or her patrol district. He knows the habitual offenders, the neighborhood leaders, the problem addresses, and the nooks and crannies of the neighborhood he patrols. It's often the time in an officer's career that he does his best police work, as quality of arrests replaces quantity of arrests. In sports, an athlete would refer to it as "being in the zone."

I was now at this point. It was 1998. With Stinky retired and the successful prosecution of the Josiah Ward case completed, I had entered the prime of my career. I had seven years of eventful patrol experience under my belt in Grand Rapids, in addition to my time with Montcalm County.

After about fifteen years, the prime of a street cop's career quickly fades. From then on, a patrol officer focuses on one thing and one thing only: pension. That doesn't mean the street cop evades his responsibilities after fourteen years on the job. It just means priorities change; he has experienced the first go-round with burnout and the battles of past wars now make it difficult to buy into the company's latest brand of new-fangled policing. He can become set in his ways and cynical. By this stage, the die has been cast. Most officers by this point are aware that they are usually closer to the end than the beginning of a career, which tends to alter priorities.

These time frames, of course, are not applicable to everyone. I've known guys who never calmed down, never stopped chasing taillights (or anything else that moved), and never seemed to understand what the job was really all about—even 25 years into their careers. On the other end of the spectrum, there were some officers who spent their entire careers taking the path of least resistance from the day after they got off probation.

A great illustration of the officer in that prime "zone" occurred when I was in my final year at GRPD—and admittedly well past my own prime. Officer Tom Warwick was (and still is) in this phase of his career. Tom was at police headquarters on his day off to attend court. While walking from the police department to the courthouse, Tom spotted a subject hurriedly exiting a downtown store-front bank with money falling out of his pockets and a handgun in his waistband. Before the bank could even activate its alarm, Officer Warwick nabbed the guy without incident, recovering all the cash and the weapon. He arrested a bank robber before the robbery had even been reported!

When an officer is in his or her prime, the combination of being acutely aware of his surroundings, intently observant, and having the knack for being at the right place at the right time seems to happen with much more frequency than at other stages. Faced with a similar situation, a rookie officer might have been in too much of a hurry to get to court on time and would not be as observant. The older officer would've skipped going to court altogether and would not have been in the area!

An officer's prime typically is also the time when most decide whether to pursue promotion and are aware of where they stand in the department's scheme of things, yet all doors are not yet closed. Some choose to move into management, others take the difficult path of being a union advocate, and others decide to keep their heads down and be "a regular Joe" who does his or her job and goes home.

I chose the most trying road and became a union steward. Throughout the 1990s, I became disgusted with the way patrol was viewed by management. We were the front-line people who took the greatest risks, worked the most difficult hours, and received the bulk of grief from the public. Despite this, a career patrol officer was almost looked upon with condescension by the powers that be. Management at that time nearly always promoted people from specialized units, all but ignoring the street cops. Whenever command had a new pet project, they robbed officers from the street to staff it—no matter how short it left patrol or how it affected emergency response. I wanted to do something about it. I was young and idealistic enough to think that I actually could.

I also could not tolerate the sellout one had to endure to seek promotion. I think if any police officer gives an honest assessment, he or she will conclude that every officer should put in ten years or more on the street before seeking promotion or lateral transfer. Any earlier than that and the officer doesn't have enough time on the street to fully understand patrol and digest all that it encompasses. However, the path to GRPD promotion was (and is) to get off the street as soon as possible and get noticed by a command unit sponsor. No thanks.

My unpretentious, working-class upbringing led me to gravitate more toward being an advocate for the rank and file, rather than choosing the promotional route. I began as the night shift union steward and later became dayshift steward during this time of my career.

This was a big decision. I was still held in relatively high esteem by management at this point. I was not a rising star, but I hadn't been pigeon-holed yet. I knew that if I got heavily involved in the union, bridges could be burned that could later have led to promotion or choice assignments.

Comfortable on the street

By now I was comfortable on the street. I had responded to thousands of calls and was confident in my abilities. I rarely needed supervision and I had an uncanny ability to correctly assess situations in short order. I was a good judge of character when sizing up citizens. I was also beyond the youthful attitude of "it's us versus them" and I didn't take confrontations personally. I could see the various shades of gray in policing.

Perhaps this is best highlighted by an incident that occurred when I had about ten years in with the department. I responded to a purse snatching of an elderly woman which happened in the parking lot of a strip mall in the East Service Area. The description of a black male in his 40's with a stocky build was broadcast by dispatch, along with a clothing description. I was close and arrived on scene within a few minutes of the dispatch.

Sure enough, I located the suspect behind the strip mall rummaging through the contents of the stolen purse. His age and prison muscles made me immediately think he was an ex-con. His mannerisms and appearance led me to believe that this wasn't his first run-in with the law, prompting me to conclude he would flee once he saw me. I tried to roll up on him without being detected, but when I got within 30 or

40 yards, he spotted me and took off on foot. The longest foot pursuit of my career ensued.

The perpetrator had a big head start on me. He ran for all he was worth behind the strip mall and through a brush-filled vacant property. He then ran onto a public golf course as I slowly gained on him. Imagine the surprise of the mostly elderly golfers as a purse snatcher and uniformed police officer ran past them on the various greens! I was around 34 years old and was far from being in the best shape of my life. However, the perpetrator was about ten years older than me and his former prison muscles were no longer toned. This allowed me to keep up.

Slowly I gained on him as he led me on a zig-zag course along fairways, hazards, and in between golfers. The golf course was huge and landmarks non-descript, making it difficult to provide my precise location to responding units. This wasn't going to be the type of foot pursuit where other officers could converge on the suspect along with me. The other guys couldn't find me. This was going to be me versus the purse snatcher in a heavyweight tilt for this guy's freedom.

Finally, as the suspect led me into a small wooded thicket, I caught up to him. All told, we covered over a mile after all the twists and turns. Giving him my best Wyoming Park football tackle, I lunged my shoulder into his back as I wrapped my arms around his midsection from behind. We were both exhausted and he tumbled to the ground like a tree struck by lightning.

The fight was not yet out of him, though, and he continued to resist my attempt at handcuffing him. He was dead tired, but he was still a lot bigger than me and he had the added motivation of losing his freedom for a very long time.

I was so tired and gasping for air that I felt like I was going to throw up, but I still hung on to the suspect. We were both completely spent when the exhausted perpetrator turned to me and pleaded in complete exasperation, "Let's rest a minute." And we did! For a minute or two, he stopped fighting me and I stopped trying to handcuff him. We just lay there catching our breath in this secluded patch of woods. It reminded me of the story from World War I when troops from both sides called a cease fire and sang carols on Christmas Eve.

After our short respite, I finally got the best of him and managed to put the handcuffs on him. We both felt like we had run a marathon as I slowly led him hundreds of yards back to my patrol car, with both of us hunched over and feverishly trying to regain our breath.

I recall this incident because it illustrates the lack of malice between the two of us. It demonstrates the restraint of the professional officer at his peak. The purse snatcher knew I was doing my job. He was doing his best to get away (he was an ex-con on parole), as he knew a long prison sentence was in the offing. I also didn't take his flight as an affront to my authority. Both of us knew the line: I had to catch him, but used no more force than necessary to make the arrest. Conversely, Mr. Purse Snatcher never tried to assault me, nor did he attempt anything more than avoidance of capture. If the Marquess of Queensbury Rules applied to police fights as they did to boxing, this was an example in which we both complied.

The scenario reminds me of the old Warner Bros. Looney Tunes cartoon where Sam Sheepdog and Ralph Wolf beat the hell out of each other throughout the cartoon. Then the whistle blows at the end of the day and they stop fighting and simply say to each other, "See you tomorrow, Sam" and "See you tomorrow, Ralph." It was just business. It wasn't personal.

At this stage of my career I could determine which part of the state a car was from just by looking at the letter configuration of license plates. Each Michigan Secretary of State branch is given an allotment of registration plates that begin with the same series of letters; all combinations of these letters and corresponding numbers are assigned to people registering their vehicles. In my prime, I could recognize these letters and tell from that alone if the car had been registered in Grand Rapids and in which area of the city, or if it was from out of town—without even running the plate through the Secretary of State computer network. When an officer is at his best, he has that sort of mental acuity.

Confidence reigns supreme when an officer is in the prime of his or her career. Once I responded to a big-box appliance store on a disgruntled customer refusing to leave. The store manager reported that the customer would not leave after a civil dispute did not get resolved to the customer's liking. I noted immediately that the guy appeared odd. He looked like a gypsy or transient. After the manager again ordered him to leave the store, I informed him he would be arrested for trespassing if he refused to go.

Now cornered, the guy was caught between backing down or making a stand that would lead to his arrest. I could almost see the wheels turning in his head. Suddenly, he concocted a third option. He stood up straight, kicked his heels together, and feigned a fainting spell as he dropped to the ground and pretended to be unconscious.

Faking a health crisis isn't uncommon among those trying to avoid jail. However, usually the preferred method is pretending to have chest pains or claiming to have swallowed drugs. Play-acting a state of unconsciousness was a new twist.

Undeterred and not buying his phony health crisis for a second, I asked the staff to bring me a flat cart. My partner and I loaded the flopper onto the cart and wheeled him toward the front entrance where our cruisers were parked—as if we were simply wheeling out a big screen TV. Store customers turned into curious spectators as I steered the suspect-adorned flat cart through the various aisles. As I reached the line at the register, I asked one of the amused customers, "Sir, did you order an asshole from the stockroom?" He burst out laughing. A rookie officer would likely have been totally flustered when faced with a similar situation and turned it into a major production.

When a street cop is in his prime, he works in crisp coordination with his fellow beat cops. There is an almost unspoken synchronicity, where each officer knows how the other will respond. Each officer knows the other's way of doing things and his or her likely next move.

I recall a time when I was on nights on the northeast end working a two-man car with Chad Kooyer. Chad was my favorite guy to work with. Chad is highly intelligent and detail-oriented. We had similar attitudes, interests, and policing styles. Eventually this led to each of us having the ability to know what the other was going to do before he did it, like an all-pro quarterback and his favorite receiver working in perfect tandem.

On this night, Chad and I had detained a couple of juvenile curfew violators in a quiet residential neighborhood. While we were dealing with the two kids, a call came in the same neighborhood of a suspicious subject on a bicycle who had been seen trying to get into houses. Seconds after the broadcast, we saw the suspect on the same street, but behind us. Chad was driving and I was in the passenger front seat. The element of surprise was going to be critical in us having any chance of grabbing this guy before he took off, so we could not turn the patrol car around.

Chad instinctively put the cruiser in reverse and quietly and slowly backed up toward the suspect with the cruiser lights off. Without prompting, I grabbed my door handle and confirmed, "I'll get ready with the door!" Let's just say the door was used in what I'll refer to as a "dynamic application of a takedown technique of a bicyclist" and we collared the burglar without pursuit. The whole thing took a matter of seconds. The juvenile curfew violators in our backseat looked on with pleased amazement at the perfect coordination of efforts between both officers. I knew what Chad was doing and he knew how I would respond without any spoken word necessary.

During this stage of a career, the prime-time street officer can relate to the citizens on his beat better than at other stages. This is again due to the officer being young enough to relate to younger residents, but old enough and respected enough to not be taken advantage of nor intimidated.

There was an incident where I observed a juvenile firing a revolver into the air in the Creston Plaza projects on the northeast end. A foot chase with the subject ensued. I lost sight of him briefly, but relocated him moments later. I eventually caught him and took him into custody, but he had ditched the gun during the time he was out of my sight. He wouldn't admit to having had the gun, even though I had seen him shooting it.

This kid had seen me patrol his neighborhood for many years, so I had some credibility and rapport with him. I calmly appealed to his sense of decency, hoping to get him to fess up to where he had dropped the gun. I explained to him that there were many young kids living in the projects. I reminded him how tragic it would be if a small child, maybe even his little brother, found that gun and shot someone. Finally, the guilt trip had its desired effect. He wouldn't admit to having the gun, but he informed me that I might find it behind the front tire of a particular car in the lot. I returned there and, lo and behold, found the gun right where he had described it.

My best asset as an officer was my ability to quickly and usually correctly assess a situation and read the players involved. My next best quality was my communication skills. Despite being an introvert, I always had the ability to speak well with others and to articulate my point in a convincing way. This included not only coworkers, but also citizens from all walks of life. I could be verbally forceful when I needed to, but I could also put citizens at ease.

Weaknesses also present

My weaknesses as an officer were apparent to me by now as well. I was not one of those officers with great ability to remember names and faces. I knew some guys who could meet a person one time and remember all pertinent information about the person from that point on. That was not me.

There were also officers who had an amazing knack for positioning themselves perfectly to catch the bad guy (or woman). GRPD officers Mike Lafave and Brian Grooms were the best I ever saw at this. Those two guys had remarkable skills that seemed to always make them perfectly situated when a major crime occurred, and they usually got their man. I never developed the skill to anywhere near the level that these guys did. I did become a very competent patrolman, however. I just was never the guy with the steel trap mind or the officer who had a nose for the bad guy's next move. But I learned how to compensate for my shortcomings and maximize my good qualities.

69

I remained a field training officer for the early part of this period. On one occasion, I was training a recruit when we came across two guys fighting in a parking lot. It had been a busy summer night, so my recruit and I were attempting to eat our lunch on the fly between calls. I was in the middle of downing mine when we spotted the fight. The rookie was startled when I exited the cruiser while still eating an apple, as the fisticuffs raged in front of me. I could see that this was clearly a case of mutual combat, with both parties willing participants. I assumed a position similar to a referee monitoring a boxing match with the apple portion of my lunch still in hand. Once the disorderly subjects had spent all of their energy, I asked each of them if the dust-up had resolved their grievance. When each exhaustedly nodded in the affirmative, I ordered them to shake hands and sent them on their way—while still nonchalantly munching on my lunch.

My trainee was impressed by the casual, but perfectly practical, resolution to the situation and also my confidence in remedying it. She chuckled and shook her head in disbelief for the next ten minutes. She had assumed we would hurriedly jump out of our patrol car, scream for backup over the radio, and then wade into the middle of the fight. She thought a trip to the jail was in the offing, with both battered combatants kicking and screaming the entire way. This would surely be followed up by an hour of paperwork to take us off the street.

That's how it is for a veteran patrol officer at this stage—not only is there confidence in his or her abilities, but also the experience that inspires well-applied discretion for solutions to problems that may not always require textbook applications of police operations. But they produce fair resolutions. Instead of taking ourselves out of service for an hour on a busy summer night for nothing more than a misdemeanor disorderly conduct arrest, we resolved the situation just as effectively.

Life changes

As well as my job was going, I was at a very difficult crossroad in my personal life. Turning thirty years old really bothered me. I had no problem turning forty, or even recently when I turned fifty years old.

But my thirtieth birthday knocked me for a loop. It regurgitated a lot of feelings that I had brewing inside me since my adolescent years, primarily the insecurity that comes with the belief that something must be wrong with me because my life wasn't like everyone else's. I was not yet at peace with a life mission that involved the proverbial path less traveled.

At age thirty, I still wasn't married. My interests and priorities were different from most of my peers. I felt like I was being left behind. My close friends were all married and most had children by now, which only added to my feelings of being the outlier. I hadn't found what I was looking for in a wife, or life in general for that matter. The women I seemed to develop feelings for were often dysfunctional women with personality defects or were party girls. Of course, these situations always ended in disaster with even more feelings of confusion.

Maybe my expectations were too high. Maybe I was too selfish and full of myself. Maybe I just wasn't meant to be married. I really didn't know at this point and it often left me confused and sometimes feeling like an outcast.

After I turned thirty and was still single in family-oriented West Michigan, friends and family were noticing and commenting. Instead of getting compliments and slaps on the back such as, "Dave, I see you're still playing the field. Good for you!" I now heard, "What are you waiting for?" or "When are you going to settle down?" Being single didn't bother me. I liked it. It was my insecurity that I wasn't in the same place as everyone else that still tormented me at this time in my life.

By now I had a new house I had built in the Grand Rapids suburb of Hudsonville. My job was demanding but going well. I was developing a reputation as a capable union representative and my hunting property was progressing as planned. The previous autumn, I had killed two bucks in the first two days of bow season.

Everything in my life should have been pointing toward happiness, or at least contentment, but I was mostly depressed and perplexed. I still often dealt with these feelings by binge drinking and carousing with good-time girls. I never got out of control and neither affected my work. I never became a drunk or sleazy "player." I was far from being the police version of Charlie Sheen. However, the partying gave me false relief from the feelings of sadness, albeit temporarily. The attention given to me by the party girls served not only as escape, but also served as an ego stroke that eased my feelings of insecurity and feelings of not belonging because I lived a life that didn't conform to cookie-cutter societal norms.

Finally, the day after my 31st birthday and in total disgust with myself, I began making the major changes I needed to make. My way of using diversions to deal with the way I felt wasn't working. It wasn't a case of hitting rock bottom. My life wasn't spinning out of control. I just needed a personal and spiritual tune-up, along with a reality check.

I finally ended my denial. I suffered from depression and I needed to acknowledge it. My feelings weren't always caused by situational external circumstances as I had always tried to rationalize in the past. No. I suffered from a condition. This was a hard thing to acknowledge when you are supposed to be a tough cop. After always being the helper, it was hard admitting that I needed help. How could I need help? I was the tough guy who could watch a man blow his head off in front of me and keep soldiering on.

I was eventually diagnosed with a form of depression known as dysthymia. Dysthymia is better known as chronic depression. Its symptoms include a long-term, low-grade form of depression. It can also make a person more susceptible to instances of major depression, which I had suffered twice before. People suffering from dysthymia often take ten or more years to seek diagnosis and treatment. It took me fifteen. Later, I was also diagnosed with Seasonal Affective Disorder, a form of depression related to low sunlight, which amplified my depression in the autumn and during Michigan's long winter.

I describe chronic depression to people as like going through life wearing ankle weights. Everything is a chore. Finding happiness by just smelling the roses is nearly impossible. I can experience joy, but it is short-lived. Bright, jubilant moments of happiness for others appear to me in muted colors. My senses related to happiness are dulled, and I do not experience them with the same intensity or fervor as others. The only time I feel normal or content is when I'm medicating my condition with alcohol, but that is clearly a dead-end street that I cannot pursue regularly and still keep my life in order.

Change needed to be more than just treatment for the biological and psychological causes of dysthymia, however. I also immersed myself in deep spiritual and inner-personal self-reflection. I concluded I wasn't living my life like the person I wanted to be.

Eventually I developed several rules that I knew I needed to live by to promote my personal spiritual and mental well-being. Really, they aren't much different than the "avoid punch and Judy" adage recruits are taught in the police academy.

First, I determined that I needed to avoid dating dysfunctional women. By this I mean broken women with personality disorders and defects. This may seem obvious to most, but there is often a rescuer quality cops possess that leads us to want to help these broken women out of their situations. These women also tend to compensate for their personality defects by consciously or subconsciously learning how to push someone's buttons and to manipulate. They also tend to be spontaneous and fun. For a structured, often-depressed guy like me, there is an appeal in that diversion or occasional "walk on the wild side."

However, dating a dysfunctional or party girl is like dabbling in crack cocaine: It might seem like pure ecstasy the first few times you partake but once hooked, life spins out of control. I learned that I can be polite and kind to them and maybe even offer advice or support, but I can't be their Jesus. I learned I cannot save them. They are not only fool's gold for me; they are my kryptonite.

Secondly, I needed to seek socialization outside of the booze and bar crowd. I consider the cop bar crowd to be kissing cousins of the dysfunctional class of women. Every bigger department has this party group of people. It includes cops, civilian employees, and cop groupies. They are the first ones to go to every police social outing, every cheap drink night, and frequent the bars that become known as cop hangouts.

Many of these people may have good qualities, do their jobs well, and are a lot of fun. But the booze and party crowd are also usually fair-weather, frivolous friends who seek only instant gratification and a good time in the moment. Many are also over-invested in the cop subculture and lead unbalanced lives as a result.

For me, these people may be good for laughs, but they are usually shallow and unreliable as true, long-term friends. Their live-for-the-moment tendencies often conflict with my personality traits and values. Commiserating with people fixed in an arrested state of late adolescent development is just not going to work for the mental well-being of a focused, goal-oriented man who subjugates instant gratification for the benefit of long-term objectives. In short, I found I can't rely on them or trust them outside of the moment. I never really joined the cop booze and bar crowd in earnest, but I had resided on its fringes at various times throughout this period of my career.

I also found I needed to keep my options open and keep my life free from encumbrances that made me feel trapped or hopeless. This meant remaining single and realizing I flourished by keeping my life simple and regimented. I do best with a structured, disciplined lifestyle whereby I control my own destiny. Things need to make sense and need to be done for a purpose. I also subscribe to the adage of "one day at a time" and don't worry about what others think. This was a hard place for me to get to, as acceptance by others had in the past alleviated some of my insecurities.

Finally, I put my trust in the Lord and in the devout belief that God never gives us more than we can handle. I try to follow his rules and seek out his plan for me. I concluded that God has a different mission for all of us, and just because mine may be different from friends and coworkers didn't mean there was something wrong with me.

My intent with this book is not to preach to anyone. This book is not intended to be about religious conversion or inspiration. I mention my devotion to faith only because it is a large part of my well-being—a well-being that I didn't achieve until this period of my life.

It is also a worthwhile side note to point out that I have observed a common theme over the years with officers who fall into corruption or suffer ethical lapses. In addition to partaking of "punch and Judy," these officers have been mostly devoid of religion in their lives to provide them with a moral compass, as well as the divine grace that serves as succor in a career filled with battling evil and tragedy.

I was also very fortunate in my spiritual life to have cultivated a friendship with our police chaplain, Father Dennis Morrow. Fr. Morrow at times rode with me on patrol. I could always seek his counsel during periods of spiritual confusion. Just being in the presence of such a holy man had a calming effect on me during difficult times.

I spent much of 1998 and 1999 applying the changes I was determined to make in my everyday life. Instead of going to police social functions, I spent my days off socializing with my non-cop friends. I rediscovered my boyhood love of fishing, making it my goal to explore all the lakes within thirty miles of my cabin.

I stayed away from the bar flies and cop groupies, even if it meant going long periods without dating at all. I really became comfortable with my own company. I went to union meetings and social responsibilities associated with my union functions. This did include occasional meetings at the cop bars to rub elbows with members, but it was done for that purpose and not solely as a social outlet.

In the fall, I submersed myself in my usual hunting, but also in following sports. I had been a big fan of University of Michigan football since the Bo Schembechler days. By 1998, some skinny kid from California named Tom Brady was battling Michigan high school football and baseball standout Drew Henson for the starting job at quarterback. I'm not too proud to admit that, back then, I favored local hero Drew Henson. As the years went by, however, Tom Brady became my favorite athlete. I greatly admired his strict, disciplined work ethic and unrelenting pursuit of becoming the best athlete he could possibly be.

I became an avid reader again, often focusing on books about history or politics. I found solace in the biographies of great leaders. One of my favorite books was Henry David Thoreau's *Walden*. Thoreau seemed to struggle with same life questions I did. I could completely relate to the rugged simplicity of his lifestyle, which also included similar intense introspection.

Ever since working at the theater as a teen, I also found movies to be a great diversion and at times inspiring. I liked uplifting movies like *Rocky* or *Apollo 13* as much as anyone. However, the movies I related to most were films such as *Unforgiven* or *Raging Bull*, where the characters were flawed or full of contradictions. I could identify with characters who had to overcome a dark side. Cinema supplemented my reading and helped solidify my commitment to the changes I had made in my life.

I'm not asserting that the rules I outlined or my lifestyle should apply to everyone. These rules are what I needed to subscribe to for my mental and spiritual well-being. Just like as a cop I recognized my strengths and weaknesses, I acknowledged the same in my personal and spiritual life. Now I began attempting to accentuate the positives and minimize the weaknesses in my personal life—or at least the temptations that lead to my weaknesses—just as I had done as a police officer. I am programed in a way that these rules kept me on the straight and narrow. I've found that when I abide by these personal principles, my life flourishes. Things make sense. There is no cure for dysthymia, but when I stick to the rules, it becomes manageable.

I wish I could say that I always followed these tenants from this time forward. Mostly, I have. But there have been a few times when I could rationalize bending the rules, even at the end of my career. I quickly found, however, that there can be no cutting of corners. When I cut corners, it's like dancing with the devil and the devil always leads.

Changes at GRPD

At GRPD, the long reign of Chief William Hegarty ended with his retirement. Hegarty had been police chief since the early 1980s. For officers of my generation, he was the only chief we had ever known. In 1998, Harry Dolan became chief of police. Dolan was a New York City native who came to Grand Rapids from a small town named Lumberton in North Carolina. Chief Dolan had made his bones by promoting community policing. He had a very different managerial style than Chief Hegarty. This naturally planted seeds of conflict with the union as Dolan attempted to implement his plan, sometimes in contradiction to our contract and established past practices.

Our union president at the time was Ed Hillyer. Ed was a pit bull and was perfectly suited for the labor struggles we had going on then. I tried to be an active steward and help Ed with numerous innovations that gave our union the teeth it needed to handle the battles at hand. One such thing was helping Ed get a union political action committee started.

I also lobbied hard to get a more sophisticated union newsletter in place to assist us in communicating our message to members and city leaders. I served as editor of the newsletter. We incorporated editorial-style articles critical of department policies that we felt were harming our members and the community. We used the talents of some of our artistic members to draft political cartoons lampooning the chief's anti-worker ideas.

The new union newsletter was highly controversial and at the same time very effective. One issue even became the lead story on the local evening news and on the front page of our local newspaper, *The Grand Rapids Press*! It had accomplished my goal of giving us a larger profile and it gave the administration pause before unilaterally imposing its will on our members, lest they endure the wrath of our next newsletter commentary.

The place I was at made me approachable to both the young guys and the veteran officers regarding their union matters. I had been around long enough that I could relate to the interests of the older officers, but I was young enough where the bulk of my career still hung in the balance. I was able to advocate for all members.

Involvement in departmental politics led me to a short-lived stint on the GRPD Board of Awards. The board was intended to represent a cross section of officers and command personnel for the purpose of awarding deserving employees with commendations for outstanding work. The board also selected the Grand Rapids Police Department's Officer of the Year. Unfortunately, over the years the board had largely eroded into a group that did little more than conduct a popularity contest. The recipients of most awards—especially Officer of the Year—were almost always "the beautiful people." The winners were nearly exclusively people in specialized units or those on the fast track to promotion. On the rare occasion that a real cop was selected, it usually was late in a career and was more of a lifetime achievement award given to a patrolman near retirement and who was no longer a threat to the powers that be.

Real cops viewed the Board of Awards as a joke. I wanted to work toward changing this. I took great pride in pushing the board hard to select Chad Kooyer for 1997's Officer of the Year. It wasn't a payback to a friend; it was truly deserved. Chad embodied the conscientious and dedicated officer, but it was much more than that. Patrol needed one of its own to receive the highest award to restore a modicum of legitimacy to it. Eventually, largely due to my relentless prodding, the board came to recognize how deserving Chad was and selected him as Officer of the Year.

The annual banquet at which Chad accepted the honor was the only awards banquet I attended in my 26 years. I was quickly replaced the next year and the Board of Awards returned to largely being a popularity contest that might as well have been picking a high school homecoming king and queen.

The prime of my career as a police officer was productive. I did some good police work and got involved in the department's inner workings and politics. My career path was now established, for better or worse. I also righted the ship in my personal life.

Admittedly a complex man often haunted by internal emotional conflict, I have many times struggled with God's mission for my life. The 1990s turned into the new millennium. By 2005, I may have been leaving my prime as a street cop, but I was about to enter a new career phase that became as much of a calling as the one I had fifteen years earlier that led me to police work. For the next half decade, I never doubted my life's mission. I was about to enter the most demanding, but rewarding, years of my career.

6

"Union Boss"

...But my ethics are very simple. Live and let live and those who try to destroy you, make it your business that they don't and that they have problems.

—James R. Hoffa

In a culture that puts too much emphasis on celebrity and fame, it's easy to miss the giants who live among us. Bruce Harvey is one such person. Bruce is a politically-streetwise labor leader who was the man behind the scene in many Grand Rapids political campaigns in the 1990s and early 2000s. A Vietnam veteran, Bruce became a union truck driver and eventually worked his way up to business agent and political director for Teamsters Local 406 in Grand Rapids. Bruce had a brilliant mind for politics and organizing. In deference to his great talent as a grassroots kingmaker, I referred to him affectionately as "The Godfather."

He had a natural gift for connecting with people. Due to his down-to-earth personality and tremendous gift of gab, Bruce could persuade and inspire people as he simultaneously instilled confidence in them.

Bruce never forgot where he came from and he never sold out. He really cared about the common working man—even police officers who were not members of the Teamsters. He was quick with witty, folksy quips that contained a common man's touch such as, "Of course Republicans are pro-life. They want you to be born so they can spend the next eighty years kicking the shit out of you!"

Bruce Harvey and other local union leaders created a loose-knit conglomeration of West Michigan unions that became known as Friends of Labor. Its goal was to get organized labor a seat at the political table in the ultra-conservative, Republican Grand Rapids area. Bruce pointed to how, for generations, city and county commission policy was driven by the financial interests of several wealthy families and how these families wielded undue influence over public policy. Through their vast political power, they controlled the appointment of department heads, government contracts, and city and county financial coffers.

The dominance of this Grand Rapids political machine had largely been unchallenged since the wealthy furniture moguls, along with influential Dutch Christian Reformed Church leaders, successfully beat back the Grand Rapids Furniture Strike of 1911. During the strike, both the bishop of the Catholic archdiocese and the city's mayor supported the workers, much to the dismay of the furniture barons.

The strike led to a Grand Rapids City Charter revision that put in place a weak mayoral system of government headed by a city manager, who essentially ran the city. By keeping the mayor weak, it ensured the wealthy industrialists that no single rogue mayor could be elected by future worker uprisings, and thereby steer city government against their financial interests. The city manager would be appointed by a vote of the city commission, and the rich families always kept a majority friendly to their interests in control of the commission. This was a guarantee that the appointed man who effectively ran the city, the city manager, was always theirs.

Friends of Labor sought to end the wealthy establishment's nearly 100-year reign. Bruce Harvey knew that the changing demographics and voting trends favored unions—especially within Grand Rapids proper. All that was needed was development of a farm system of candidates and a sound grassroots operation to educate voters and get them out to vote.

Over two election cycles ending in 1999, Friends of Labor-endorsed candidates prevailed in city commission elections and secured a slim 4-3 majority on the Grand Rapids City Commission. Bruce's plan had worked perfectly. The election of a labor-friendly city commission was a major coup in Grand Rapids politics. For the first time in nearly a century, the powers that be in the city no longer had a virtual rubber stamp for anything they wanted to do.

This history lesson is relevant to GRPD because we were about to be thrust center stage into a major political showdown between the city's big-money power structure and the fledgling labor-friendly majority on the city commission. New police chief Harry Dolan was hoping to decentralize the police department and his proposal was about to shake the very foundation of Grand Rapids politics.

Dolan's plan involved purchasing a vacant downtown department store and using it as the new police headquarters. There would also be five smaller substations scattered throughout the city. The proposed new headquarters was owned by multi-millionaire and Republican Party activist Peter Secchia, one of the big-money businessmen who ran Grand Rapids. Rumors in local political circles claimed Dolan was hired primarily because city bigwigs recognized that Dolan's decentralization plan would allow Secchia to unload his white elephant vacant building to the city, as well as razing the current police headquarters to allow for construction of a new convention center.

Our union, the Grand Rapids Police Officers Labor Council (GRPOLC), recognized early on that Chief Dolan's decentralization plan would be a disaster for the city. It called for spreading out police personnel over six separate buildings. It was going to be a costly endeavor with no assurance that police services would be any better. In fact, we contended that the proposal would weaken our effectiveness by fracturing investigative units and producing potential duplication of efforts. It also risked increased difficulty in sharing information and intelligence because investigators would be spread across the city and no longer working in a coordinated effort. The enormous estimated cost to taxpayers for the decentralization plan varied from $29 to $34 million.

The GRPOLC Executive Board and its members were nearly unanimous in our opposition to Dolan's plan. I never saw our membership more united. Even the chief's own command staff privately opposed his proposal. Of course, in typical command fashion, they were too timid to publicly voice their opposition as it might hurt their careers. As usual, the fight to stop Chief Dolan's decentralization debacle would fall on the shoulders of the rank-and-file union members and Bruce Harvey's Friends of Labor.

GRPOLC Chief Steward Ed Hillyer served as a fantastic front man. He effectively communicated our position in the media and in various public forums held around the city. I, along with GRPOLC Political Action Committeeman Karl Holzhueter, worked behind the scenes with Bruce Harvey in lobbying the city commission to defeat the measure. The chief and City Manager Kurt Kimball were not going to back down from the proposal, no matter the validity of our arguments and despite growing public backlash. The proposal would come down to a contentious vote of the commission and would be the first test for Friends of Labor's slim new majority.

In the end, Chief Harry P. Dolan's plan to decentralize the police department was rejected in a dramatic 4–3 city commission vote. Friends of Labor-endorsed commissioners James Jendrasiak, Rick Tormala, Robert Dean, and Scott Bowen all voted against the measure. They became known as "The Gang of Four" in Grand Rapids political lore. It was one of the few instances in recent decades in which the big-money Grand Rapids political machine sustained a stunning and unexpected public political defeat. It was David slaying Goliath. I absolutely loved it! The process solidified my commitment to the union and an already apparent devotion in me to stand up for the underdog, the working man.

Chief Steward Ed Hillyer remained our union president for several more years until he retired in spring 2005. By this time, I was an experienced union steward and most considered me the heir apparent to the top post when Ed retired. I agreed to finish out Ed's two-year term. I really had no plans to be president beyond that. Fate had different plans, however, and I would serve as union president for nearly six years.

I have a very different personality than Ed Hillyer. Ed and I agreed philosophically on most things, but Ed was a more natural people person. While sometimes known for having a hot temper, Ed enjoyed people and the social aspect of being in a union leadership position.

I was the classic introvert. I was social, but much more guarded and reserved. I like people, but as I'm fond of saying, "no one in particular." With my personality type, it was much more stressful for me to serve as a front man and handle the constant interactions. It was a little like trying to put a square peg into a round hole.

Being union president is also the hardest job at the police department. It involves being the primary advocate for working conditions, wages, pension, and disciplinary representation for over 300 members of the department. The laws and financial coffers naturally favor the employer, making the union president's job a constant uphill battle. The union president is the point of the spear when dealing with police management and City Hall. He is a lightning rod for confrontation and conflict resolution. Staring down management is hard enough. Trying to keep 300 mostly alpha-male members armed with guns happy is indeed a herculean challenge!

The union president naturally serves as the face of the union and media spokesperson, meaning it is a very public job, especially in times of controversy. This again goes against the grain of a loner/introvert—even a very outspoken one.

All of the president's union duties are done while still working as a full-time police officer. The union and city never agreed to allow the role of union president to be a full-time position as some cities do, although it clearly takes up huge amounts of time. This creates a dilemma for the union president, who must juggle all the union responsibilities while still dealing with the trials and tribulations of being a street cop. I remember on numerous occasions being on the phone with the city's Labor Relations Department while simultaneously driving to emergency calls. For obvious reasons, the combination of working two full-time, high-stress jobs is extremely taxing and leads to a high burnout rate. The union president has a short shelf life. Nonetheless, I truly enjoyed it.

I believe I had a real talent for serving as an effective advocate for our members. I think this came as a result of my modest upbringing, which was devoid of any access to social privilege. All I had ever accomplished was by the sweat of my own brow. I also had an anti-establishment rebellious streak and channeling it for the benefit of my fellow cops was a great way of using it. Squaring off with management and the powers that be to ensure rank-and-file police officers received the treatment and compensation they deserved was to me just as virtuous as being a police officer. In some ways, it was much more so.

I have often said in frustration that GRPD is the greatest job in the world for the 15 percent or so of those deemed "the beautiful people" by management. For the rest of us, it is as trying as a prison sentence but with weekend furloughs—our days off. It's a place where the hallowed few continue to walk between the rain drops, while the majority of the grunts do not get the notice or consideration they deserve. As police officers we have a profound sense of right and wrong, but in the inner workings of the department there was little justice at all. That same chosen group continued to get the choice assignments, promotions, and accolades, while the majority remained stereotyped with their careers stymied. The union presidency offered me a bully pulpit to fight back. If I couldn't change the culture of the good-ol'-boy network, I could at least bring its injustices to light.

These injustices aren't limited to intra-departmental strife. It affects the public as well, and the union president is critical in communicating mutual interests to the citizens. The whistleblower component of police unions plays a vital role in providing citizens with an invaluable perspective outside of the spin produced by government administrators.

This is why people working in the private sector should be concerned about the way public employee unions are currently under attack. Right-wing state legislatures and governors are putting on a full-court press to eliminate collective bargaining, implement right-to-work legislation, and prevent dues collection through payroll deduction.

However, the citizenry should know how important public employee unions are to their safety and quality of life, even if the citizen is not a member of a union.

Police unions are the watchdogs that keep chiefs and city government leaders from having *carte blanche* to craft a message or policy to the public without checks or balances. It is typically public safety unions that bring to light staffing issues that may threaten public safety, defective or inadequate equipment, or policy follies that waste citizens' tax dollars. As a politician friend once said to me, "When I really want to know what's going on at the police department, I don't ask the chief. I talk to the officer who lives down the street." A strong public-sector union is one of the checks and balances that keeps local government honest.

Moreover, the effectiveness of collective bargaining has led to wages and benefits that attract talented people who have been critical to the professionalization of modern policing. The citizens are better served because of the strides made in recruiting college-educated police officers who previously went into other fields that paid more.

Union boss in tough times

The time that I spent as union president were during the most tumultuous in Grand Rapids PD's history. By 2005, the economic slowdown that foreshadowed the Great Recession of 2008 was already apparent in rust-belt states like Michigan. The auto industry had slowed to a crawl, impacting parts suppliers in West Michigan. The slowing economy led to a lower demand for office furniture, hurting Grand Rapids furniture makers. Outsourcing of Michigan's high-paying manufacturing jobs became rampant. Factories were closing everywhere.

These factors, combined with Michigan's switch to a tax system via a 1990's ballot proposal that made state tax revenues more dependent on oft-fluctuating sales tax instead of the more stable property tax, made for a constant struggle for the legislature to balance the budget. They usually accomplished this by slashing something known in Michigan as "statutory revenue sharing" for local governments. The word "statutory" is synonymous with "law." The law-making legislature would simply change the law each fiscal year to modify the formula that would subsequently reduce revenues that would be returned to the cities.

Local governments that had been promised these revenues were then left scrambling each fiscal year when the State of Michigan balanced its budget on the backs of the cities and counties. These factors combined to put Michigan police departments in a financial jam long before the Great Recession hit the rest of the nation and the world. By the end of 2010, Michigan had 1,000 fewer officers statewide than it had on Sept. 11, 2001.

With this backdrop in place, I was thrust into the role of union president. I could immediately tell we were entering uncharted territory. Our union looked to conserve and better utilize its financial resources amid rapidly declining membership numbers. One thing I recognized was how much money we were sending to the state labor organization. It became quite apparent that we were a big enough organization to strike out on our own and become an independent union. Our executive board began to take a serious look at this possibility.

Secretary-treasurer Greg Hillary and I gamed out numerous worst-case scenarios that we could encounter financially if we became an independent union. We costed out the expense of securing our own attorney who would work exclusively for us. Finally, we concluded that we could endure all the potential doomsday scenarios if our union went out on its own and without the umbrella of the state organization. We made the case to our members, who overwhelmingly voted to become an independent union. The Grand Rapids Police Officers Association (GRPOA) came to fruition on July 1, 2007.

The evolution of our union to an independent one allowed us to devote all our members' dues to our interests. We were no longer using our members' dues to subsidize smaller bargaining units represented through the state organization. This became important in weathering the approaching storm of the 2008 economic collapse.

However, it also put a tremendous amount of pressure on me. I was now the sole person held accountable for union actions. There was no more deferring to a higher authority for counsel at the state level. There could be no more passing the buck.

We were already in contentious contract negotiations with the city. However, our new union was put to an even greater test just eight days into its existence. On July 8, 2007, Grand Rapids Police Officer Robert Kozminski was tragically killed in the line of duty. "Koz," as he was called, was gunned down by a cowardly assassin named Jeffrey VanVels. VanVels had lay in wait for Officer Kozminski as he responded to a domestic call involving VanVels and his wife. The killing made no sense at all. The killer had hidden in a detached garage and shot Koz in the head with a shotgun as Koz walked behind the house. Koz never saw his killer and had no chance to defend himself. He was 29 years old and had a four-year old daughter.

I received the call from our third shift steward in the wee hours of the morning while up at my cabin. It was the worst telephone call I had received in my life. I immediately left and headed back to Grand Rapids to assist in any way I could.

A death in the line of duty is the most difficult thing a police department can endure. It also shakes the local community. It reminds the community that if those who are dedicated to protecting us can be senselessly killed, we are all vulnerable.

As union president, I wanted to make sure everything was handled correctly. There were officers who had been on scene and needed representation, along with compassion and comforting. As rocked by the death as I was personally, I knew I had to be a strong leader now more than ever. I was a veteran officer and the younger officers would be looking to me for calm guidance. My responsibilities would not pause for bereavement. Showing great composure would be critical. This was no easy task because I was just as shaken as everyone else.

Over the next couple of weeks there was a tearful funeral. There were reports to be written by members who had been at the scene and were grief-stricken and running on nerves. There had been a controversial discharge of a duty weapon by a member in the chaos at the original scene. There were media interviews. There were debriefings and coordination of various police support organizations, federal benefits, and charities to benefit the family of Bob Kozminski. And I had to work twelve-hour days as a patrol officer while all this going on.

When all was said and done, the Grand Rapids Police Officers Association and GRPD command came together as never before. We put past differences aside and did everything we could to honor our fallen officer and help the Kozminski family. It was Chief Harry Dolan's finest hour. Jeffrey VanVels was later convicted of first-degree murder and sentenced to life in prison without parole.

Things remained tumultuous, however. I went from the tragedy of Koz's line-of-duty death directly into the most arduous labor dispute in our department's modern history. The city demanded draconian concessions in contract negotiations. Negotiations went on for over a year with little progress made. For the first time since 1980, we reached a bargaining impasse that led us to pursue arbitration in autumn 2008.

Binding arbitration means that a third-party arbitrator agreed upon by both the employer and the union settles the issues of impasse. Arbitration is always dicey. Doing so assumes that the arbitrator will be impartial and understand the minutia of complex issues of impasse that were often years in the making. This is further complicated when a person renders his or her decision without the benefit of having the full knowledge of past labor relations between the two parties. The arbitrator walks away in the end and the union and employer have to live with the consequences.

We couldn't have gone to arbitration at a worse time. While we were having hearings, the stock market crashed. The country sank into the Great Recession. These events and the projected reduced tax receipts bolstered the city's claim of an inability to pay.

The arbitration decision was a mixed bag, with the arbitrator, Hy Grossman from Flint, ruling for the city on the biggest issue of retiree health insurance. We were awarded our last best offer on wages and a pension enhancement. Neither the union nor our members were happy with the decision.

The bitter process showed me the ugly side of people. As much as I care about my police brothers and sisters, many of them live in a bubble and have unrealistic expectations. Some believe that because they put their lives on the line, they should be exempt from the effects of a devastating economy. While this is an idealistic notion, it simply isn't reality. Some members failed to notice what was going on around them. Factories were closing all over the place. Manufacturing jobs that had been paying $30 an hour now payed $14. Many companies offered no health insurance coverage at all, much less retiree health insurance.

Still, the fact that our members took no wage increase in the first year of the new contract and non-vested employees were forced into a new retiree health insurance system, led many to lash out at the bargaining team and me personally. They failed to realize that while I was a master at playing the hand I had been dealt, the city still owned the casino and the house usually wins. There were limitations to what I and the union could do. I regularly had the point driven home that one sees a person's true character in hard times.

Despite this, I got creative and did the best I could for the members to limit the impacts of the recession on our members' paychecks. I petitioned the Grand Rapids Civil Service Board to conduct a job reclassification study to assess our compensation levels due to increased job responsibilities. The reclassification yielded a small wage increase that helped offset the 0 percent we endured in the first year of the contract. I was also successful in negotiating a freeze in our pension contribution rate in exchange for a longer pension smoothing period. When all was said and done, GRPOA members weathered the recession better than most Michigan workers due to hard work and thinking outside the box.

Things were only going to get more difficult, though. For the first time since 1970, the Grand Rapids Police Department laid off officers in 2009. We were already running short-handed, as budget constraints had led to many unfilled positions created through attrition.

Kevin Belk had by now assumed the role of police chief after Harry Dolan left for Raleigh, North Carolina. Belk was a career inside person. He had almost no experience on the street. A pure technocrat with little charisma, speculation was that Belk was essentially awarded the job by soon-to-retire City Manager Kurt Kimball for being a faithful sycophant for city hall. He simply did not have the force of personality to rally the public to more vocally oppose police layoffs.

Despite a modest upbringing in Grand Rapids' Black Hills neighborhood, Belk had little sympathy for the union and its rank-and-file members. Kevin was only for Kevin. He was a self-centered company man through and through. Chief Belk was a control freak and micromanager. Any union power was viewed by him as an impediment to his unilateral control, and he clearly resented it. Belk was one of those people who often seemed to enjoy arguing. If you said something was white, he had to say it was black. However, he knew who his bosses were at City Hall and he always dutifully genuflected to them.

Despite his disdain for the union, I met with Chief Belk regularly. I think we eventually forged a mutual respect. I tried to head off the pending disaster of layoffs by discouraging hiring more officers throughout 2008 and 2009. While I would've liked more officers on the street as much as anyone, I was acutely aware of the precarious financial position the city faced.

I was concerned about how the prospect of layoffs would impact the department's morale. I knew layoffs would be extremely divisive. I did not want to see our members given the ultimatum of taking huge concessions or the city putting police families out of work. However, Belk and Training Unit Lieutenant Dan Lind were determined to fill as many open positions as they could. Consequently, they followed through with hiring despite the economic realities that existed during this deep recession. I was told by some of the new hires that Lt. Lind had told them there was no threat of layoff. This assurance prompted several recruits to leave secure positions in other departments. The department was making promises it could not keep.

Twenty-five officers were laid off with the possibility of more looming on the horizon. To put this in context, most cities the size of Grand Rapids averaged 16.1 sworn officers per 10,000 residents. Grand Rapids had only 14.6. A Safewise Security report analyzing 2014 FBI Crime Reports and census data concluded that Michigan police officers were the most overworked in the United States. An already understaffed department would be stretched even further.

Things became ugly around GRPD. I worked hard with the chief and human resources to save as many positions as possible. We saved several jobs by creating a desk officer position in place of college interns. We looked at putting displaced officers into unfilled civilian dispatch positions.

Despite these efforts, I realized that these moves were only temporary fixes that put a bandage on things and would not get everyone back to work. More revenue would need to come into the city's coffers in a big hurry to solve the larger problem. I publicly proposed a dedicated millage at a city commission meeting. I worked with the new city manager, Greg Sundstrom, and other city leaders and they agreed to a modified version of what I had proposed, opting for a modest temporary city income tax increase proposal. The promise to the voters was that all laid-off police officers would be recalled, and ten new community officer positions would be created.

Meanwhile, a few of our members facing layoff became downright nasty. They began blaming me and the union for losing their jobs. I had been the only one sounding a cautionary warning against hiring these officers in the first place, and yet I was the one receiving the blame! Attempting to humiliate me, one member read a long, rambling and disjointed vilification of me at a union meeting, at one point comparing me to Neville Chamberlain's appeasement of Adolf Hitler before World War II. I think if he had another two minutes, he would've blamed me for everything from the Kennedy assassination to 9/11! But in typical GRPD fashion, this guy was promoted shortly thereafter. He is now a captain. Go figure.

Another young guy sent out a department-wide email berating me for not making more concessions to the city to save his job. Apparently, all that mattered was *his* well-being and to hell with everyone else. He wanted his job, so he thought I should give up everything the union had fought for during the past 40 years to get him his job back. These people should not have been hired to begin with if the chief and city management had been acting responsibly, but now I was supposed to make any concession needed to save his job.

I tried to take it all in stride. I recognized from years of working in the inner city that the loudest person in the room is usually the weakest person in the room. Like it's been said that "profanity is the effort of a feeble mind to express itself forcibly," I realized the unprovoked attacks were the only vehicle these disgruntled members felt they had at their disposal. They needed a fall guy, and I became that person. They showed their asses in their anger and ignorance. I wasn't going to show mine. I forgave them and remained dignified, recognizing that this was the league I played in.

I must admit, though, it hurt. I desperately wanted to respond by saying, "Listen, you spoiled brats! The world does not revolve around you. I'm not going to ask 300 members to give back pay and benefits that took generations to accrue to help you further delude yourself in your vain sense of entitlement!"

Instead, as I often did when attacked either personally or as a police officer, I tried to refer back to my faith. I did not retaliate. I needed to avoid being vindictive because there was too much at stake.

Most GRPOA members, however, were a tremendous asset during this time. They volunteered to go door to door handing out literature supporting the tax increase. Many volunteered to work at a GRPD open house for the public that helped show citizens operational aspects of the department and how their tax dollars were being wisely spent.

I secured Friends of Labor support for the tax measure. I spoke on several local radio shows to garner public support. The GRPOA purchased a large newspaper ad to further make the case that the tax hike was necessary. I attended public meetings held by the city and engaged in question-and-answer sessions. It became the sole focus of the union to get the tax proposal passed and our members back to work. Chief Belk, to his credit, had been good at number crunching and helped to save jobs behind the scenes. Unfortunately, he was basically missing in action when it came to public lobbying for the tax increase. This was noticed by the members. It became apparent that the GRPOA, led by me, would again need to spearhead the effort.

This was also the time of the rise of the so-called Tea Party Movement. An organized group consisting mainly of Tea Party members calling itself Grand Rapids Advocates for Sensible Spending became the chief opposition to the tax proposal, along with the Grand Rapids Area Chamber of Commerce, which was little more than a tool of the big-money Republican establishment. The prospect of passage appeared slim.

We made the argument that the average Grand Rapids taxpayer would see a weekly tax increase that amounted to about the price of a cup of coffee. This wasn't going to be a huge drag on citizens' wallets. However, the group of retreads that made up the Tea Party group instead wanted to make the measure a referendum on employee pay and pensions. They really embarrassed themselves. They came across to me as a sad, ignorant rabble of life's also-rans intent on taking away our benefits more out of jealousy than out of principled concern for the taxpayers. They attended every informational meeting, often trying to bully and trip up the speakers and making it difficult for other citizens to engage in the meetings, further hurting their cause.

Finally, it was time for citizens to vote on the tax plan. I was elated when the measure passed, even though it was by a razor-thin 200 votes. I was later told by a local political historian that the passage of the tax increase was the only occasion in Grand Rapids history where voters passed a tax hike during a recession. It was a huge win for the GRPOA and the citizens. Our laid-off police officers were going back to work! I had worked very hard for that outcome. I had exhausted all the political capital I had accrued in over a decade of political activism. To illustrate how thankless the job of union president is, however, not one of the recalled officers ever thanked me. That's just the life of a union leader.

In the aftermath of the vote, a *Grand Rapids Press* reporter tried to box me in by asking if the GRPOA would also accept concessions in upcoming contract negotiations to better ensure no future layoffs would be necessary. I knew negotiations would again be tough, but I was not about to put anything on the record that could be used against us by the city. Instead, I gave a generalized answer to the effect that, "we intended to bargain in good faith and everything was on the table, but I was not prepared to say concessions were in the offing." This prompted a local conservative radio show host to refer to me as "a typical union boss." It made me chuckle.

Paying for the role of union boss

That term "union boss" seems to be part of the new Republican lexicon proffered by their propagandists and candidates to insinuate a negative connotation about any union official. The term is intended to conjure up shady images of smoke-filled rooms and heavy-handed double dealing. If they only knew I was just common guy from Wyoming Park who liked to drink cheap beer around a camp fire! My effectiveness was based on the strength of my and the union's arguments. I was able to rally our members and the public because I was genuine. I was authentic. I was one of them. I was hardly a threatening "union boss" or part of any political machine.

My time as union president was extremely rewarding. I really believe being a protector for those who protect us all was part of God's mission for me. I take great pride in the fact that I was an effective advocate. I paid a heavy price for it in stress and greatly reduced intra-departmental opportunities, but it was worth it. It was an honor that our members trusted me with such an important responsibility at such a critical time. I found it flattering that my good friend and eventual F.O.P President, Paul Johnson, often referred to me out of respect as "Dave Hoffa," in obvious deference to the legendary Teamsters leader.

I have always admired great leaders. Throughout my modest upbringing, I wondered how I would measure up against the greatest minds in local government and politics. I found out that I could more than hold my own against the wealthy West Michigan establishment and its surrogates, despite having the odds stacked steeply against me. Seeing how politically stacked the odds are against the common man also made me much more sympathetic toward causes related to social justice. The entire experience gave me great confidence and a profound sense of purpose. I believe that, even now, I'm more remembered for my tenure as union president than anything else I did at GRPD.

The time as union leader also alleviated a lot of my personal insecurities. I finally felt like I really fit in. Even though a lot of the work was confrontational and far from being a lovefest between me and the city or the GRPOA members, I learned I was mentally and emotionally tougher than most people. My strong will could not easily be shaken. Things that would reduce others to emotional shambles only strengthened my resolve. I now felt I had proven myself in my own mind.

I never again felt like there was something wrong with me because my life was not like everyone else. My mission was different, but it wasn't indicative of some defect. Being union president allowed me to realize I had some of the same qualities as the strong figures in history, sports, and cinema that I had always admired, albeit on an admittedly much smaller and less significant historical scale.

It is still a great source of pride when I see some of the causes that I championed years ago continue to help not only the GRPOA members, but have also become the gold standard for other bargaining units throughout West Michigan. I feel all the grief was worthwhile when I see a fellow cop now able to retire with a more secure standard of living than his predecessors, due at least in part to things I bargained for. The political action committee I helped establish nearly 20 years ago also still flourishes, and the GRPOA endorsement remains one of the most sought after in local Grand Rapids political contests. The temporary city income tax increase I proposed back in 2009 was later made permanent by voters and will help stabilize city budgets for years to come.

As 2010 was ending and with our laid-off members back to work, I began to realize it was time for me to move on from the role of union president. The membership was now mostly a lot younger than me. It was becoming harder for me to relate to the younger generation and I was no longer at the stage in my career where I could bridge the gap between the interests of both the young and older members. I would sometimes gaze out at the membership from behind the podium at union meetings and realize there were more strange faces in the crowd than friendly ones. We were also about to enter into another difficult round of contract negotiations. Mostly, though, I was just spent. I was tired and very run down. In fact, the union presidency was so encompassing that I have little recollection of the thousands of police calls I responded to during that time.

My generation of union leaders and politicos were now gone. Bruce Harvey had retired from the Teamsters. Without Bruce, Friends of Labor was a shell of its former self and would soon disband. None of the "Gang of Four" were still on the city commission. Bruce had always told me, "You will know when you are done." I now understood what he meant by that. It was time for the next generation to step up and assume union leadership. I stepped down as president of the Grand Rapids Police Officers Association on January 1, 2011. I was entering the later innings of my police career.

7

Death, Lies, and Videotape

The problem with the media is that if you talk to it, it will use things against you. And if you don't talk to it, it will use things against you.

—Lauren Klarfeld, writer/columnist

Almost nothing in American society today is more controversial than police use of force. With the advent of modern technology, it is common to turn on the news or surf the Internet and see many of these incidents captured on video. Media coverage is usually quick to frame such incidents in a manner that maximizes shock value and controversy. Patrol officers are often thrust into the resulting firestorm to a greater degree than anyone else. The street officer is not only most likely to use deadly force, but is also the most impacted by policy changes related to its use, public reaction, and media scrutiny.

As I entered the latter portion of my career, local and national scrutiny over use-of-force incidents was on the rise. I had handled tens of thousands of calls by now. I was well aware of how much a street cop's perspective on use-of-force incidents could vary from those of the media or community leaders.

By this point, readers may be wondering if I, the author, ever used deadly force to kill someone in the line of duty. I did not. I came close to shooting two different subjects and was likely justified in using deadly force in a third incident, but thankfully did not have to. I confronted scores of armed subjects, mentally unstable people, and suspects intent on assault or resistance to arrest. Any of these confrontations could easily have led to deadly force situations, but fortunately did not. I did use non-lethal force via kicks and strikes, impact weapons, or chemical sprays several times. However, on two occasions I was within an eyelash of pulling the trigger of my duty weapon.

Potential deadly-force incidents leave an indelible imprint on the mind of the officer. Whether the officer pulls the trigger or not, details usually remain etched forever in his or her memory in vivid detail.

The first incident happened in 1992. I was investigating an assault call on Grand Rapids' West Side with Officer Mark Worch. We were both young officers. I had about a year on at GRPD and Mark had started in the recruit class right after mine. As we were attempting to initiate contact with the parties involved, an enraged woman came charging down a steep flight of stairs from a second-floor apartment while simultaneously swinging multiple knives. The woman was brandishing knives in both hands as we stood on the landing at the bottom of the stairs. She was screaming something unintelligible at the top of her lungs. It was unknown to us at the time, but she was actually the person who had called police and was the alleged assault *victim*.

Both of us immediately drew our sidearms and pointed them directly at her while giving verbal commands to drop the knives. She ignored our orders and stormed down the stairs while still waving the knives. We both were within a fraction of a second of shooting the woman to stop an imminent and potentially deadly assault on us. Instead, the woman dropped the knives as she neared the bottom of the stairs at the last possible moment before I pulled the trigger. The knives fell from her hands and bounced around at my feet on the landing. Neither of us ended up discharging our weapons. I don't think the time from when we were first confronted by the armed woman until she dropped the knives was more than five seconds.

We arrested her for felonious assault on a police officer. Surprisingly, the next day she convinced the detective and prosecutor that she had mistaken Officer Worch and me for the perpetrator of the earlier assault. She thought the assailant was returning to harm her again and she claimed she was merely defending herself. She was not prosecuted for her knife-wielding charge at us.

The version she gave to detectives was hard for us to believe. Mark and I were in full police uniform. We are both white males and the actual perpetrator was a black female. It's difficult to fathom that two white males in police uniforms could have been mistaken for a lone black female, no matter how scared or upset she may have been. Nonetheless, the subject who came within a split second of being shot and who was within feet of being able to stab or slash us with multiple knives, was never charged.

I learned many things from the encounter, as brief as it was. It was a major test for a still young officer. It proved to me that I could react quickly in the face of a quickly-developing and unexpected threat. It also showed me that I could still exercise restraint when faced with a deadly threat.

The second incident came many years later while I was working on the southeast side of Grand Rapids. I was dispatched on a report of a black male juvenile walking on the sidewalk flourishing a semi-auto handgun. I arrived on scene before any other officer and spotted a juvenile about 12- or 13-years-old waving around a black semi-auto pistol. I quickly exited my patrol car and drew my .40 caliber Sig Saur duty weapon. I immediately pointed my gun at the suspect, identified myself as a police officer, and ordered the kid to drop the gun.

Instead of dropping the gun, he began raising the handgun from down near his waist and started to point it at me. I was about to shoot but paused for a fleeting fraction of a second. The juvenile dropped the handgun just as I was beginning to put pressure on the trigger. I was able to pull up and quickly secured him with no shots having been fired. An inspection of the kid's weapon revealed it was an Airsoft pistol. It wasn't even a real gun.

Airsoft guns are a street cop's worst nightmare. For those unfamiliar with them, they are pellet guns designed to be precise replicas of actual firearms. The manufacturer places a bright red tip on the end of the

99

muzzle to signify that it is not an authentic firearm. However, it is common for people to remove the red tip from the end of the barrel, making them appear exactly like the real thing. That is what the kid had done in this incident. With the red tip removed, adolescent "gangster wannabes" try to gain street cred with their friends by feigning they have a real gun. Others are successful in using Airsoft's realistic detailing to bluff unsuspecting victims in robberies.

I once had an Airsoft gun turned in to me by a concerned apartment manager who had found it in a heat vent after a tenant moved out. It was so realistic that I'm not too proud to admit that, despite having a fairly good knowledge of firearms, I was halfway downtown to turn it in before I realized it was a fake!

I'm not sure why I paused that split second before shooting the kid with the pellet gun. I certainly believed it was real at the time. Maybe it was poise under pressure. Perhaps it was confidence in my ability to fire at him before he could shoot me. Maybe it was divine intervention looking out for both of us. I really don't know. However, I must admit that even though my life was potentially in jeopardy and I was in the middle of a huge fight-or-flight adrenaline dump, it crossed my mind in the moments afterward what a huge controversy it would have been had I killed a 13-year-old African American kid. That should not be a factor in a police officer's decision about defending his life, but it sometimes is an unfortunate reality in these times.

This is important for the public to realize: White cops are not a trigger-happy bunch of prejudiced bullies chomping at the bit to shoot minorities at the first possible moment of justification. The exact opposite is true. We go to great ends to avoid taking a life. Deadly force is used only as an absolute last resort. I never met a single police officer who wanted the sobering reality of taking a life on his conscience.

However, if a citizen went strictly by the sensationalized news coverage prevalent today, one could conclude that officers—especially white male officers—are looking for any reason to shoot any person of color. At the very least, in a thinly-veiled snipe at a white officer's courage, it is implied over and over that white officers overreact out of fear of blacks.

Research, however, simply does not support the narrative of white officer bias in deadly force incidents peddled by the media. A 2016 study conducted by Harvard economics professor Roland G. Freyer Jr., an African-American researcher, found that white officers were actually 20 percent *less likely* to use deadly force on black citizens than white citizens. In his extensive research, Professor Freyer analyzed 1,332 police shootings between 2010 and 2015 in ten American cities before drawing his conclusions. White perpetrators were also *more* often shot by police without having first attacked the officer. Professor Freyer found that black and white civilians shot by police were equally likely to have been carrying a weapon.

In fairness, the study also concluded that African Americans were more likely to have other types of force used on them such as handcuffing (if one considers that force), hands-on defensive tactics, impact weapons, or pepper spray. However, the study does not conclude one way or the other if this is the result of racial bias.

It could very well be that the disparity in use of non-lethal force is the result of more complex social conditions rather than an indication of racial bias. Are poor people, who are disproportionately black in urban areas, not getting adequate access to mental health and substance abuse treatment? A subject under the influence, or one who is mentally unstable, is far less likely to obey police commands and is more erratic in their actions. Both factors are precursors to the need to use force. However, few studies take such social or economic factors into account before drawing conclusions.

The last thing a police officer wants to go through is the public and intra-departmental scrutiny involved with the use of force—especially deadly force. We live with the possibility that a deadly-force encounter could happen on any given day, but we also know it will be a life-changing event we hope to never experience.

I would never hesitate to use deadly force to protect my life or the life of another. But I never went into a shift hoping it would happen.

Going back to the incident with the juvenile and the Airsoft pistol, we did not charge the teen who pointed the pellet gun at me. It was not even a functioning pellet gun. With the Airsoft pellet gun not being a real firearm and with no discharge having occurred, there was no crime.

It is important to note that in the two potential deadly-force incidents I was involved in, subjects who were on the cusp of being shot were not charged criminally when the dust settled. This demonstrates how quickly a use-of-force decision must be made in each circumstance. It shows how things appear very differently when all facts are known— but these facts are not usually known to the police officer forced to make a life-and-death decision in milliseconds.

In the knife-wielding incident, it is easy to see how the media could have seized on the narrative that it was the black female *victim* shot by overly-aggressive police. In the second instance, tremendous media scrutiny would have likely concentrated on the facts that the subject was African American, was only 13 years old, and didn't have a real gun.

Thankfully, I did not have to use deadly force in either harrowing experience. However, knowing what I was facing and what I knew at the time, could any objective person blame me if I had? It is easy to rush to judgment when assessing actions of a police officer making snap decisions amid chaos, confusion, fear, limited information, and adrenaline-induced tunnel vision.

As a union steward for many years, I provided representation in the aftermath of numerous officer-involved shootings. In each incident, both internal investigation and prosecutorial review found the shootings justified. In all cases the officers involved acted heroically in the face of enormous, life-threatening circumstances. I viewed representation and personal support on these occasions to be the most important aspect of my steward responsibilities.

However, the story for the officers involved doesn't end after a shooting is ruled justified. If police critics could see the emotional impact in the hours, days, weeks, and sometimes years following a deadly-force incident, they would perhaps change their perception of a police officer's attitude toward using deadly force. Critics don't see the officer shaken to his core. They don't see the inability to calm down—sometimes hours after the event. They don't see the intense introspection and second-guessing of actions, even when the officer had no other choice but to act in the way he or she did. They don't know about the sleepless nights—sometimes followed by nights of bad dreams when sleep finally does arrive. Critics don't see lives changed forever and careers sometimes cut short by ensuing PTSD. I have seen all that and more.

When the use of force turns controversial, I believe the public and media often make the mistake of putting too much emphasis on incidents captured on video when drawing conclusions. Without question, video is a huge piece of evidence—but it should not be the only piece. Whether incidents are captured on police body cameras, in-car video, or by passersby, video images cannot recreate the totality of circumstances involved in these incidents.

A video camera does not capture the officer's mindset. It cannot detect fear. It does not understand the events leading up to the use of force. It cannot alert a watcher to the history of the recipient of force, nor the one delivering it. Most important, video does not capture perception or emotion. The officer who lives through the incident sees it only in real time. He does not have the benefit of slow motion or frame-by-frame review. As a former college football player once told me, "The game looked completely different to me on Monday morning when I was watching game film than it did when I was playing it on Saturday."

The Rodney King case

The shortcomings of video footage are further exacerbated when the video is edited or only portions of the incident are shown. I was a rookie when America got its first real example of this in 1991 with the Rodney King incident. The video in that case was often heavily edited by media outlets and condensed to an 82-second clip that showed the most intense moments of the incident, when another 20 minutes of film existed. The 82-second version was shown over and over. After the repeated exposure of only a small portion of the tape, most of the public had already made up their minds about the incident: The LAPD cops had obviously brutalized poor Rodney King, who was also referred to as merely a black "motorist" in most news accounts.

The benign term "motorist" implied King had simply been out on a harmless Sunday afternoon drive. In actuality, he had risked thousands of innocent lives by first leading police on an eight-mile, 110-mph chase through the country's second largest population center. The media rarely mentioned King was a convicted felon, was driving while intoxicated, and displayed behavior consistent with someone on the drug PCP.

When people viewed the 20-minute video in its entirety, the Rodney King incident looked markedly different. However, few people ever did. Viewers of the entire tape can see King refusing to comply with lawful police orders. King is observed not only failing to comply, but also lunging at officers. Officers are also seen pausing before delivering a series of baton strikes to assess and evaluate the effects of the force and King's continued non-compliance, which is not consistent with a loss of control. The blows used were also consistent with PR-24 baton training, which was the impact device used by LAPD at the time.

At the trial of the four LAPD officers involved, the seemingly damning videotape ended up being the most valuable piece of evidence used by the defense to secure acquittal for Sgt. Stacy Koon, Officer Theodore Brisenio, and Officer Timothy Wind, with the jury hung regarding Officer Laurence Powell's guilt or innocence. A seemingly slam-dunk conviction wasn't so obvious when the totality of circumstances was presented to the jury. The problem was that an overwhelming majority of Americans never saw the entire Rodney King tape as the jury did. They already had made up their minds.

The continued media presentation of police video in edited forms and devoid of full context, such is in the Rodney King case, is at least partially responsible for the public's increased cynicism toward the police. I am not one who buys the Trumpian claim of "fake news" whenever a critical story comes out. The real problem we have in this country with regard to police actions is not fake news, but is better described as "sensationalized news"—coupled with bias.

Anyone who has worked in law enforcement knows police video, whether it be body cameras, in-car video devices, or citizen cell phones, exonerates far more police officers than implicates them in wrongdoing. There are significantly more false citizen complaints brought to light than sustained incidents of police misconduct captured on video. However, this is rarely acknowledged or reported on.

The relatively new phenomenon of the 24/7 cable news networks, the struggle for survival of traditional print newspapers, and evolving news sources found on social media and phone apps are all in huge competition for viewers and advertising dollars. Controversy means more mouse clicks, higher TV ratings, and more papers sold. In a saturated news market with more media outlets scrambling for a relatively static number of news consumers, the competition is fierce. Outrage keeps viewers riveted. The more controversy or conflict that can be brought to light, the more the news story thrives.

The necessity for short segments to fit more news into the allotted time, perhaps combined with the added shock value of showing only the most intense images, often does not come close to presenting an accurate accounting of the event. There is also nothing from media's perspective that sells better than a racial component to the story. These factors converge to make the media's presentation of police video clips something that should be taken as only a portion of the story; the viewer simply is not getting a full contextual view of the incident.

Evidence of media bias was more recently on full display with the unrest in Ferguson, Missouri. I remember scanning the cable news channels at the time of the Ferguson riots. I could not believe the forum these networks gave to criminal rioters. Those rioting were all but elevated to martyrdom status. People who had participated in the near destruction of their own neighborhoods were viewed almost as civil rights activists instead of what they really were: criminal opportunists of the worst kind.

I think many of the media talking heads covering the Ferguson riots thought they had their generation's version of Selma in their midst. They seemed to believe they were simply covering an act of civil disobedience or protest. Many commentators appeared to have bought hook, line, and sinker into the notion that the Ferguson rioting had exposed the rage associated with systemic and institutional police abuse of minorities. They became social crusaders spotlighting the underprivileged minority community's victimization by out-of-control cops, rather than objective journalists. I'm sorry to break the news to those in the media who were duped, but you were not sticking up for a modern-day Rosa Parks. Instead, you gave credibility to the scoundrels who would've stolen Rosa Parks' purse while she fought for her seat at the front of the bus.

I am not defending all police conduct in Ferguson. I think that the police department had an obvious problem, evident by the way the justified shooting of Michael Brown by police caused such an uproar. In most communities, the police shooting of a violent criminal who had already stolen from a local business after manhandling the clerk and who was now attacking a police officer would not lead to such outrage and rioting. Clearly there were long-standing police-community tensions that boiled over. However, the national media was complicit in not bringing all of the facts surrounding Brown's actions to light and explaining why the shooting was justified. The coverage in some ways helped fuel the riots.

I spoke to a social worker at a local juvenile correctional facility at the time of the Ferguson rioting. His statement on the media coverage was prescient when he disgustedly said that the voiceover at the top of the hour on CNN should not be, "This is CNN," but instead should have been, "This riot is brought to you by CNN."

Sgt. Stacy Koon, one of the defendants in the Rodney King case, correctly testified at his trial that, "sometimes police work is brutal." Using force never looks good. It's not a pleasant thing. Battling people with little regard for authority and intent on thwarting the law at any cost sometimes is not pretty. Police officers do not work in the controlled environment of an office cubicle.

No single shift or citizen interaction is ever predictable for a patrol officer. The fact that some of the brutality that is part of human conflict is now more regularly captured on video devices should not be misinterpreted to mean police are more violent or are out of control.

To the contrary, police officers today have never been better trained. Rules for the use of force have never been stricter, nor more scrutinized. John Q. Citizen is just now seeing, through the proliferation of modern technology, what officers have had to face since the time of the Roman centurions.

Nationally, there is a slight upward trend in the number of officer-involved shootings, although numbers declined from 2015 to 2016. However, the uptick in police shootings is not radically disproportionate from nationwide population increases. I think it is important to also consider the change in criminal trends that may impact the increase. While homicide rates may be down nationally, there is an increase over the past decade in "suicide by cop" incidents, which may skew the numbers. Suicide by cop was something rarely seen when I started in 1990.

Personally, I have also noticed an increase in the number of deranged people in society today who have a "take no prisoners" attitude. It is apparent that more and more people are willing to go out in a deadly blaze of glory. Clearly, people with this mindset are more likely to engage in a deadly confrontation with police. These deadly encounters also translate to an upsurge in police shooting numbers. However, I am unaware of any study that quantifies the effects of the deranged, suicidal individual or the mass shooter on police deadly-force incidents and its impact on overall police deadly-use-of-force numbers.

Despite all of these factors, the chance of a citizen of *any* race being killed by police remains astonishingly low. The Bureau of Justice estimates that 62.9 million people in the U.S. had contact with police in 2011 (the most recent year for this data). This only accounts for citizens ages 16 or older, so the actual number of citizen contacts is significantly higher. Only 957 people were killed by police in 2016 in a country of nearly 330 million. Put another way, there was only one fatal shooting for every 65,794 citizen contacts with police—and that is using the assumption there were only 62.9 million police-citizen contacts. No juvenile contacts under the age of 16 were counted. For example, the 13-year-old with the Airsoft gun cited earlier in this chapter would not even count in this example as a police contact.

The number of police-citizen interactions is dramatically higher and the chances of being killed by police is actually even lower when that factor is considered.

An article published in the Minneapolis Star-Tribune in June 2017 listed the nationwide percentage of *arrested* subjects killed by police at 0.01%. They concluded in the article that, "What this means is that the probability [of being killed by police] is so low—roughly 0.01% percent in each case—as to be virtually nonexistent." Obviously, the chances of being killed by police are much lower yet during run-of-the-mill police contacts with no arrest involved. Milwaukee's then police chief Edward Flynn put it succinctly in a 2014 Wisconsin Public Radio interview. Referring to fatal police shootings, Flynn said, "it's an extraordinarily rare event. But the fact is, (in) 2012, there were 12,197,000 arrests in the United States ... and there were 410 uses of deadly force." That equates to one fatal police shooting in 0.000003 percent of all arrests.

Sadly, statistics such as these are rarely cited by news outlets. Most of the media never report on the infinitesimal chances of a citizen being killed by police, despite having vast resources and research tools to explain it to the public in simple-to-understand terms. They instead choose to profit from the false narrative that innocent citizens—especially black males—are routinely killed by racist, trigger-happy police. The misconception this irresponsible reporting creates only makes the street cop's job that much harder.

Back home in Grand Rapids, GRPD made 10,167 arrests in 2016—my last full year as a police officer. Out of the over 10,000 arrests, plus additional citizen contacts totaling more than ten times that number, no uses of deadly force occurred. Grand Rapids may not have the population sample size of New York or Los Angeles, but it is hardly Mayberry RFD either.

Another myth that needs to be exposed is the misconception of a "police brotherhood" that protects the bad apples in use-of-force incidents. Urban legend has it that cops are part of this large fraternity that has taken a sort of mafia-like oath of "omerta" to remain silent and look the other way in the face of misconduct by our colleagues. This is so incorrect it's laughable. While it is true there is an intense sense of duty to back each other up and to ensure everyone gets home safely, the thought that anyone is pressured or encouraged to remain silent when misdeeds occur is complete fiction. Not only do today's police officers value the reputation of their profession but, from a self-preservation perspective, few people are going to jeopardize their freedom, career, and family's livelihood by turning a blind eye to transgressions by co-workers.

When I was a union steward, I always emphasized the need for honesty in all internal investigations. My mantra was, "They may forgive the sin, but they won't forgive the lie." Police officers know that lying in an internal investigation is grounds for dismissal. People aren't going to sacrifice a career they worked so hard for to cover up a criminal act by someone else.

For example, we had a major controversy in Grand Rapids in 2016 shortly before I retired. A local assistant prosecutor drove the wrong way on a one-way street while allegedly intoxicated, causing a traffic crash with injury. The responding patrol officer, street sergeant, and desk lieutenant conferred via telephone and decided to simply issue the assistant prosecutor a traffic citation for the wrong-way-on-a-one-way street violation instead of arresting him for drunk driving. The officers did not know that their phone conversation discussing the incident was captured on a recorded departmental line. The recorded call contained an embarrassing exchange between the officers as they colluded to help minimize the charge the prosecutor received.

The unequal treatment given to the prosecutor by these officers was somehow brought to the attention of a local TV station, and the ensuing firestorm was harsh and unrelenting for several weeks. There were media assertions of police conspiracy and cover-up. The officers involved received enormous public criticism. The lieutenant involved was fired. The sergeant was demoted, and the patrol officer suffered a long suspension.

At first glance, this incident seems to prove the claim of a "police brotherhood" protecting its own, right? In reality, all of the controversy was because these officers essentially gave an assistant prosecutor a break from a misdemeanor traffic charge to a civil infraction traffic charge. Poor judgment? Certainly. In the end, one career ended and the others suffered life-changing scrutiny and criticism. Now, after seeing what these guys went through after making the poor decision to minimize a misdemeanor traffic offense, does anyone really believe there is a secret police brotherhood covering up unjustified shootings akin to murder or manslaughter? It's not very likely.

The so-called "police brotherhood" is actually more of a support network than the mistaken idea of an unspoken code of silence. Ironically, it is quite similar to that of the minority community whereby minority leaders rally around their own in instances of controversial use of force to ensure justice is served. Similarly, cops also circle the wagons in a sense of kinship and strive to make sure treatment of the officer involved is fair and not politicized. In a strange way, we, too, are minorities. After all, there are only 300 police officers in Grand Rapids out of 200,000 people. This support of fair treatment, or affording a fellow cop the benefit of the doubt, should not be mistaken for a secret, nefarious pact to turn a blind eye to misconduct.

Media coverage and some in black leadership positions are often quick to assert race was involved in any controversial use-of-force incident. Not every use of force needs to have racial connotations. It is appalling to suggest that police officers, thrust into harrowing decisions requiring quick assessment and action, base their decision to use force on the subject's race. In many incidents, the officer only has time to ward off a dangerous threat, not assess skin color.

However, whenever a controversial use of force becomes newsworthy, the media will *always* mention the officer's race during coverage if it involves a white male officer. Only rarely is the officer's race mentioned if the force is delivered by a minority officer. It's just not as good of a story in those instances.

I spent nearly twenty years of my career risking my life in predominately minority neighborhoods—neighborhoods I did not live in. Yet each day I put myself at risk for people who mostly did not look like me, did not share my ethnicity, and were not my neighbors. Nonetheless, I served these neighborhoods knowing that every day could be my last and with a willingness to die if need be for those citizens. I contend this is the definition of color-blind dedication. I'm far from being an isolated example. There are thousands of officers just like me.

"Militarization" debate

While much of the news coverage is biased, there is an aspect of modern policing that has justifiably received media scrutiny in recent years. Some refer to it as "the militarization" of America's police forces and I think there is an understandable correlation between citizen mistrust of the police and the evolution in police tactics and equipment.

When I started at GRPD in 1991, patrol officers still carried .38 caliber revolvers. When I retired, sidearms were 9 mm semi-auto handguns. Officers were also trained in and were carrying tactical .223 rifles in each patrol car. In 1991, tactical responses to critical incidents involved SRT officers responding in a step-van that looked like an old bread truck. By 2017, the Special Response Team had an armored vehicle called a "Bear Cat" to respond to serious incidents. Clearly, there has been a significant increase in police firepower and an upgrade in critical response incident equipment over the past 26 years.

Tactics and training evolved dramatically as well. Officers were trained in use of contact and cover, tactical rescues, and felony traffic stops that limited the exposure of officers to potential threats. Training included response to active shooter scenarios. These were positive developments. However, it can give the public, largely unaware of the reasons for this tactical evolution, the feeling that the police are intimidating.

While equipment, tactics, and training have evolved, police departments have often failed to educate the public in their usage and purposes. Changes in citizen interactions with police have resulted from the tactical changes that are sometimes misunderstood. This became apparent when I had level-headed friends, who were consistent supporters of the police, call me and ask, "What is the police department doing driving a tank down my street?" They were referring to the

Bear Cat. Eventually, these friends came around to the benefit of such equipment, but were initially taken aback until I explained it to them.

Police responses to possible threats have also changed dramatically over the last quarter century. Perhaps the best example of this comes from an incident told to me by one of my former sergeants, Jerry Rauwerda. Jerry was the best sergeant I ever worked with. He was, without question, a real cop. A large man with a booming voice and imposing physical presence, Jerry was a true tough guy who had grown up in the city's tough Black Hills neighborhood. In all the years I worked with him, I never saw Jerry get rattled. He always knew how to handle things regardless of the situation. Jerry spent his entire career on nightshift patrol and was a tactician with common sense. He was legendary around GRPD for intervening over the radio and sarcastically asking, "Did you try knocking on the door?" when he saw officers making mountains out of mole hills on certain calls.

Jerry once responded to an incident where a mentally troubled, former combat veteran donned his full military uniform, grabbed his rifle, and proceeded to march up and down his quiet residential street believing he was once again in the army and on sentry duty. Jerry responded by driving right up to him and speaking to him with a degree of nonchalance. He calmly informed the delusional veteran that he was now relieved of his duties and could stand down. Jerry confiscated the rifle for safekeeping, petitioned the subject for a mental evaluation, and the situation was resolved, no fuss no muss. Few residents, sound asleep in the middle of the night, even knew of the threat to the neighborhood.

Today, a similar situation would result in an enormous police response. Neighborhood blocks would be cordoned off. Special Response Teams would be summoned along with negotiators and stand-by medical units, and traffic rerouted to keep citizens as far away as possible. If practical, houses in the area would be evacuated. Officers would address the subject only from locations of cover and the disturbed person would not be approached until all options from behind fixed cover were exhausted; they would then proceed from behind bullet-proof shields.

This modern approach may be the best way to respond to such a situation to limit the risk to both citizens and responding officers. However, the overwhelming and highly coordinated response may appear intimidating to citizens unaware of its purpose. It also causes a huge disruption in the neighborhood. I've heard it described by some as, "the appearance of an occupying force."

I must admit that the old-school cop in me gravitates toward the way Sgt. Rauwerda handled the situation so many years ago. But I realize this way of doing things is over now—for better or worse.

Those who enter police work realize there is an expectation of reasonable risk to one's safety. But sometimes, in efforts to minimize this risk to almost zero, modern responses leave citizens with a negative opinion of the police.

For example, it is now common practice to conduct what are termed "high-risk stops" whenever there is an elevated possibility of danger in a traffic stop. High risk or felony stops are designed to protect officers from ambush when stopping potentially dangerous suspects, and allow for officers to better control vehicle occupants. Such stops involve ordering subjects out of the vehicle one at a time and having the subject walk backward toward officers, who have guns drawn behind cover. The occupants of the vehicle are ordered to keep their hands above their heads until reaching the officers, at which time they are secured. This is an effective way of preventing officers from being shot while walking to the suspect's vehicle. High-risk stops can indeed be a valuable tactical tool.

The problem is that the stops can be extremely frightening and demeaning to the occupants of the suspect vehicle. I'm not concerned about scaring a criminal who is intent on harming police officers. However, in cases of mistaken identity where the incorrect vehicle is stopped or the supposed dangerous suspect is not in the car, these stops can leave a bad taste in the mouth of the innocent occupant.

Many of us are aware of this and can sympathize. We also don't want our family or friends ordered out of their car at gunpoint just because that person may drive a vehicle matching the description of one used in a crime.

There is a fine line between a tactical response designed to protect officers and one where citizens feel harassed or humiliated. I'm not sure we have properly defined that line yet in this new era of policing.

However, citizens should realize that the modern evolution of tactics and tactical equipment does not mean they should view the police as ninja warriors hellbent on turning their neighborhoods into little battle zones. To the contrary, the intentions are to keep citizens as well as the officers safe—even if old heads like me sometimes long for the pragmatism of the old days.

Police management can assist by better educating the public about the reasons behind this evolution in tactics and equipment, and the reasons for each. Police departments also need to make sure such tactics are used only when necessary and in the proper context.

As good as this training in more advanced tactical techniques is, I believe the techniques are sometimes overused. This became very apparent in the second half of my career. Mandatory training became heavily weighted toward tactical responses. Instructors disproportionately came from SWAT or specialized units. Meanwhile, training on legal updates, communication skills, and more practical skills such as crash investigation, report writing, or crime scene investigation was limited to departmental emails or short briefings before line-ups, if addressed at all.

Younger officers, who had only been trained in these tactical responses, seemed to escalate even the most minimal threat into a huge critical incident. I don't blame them; that's how they were taught.

When I started at GRPD, we had maybe three or four of these so-called "critical incidents" per year—and that was at a time when crime rates were much higher than today. Toward the end of my career, it seemed like we engaged in three or four critical incidents per month. Whenever I saw that next-generation officer immediately go into tactical lockdown mode at the first hint of possible danger, I always harkened back to Jerry Rauwerda asking, "Did you try knocking on the door?"

However, police officers are also put in many no-win situations. There are some situations in which there are no good options. Just before I retired, Grand Rapids had another high-profile incident in the inner city in which several pre-teens were ordered to sprawl out on the ground at gunpoint by responding officers. Officers were sent to this location on a citizen 9-1-1 call of a group of black male juveniles in possession of a firearm—not unlike the incident I recalled earlier in the chapter where I nearly was forced to shoot the juvenile.

In this 2017 incident, officers did as they were trained and held the juveniles at bay with guns drawn until officers could safely check the subjects for weapons using proper contact and cover techniques. No gun was found on the juveniles. They apparently were not the correct subjects or perhaps the caller was mistaken about the gun. The incident was captured on officer body cameras.

There was a resulting local outcry from the kids' parents and some black leaders that, of course, got considerable traction in the local media. But what were the officers to do? If they ignored these juveniles matching the description given in the 9-1-1 call and these kids had been armed and had shot or robbed someone, the outrage would've been much greater. One can hear the cries now: "The police don't care about black neighborhoods and ignored a report of armed subjects!" Police would've been accused of bias and apathy for black lives. If the officers did not order the kids to the ground and take the safe approach and an officer had been killed, another horrific tragedy would have occurred. Neither scenario is good.

Late in the year, another controversy in Grand Rapids received national attention. In this incident, officers responded to a home on the city's west side based on information that a female attempted murder suspect was at the home. As part of standard operating procedure, officers ordered the occupants to exit the house.

One of the subjects ordered out was an 11-year old girl. She was briefly handcuffed and placed in a police car as part of securing the scene where a potential armed and dangerous suspect was believed to be. The fact that a child had been briefly handcuffed created a huge local uproar. Once again, officers were placed in a damned-if-you-do, damned-if-you-don't predicament. Chief David Rahinsky made things worse with media statements that were initially unsupportive of his officers. The local media then, of course, fanned the flames.

Police officers are far from perfect. We do make mistakes. However, the amount of errant police behavior that occurs is surprisingly low considering the volume of incidents investigated and the seriousness of many of them.

As tactics, equipment, and technology evolves, police need to be mindful of the effects on police community relations. There needs to be a happy medium between officer safety and empathy for citizens' dignity. However, the media also needs to be responsible in its coverage as well. The full context of police actions is imperative to accurate reporting. Leave the social crusading at home and properly report. We expect to battle the criminal element. We should not have to battle bias and sensationalism masquerading as journalism.

8

Sixty-Two Miles to Nowhere

The world is moved not only by the mighty shoves of the heroes,
but also by the aggregate of the tiny pushes of each honest worker.

—Helen Keller

There is an old saying that describes police patrol as "hours and hours of boredom punctuated by moments of sheer terror." I think most modern street cops would also throw in "and long stints of frustration and fatigue." Most civilians are unaware of what transpires during a typical day for a first responder. My friend Chad Kooyer used to describe it as, "sixty-two miles to nowhere"—sixty-two miles being what he concluded as the typical number of miles driven during an urban patrol shift.

While I worked all three patrol shifts during my career, I was fortunate enough to spend most of it on dayshift. After my stint as GRPOA union president, I remained on Patrol Unit One (dayshift) working in the inner city. I was nearly forty-four years old by now and was approaching my 20th anniversary at GRPD.

For the first year of post-union president patrol, work itself seemed easy. I had essentially been working two full-time jobs for nearly six years. Relieved of my union responsibilities, I now worked "only" as a

117

police officer. It almost felt like working part-time, even though I was still working 40-plus hours a week. By this time, I had seen almost everything. Few things that I saw on the streets rattled me. I was tired and beyond my best years as a cop, but I remained confident in my knowledge and abilities.

The absence of being at the center of controversy that comes with being union president was a big lifestyle change. It took me quite a while to adjust. For over half a decade, my life revolved around constant conflict resolution, phone calls at all hours of the day and night, and being in the middle of nearly every major incident at GRPD. I had become a reluctant adrenaline junkie of sorts, having grown accustomed to an elevated sense of stress-related anxiety and a constant mild burn in my stomach. It took me some time to get used to not being in the thick of things and to the loss of identity. I had to re-learn how to relax.

At least a day on the streets remained constant, but only in that no day is ever the same as the day before. That is both the appeal of patrol and the most difficult thing about it.

Perhaps the most challenging section of this book is trying to describe a typical day in the life of a patrol officer. The truth is, there is no typical day. Every single one is different. I can offer an average number of miles traveled or the average number of calls a GRPD officer responds to per shift. However, I can't describe a normal day because every day is a unique snapshot in time.

I think that variety is what kept me on patrol my entire career. The loner in me liked being out on the street and away from the administration. I tend to get bored easily, prompting me to sometimes wonder if I have a touch of attention deficit disorder. But the reality of each day being different helped alleviate feelings of monotony. There are strict policies and procedures that must be followed, but as long as I stayed within them there was a sense of being my own boss. This, at least minimally, assuaged my feeling of being under the thumb of the command. This was important for a fiercely independent man like myself.

There was a strange irony in that, though. A part of my personality craves order and disciplined ritual. I am always searching for the myth of permanence in my work and personal life. Only glimpses of that can be found in a job with no control over what situation arises next.

My day began with my alarm clock going off at 4:06 AM. Don't ask me why I chose that precise time. My guess is that I was trying to set my alarm for 4:05, but inadvertently skipped ahead a minute and just left it that way. I don't care how long a person gets up at four o'clock in the morning. One never gets used to it. It always hurts when that alarm clock goes off.

A quick shower preceded a breakfast of cold cereal. I never once ate a cooked breakfast before work. Cooking breakfast would take time and sleep was precious. Light morning traffic usually meant a quick drive into work and I typically arrived at headquarters about 30 minutes before my shift started at 5:30 AM.

Once at headquarters, I changed into my uniform and headed to the department's motor pool to secure a cruiser. In the last decade of my career, there was a huge push toward computerization and a march toward paperless reporting. This required a series of temperamental laptop computer logins in the patrol car, with frequent system failures that usually led to the day's first round of profanity-laced frustration. I cannot describe to you how angry most patrol officers at GRPD get on any given morning as they try to make complicated computer systems operate inside of a police car—when these systems were really intended for office use.

With blood pressure already elevated by inoperable computer technology and no one from IT available for several more hours, it was time to head to the squad room for line-up at 5:30 AM. Some departments call it "roll call" or "briefing." At line-up we were given our patrol district assignment for the day and crime reports from the previous shift. After that, we headed to our assigned vehicles to begin patrol.

I've been asked if I ever gave any thought to the prospect that I could be killed as I began my shift each day. Did I ever think that this day could be my last? I did not do so consciously. That possibility is always in the back of a street cop's mind, but was nothing I ever dwelled on. Usually I was focused on getting through the frustrations and challenges of the day at hand, one call at a time.

Most cops get to the point where they are at peace with the possibility that each day could be their last. I had a penchant for summing up the prevalent feelings regarding death and desperation of the career street officer in succinct albeit, admittedly, morbidly cynical terms. Without me knowing it at the time, Chad Kooyer found a few of my quotes profound enough (or perhaps troubling enough!) to jot them down over the years. One read, "Police officers have a certain affinity with death because the blunt finality of death jolts them out of everyday depression." Chad gave me the quote after I retired when he learned I was writing this book. I don't remember saying it, but I think it captures the deep cynicism and feelings of despair the career patrol officer feels as the years begin to take a toll and burnout sets in.

At GRPD, hitting the street meant leaving the underground motor pool parking and driving up a short ramp to street level. A responsible officer would then call in service via the police radio. Cheaters would refrain from calling in until they reached a coffee destination. I always took the responsible route.

Once I reached the top of the motor pool ramp, I never knew what awaited. Sometimes it meant getting a hot call right out of the chute while still bleary-eyed and not yet fully awake. Once, when I had barely exited the motor pool's overhead doors, a call came in about a shooting in progress in my district in which a male had just shot a female in the middle of the street. I rushed to the scene, still wiping the sleep out of my eyes, to find a woman lying dead in the middle of Oakland Avenue with a bullet hole in her head.

The information on the call indicated the victim lived just a couple houses away and had been shot by her live-in boyfriend. An apparent domestic situation had spilled out into the street where the shooting occurred. The shooter was no longer with the victim, so securing the couples' house would be critical in the event that the shooter had retreated to his house.

I requested additional officers; after locking down the potential suspect's house, the Special Response Team arrived at the scene, while I manned an inner-perimeter post. The SRT eventually entered the house and found the suspect dead of a self-inflicted bullet wound. Tragically, his young children were huddled around his lifeless body believing their dad was merely asleep. All this happened before I had the chance to grab my morning caffeine and take my morning bathroom break!

Other days, a street cop may go several hours before getting his or her first call. On those days, my routine involved leaving headquarters and getting a large diet Mountain Dew at a convenience store in my service area. This was my caffeine delivery system to help jumpstart myself so early in the morning. I do not drink coffee, prompting me to coin the corny joke that I was the only cop in the world who didn't drink coffee or eat donuts.

After that it was on to a secluded spot to go over departmental memos, emails, and other communications. It would also be a time to deal with any lingering connectivity issues with the patrol vehicle's unreliable computer system.

Mornings often involved calls regarding business alarms as people arrived for work and mistakenly tripped the alarms. Traffic issues became prevalent if road conditions were poor and as rush hour traffic picked up. During one particularly bad winter, I had my cruiser struck three different times while I was on the expressways policing other crashes.

I often felt there was a greater risk of being killed in a traffic-related crash than by a criminal's bullet when considering all the stressful driving situations patrol officers are placed in. In fact, a National Law Enforcement Memorial Fund study found that during the five-year period from 2010-2014, 272 out of 684 police fatalities in the U.S. involved crashes or officers struck by automobiles. It is surprising that even more first responders aren't killed in traffic-related incidents. We are on the roads when we are ordering everyone else to stay off them, no matter the road or weather conditions. Night shifters are out driving when the highest percentage of drunk drivers are on the roads. We go through hundreds of intersections each shift and often hurriedly traverse busy streets while responding to emergencies. For those of us working in the north, winter only complicates matters.

During the winter, it's common to go through an entire 12-hour shift with cold feet. I don't care how much money one spends on waterproof boots; within a few weeks they begin to leak. This means an officer's feet get wet at the beginning of his shift from snow and slush, and they stay that way for the next twelve hours. For the few weeks the boots don't leak, they also don't allow your feet to breathe, which causes them to sweat. Feet then become wet and cold anyway. The constant annoyance of cold, wet feet coupled with continuously exiting a warm cruiser into bitter cold temperatures is very trying for officers in the north from November through March.

Anyone who happens to be inside a police department in the winter can easily differentiate between patrol officers and inside officers by one simple tell: the patrol officers have white spots on the backs of their pant legs. This comes from our pant legs drooping onto the cruiser floorboard and soaking up salt water from our boots, which creates a condition we call "salty dogs." Our boots get snow caught in the soles. The snow has salt dropped by city plows to melt snow and ice on the streets. When the snow melts, we are left with the dirty salt water on our floorboards. That slushy salt water stays on the floorboards all day, with our pant legs constantly soaking it up.

Morning regimen

The morning regimen often includes what I used to call "putting the drunks to bed." These are the left-over night shift calls where the previous night's drunks are now completely smashed and have yet to go to bed. A lot of mornings involve responding to their drunken domestics and disturbances related to alcohol-induced stupors. Sometimes this results in the first trip of the day to the jail before the sun has even come up. Other times officers coax the last semblance of reason out of the drunk and persuades him or her to knock it off and just go to sleep.

The mornings also involve discovery of the previous night's crimes by victims as they awake and begin their day. It is common to take several larceny, vandalism, or stolen vehicle reports in the morning.

Domestic calls occur all times of the day or night, but are more frequent in the morning than the public may realize. Mornings are often when all things come to a head—the spouse who did not come home the night before, squabbling kids who refuse to go to school, or the previous night's binge that prevents work attendance by one spouse or the other are just a few things that can shatter morning familial bliss.

The thing that I looked forward to most in the mornings was my "10-7," or morning 15- minute break. It became one of the few rituals in a job that didn't lend itself to an hour-by-hour routine. I always tried to take my 10-7 at 9:00 AM, but that was never a sure thing. For about 15 years, my break was at a McDonald's on 28th Street. I usually went with my good friend and co-worker Russ Headworth.

This McDonald's franchise was owned and operated by a retired police chief from Indiana. He and his wife bought it as a retirement job. The owner was African-American and the black-owned business attracted a lot of retired black gentlemen who wished to support a business owned by one of their own.

On many days, ten or more of these old guys congregated at the McDonald's, always sitting at the same tables. I got to know them over the years. What began as a courteous but tepid coexistence, developed into warm friendships. As time went on, I often sat at the same table with these guys. I became part of the group I affectionately called "the city commission," as it seemed our little group could solve all the community's problems over Egg McMuffins. Here I was, a white guy in his 30s and then 40s in full police uniform, sitting with a group of elderly black men in their 60s, 70s, and even 80s. It didn't matter one bit.

Even though I was at a restaurant, I almost never ate. I was concerned about the high calorie count of fast food, so I refrained. I just had my next round of caffeine infusion via a Diet Coke and chatted with the regulars.

One of the challenges for a patrol officer working 12-hour shifts is eating healthy. Working days that go from 5:30 AM to 5:30 PM means being on the job during times most people eat breakfast, lunch, and dinner. If a cop eats all three meals at fast food restaurants, which is usually all we had time for, he'll pack on the pounds very quickly. To combat this, I brought a lunch. I usually ate a half sandwich, apple, and some carrots in the morning. For lunch, I had a standing order of a turkey sub at the Eastown Jimmy John's, which was relatively healthy if I avoided chips. I then had another half sandwich late in the day. I skipped a big meal when I got home, as I needed to go to bed so early. I was far from having the body mass index of an Olympic athlete, but my routine did keep me from becoming the fat cop with the belly hanging over his gun belt.

Even during these friendly contacts with citizens at McDonald's or Jimmy John's, a patrol officer has to constantly be aware that there is always a loaded gun present in every interaction—his own. It is an enormous responsibility carrying a firearm every day. An officer can never forget that he has it on his side and in plain view.

One of a police officer's biggest fears is that he or she will be disarmed and his gun used against him. I always made it a habit to have a portion of my hand or forearm touching my duty weapon as often as I could. I learned how to do this discreetly so I didn't appear threatening. Doing this allowed me to keep close tabs on my handgun and to deter any bad guy's thought of grabbing it.

But the career patrolman's expertise also includes a cache of knowledge beyond tactical operations, application of criminal law, traffic law, and public relations. I always felt that a patrol officer perfectly fits the adage, "jack of all trades, but master of none." He or she learns through experience lots of general information about numerous subjects not typically expected for a police officer to know.

The need for this information can arise at any time during a street cop's shift. For example, from policing hundreds of traffic crashes I learned how to determine if a downed utility pole belonged to the city or the power company. I could differentiate between downed power lines and phone lines; high voltage versus low voltage. I knew who to contact to provide care for injured wildlife that had wandered into the city. Conversely, I learned a method of using a dog snare to dispatch rabid or diseased raccoons that made their way into citizens' yards every spring. The street officer may go years between applications of the knowledge gleaned, but it's invaluable when the need arises.

Somewhere during the day, the street cop tries to get in a traffic stop or two. Sometimes this is because the officer witnesses egregious driving that warrants it. Most of the time, however, it's just to keep the command off our backs. You see, command is usually so devoid of any idea what real cops do that the only way their minds can assess a street cop's worth is by the number of traffic stops he or she makes.

As morning morphed into early afternoon, call volume often increased. An officer can see the city change with each hour. More people become active as the day progresses. In the inner city, each hour that goes by brings out more of the criminal element that had been sleeping most of the day. The bustle of the city becomes more pronounced. Traffic increases. Violence often does too. A patrol officer may go from a parking complaint to a bank robbery at the drop of a hat. The patrol officer then goes from tedium to a major adrenaline dump in seconds.

The question always arises from people who have never worked in the field: Do cops get scared when going to these risky calls? Of course we do! We are human beings. Who wouldn't be scared going to face an armed suspect? We are not Robocop.

The key is to be able to control the fear, as much as one can, and to keep a level head that does not act on impulse. When we do act impulsively, we want our training to kick in instinctively. Of course, all of this is easier said than done. As boxing great Mike Tyson once said about fight strategy, "Everyone has a plan until they get punched in the mouth."

I was pretty good at mastering the big adrenaline dump and fear in the moment. There were many times I arrived on the scene of a life-threatening situation and knew my life could end or be changed forever during the next few minutes. However, I never panicked and I never lost my head. I never froze. In some ways, both sports and hunting prepared me for these situations. High school football at a powerhouse like Wyoming Park was downright nerve-racking for a teenager playing in front of thousands of fans that expected you to win every week. Deer hunting taught me to keep my excitement under control when that big buck appeared. I never suffered from "buck fever" in the woods and I never unraveled or froze on the street.

For many of us career street cops, there is a constant feeling of desperation, though, as burnout sets in. With twenty years on the street, I was certainly at this point in my career. It becomes a big chore to go from one problem to the next. I once listened to a radio interview with a Catholic priest who had performed several exorcisms on people who were believed to be possessed by demons. The priest explained how exhausting the process was. He concluded that each rite of exorcism took something out of him. While police patrol isn't nearly as dramatic as battling the devil, an aspect of it does involve combating evil and it certainly wears on the officer over time.

I compare it to a drop of water and a piece of iron. Each drop of water falling on that iron bar is insignificant by itself. However, if that water drips on that iron bar long enough, it will eventually create a hole in it. It may take a thousand years, but a simple drop of water will eventually ruin that piece of solid iron. The same is true with calls and street cops. Even the most routine calls, when faced over and over and over, eventually chip away at the career street cop's psyche and morale.

It is also disheartening to hear nothing but lies and half-truths all day. "I wasn't there." "I didn't do it." "I didn't see anything." "I didn't run that red light." The process of sorting through all this deception is more grueling and frustrating than one might think. Almost every call is a small riddle or enigma that needs to be figured out to get to the truth. Once the patrol officer sorts it all out, he is sent to the next fracas and the process begins all over again. This is one reason why cynicism is so rampant among patrol officers.

There are also extremely rewarding calls. Catching a true bad guy who preys on society is one of the most fulfilling things to experience. Other times, knowing you touched a life makes all the other BS bearable. One time I had an emotionally disturbed person who was threatening to jump off Leonard Street bridge into the icy Grand River and to a near-certain death. This guy was hanging off the edge of the railing. I calmly spoke to him and established a rapport. I eventually talked him off the literal ledge.

A few months later, I saw the man again on an unrelated business alarm at the company where he worked. I didn't recognize him at first. He was now composed and completely normal. He did not at all resemble the frantically suicidal and disheveled subject I knew from the bridge. He explained to me that he had had a major depressive reaction to a medication that night on the bridge that caused the bizarre behavior. He now was on the right medication and was back to normal. He told me I had saved his life and he thanked me profusely. Knowing that you helped save someone reaffirms the original calling to police work. It sustains a cop during the times of frustration and monotony.

Chad Kooyer had a similar experience. He was sent to pick up a troubled young woman per a judge's order. The distraught female had barricaded herself in a bathroom, insisting she would go with police but only after she took a shower. Within a minute or so, Chad figured something was amiss. He kicked the door in to find the woman had stabbed herself in the chest, nicking an artery near her heart. The arterial bleed was spurting blood six inches into the air. Chad applied direct pressure to the wound and stopped the bleeding. The quick response and first aid saved the woman's life.

She later learned at the hospital that she was pregnant. The woman received proper mental health treatment, later gave birth to her baby, and settled into a productive life. Chad's actions had not only saved her life, but the life of her unborn child.

Several years later, the woman flagged down another officer, Tim Johnston, who had no prior knowledge of the call. The woman explained to Tim what had occurred on that fateful day and stated she wished to thank the officer who had responded—Chad Kooyer. Tim forwarded this information to Chad. Chad eventually stopped by the woman's house where she confirmed that he had, without question, saved her life. She also was the proud mother of a now four-year-old daughter. Later that year, the woman sent Officer Kooyer a Christmas card showing a happy and loving family of four, along with her everlasting gratitude.

In an example of the GRPD Board of Awards getting things right, Chad was awarded GRPD's Life Saving Medal several years after going on the original call. These moments when the patrol officer sees tangible evidence of making a difference don't happen often. When it does, however, it warms the soul. There is no better feeling in the world.

These things also help with what so many calls end up being: busy work. One of the biggest eye-openers in law enforcement is the realization that a lot of calls simply involve one criminal getting the better of another criminal. There rarely is a clear-cut good guy and bad guy. The "victim" is often a scumbag himself. Today's "victim" will be tomorrow's perpetrator. It sometimes seems there are no truly innocent victims.

Assault calls are a prime example. To the layperson, an assault call may sound like a classic example of a bad guy and an innocent victim. However, most assault complaints are what's termed "mutual combat" in legalese, meaning it takes two to tango. As Stinky used to say about assault calls, "There is no such thing as a real assault. It's just the loser of the fight who calls the police." Street cops spend countless hours taking assault reports from the losers of these fights, which are rarely prosecuted but consume considerable police time and resources. Very few assaults involve a poor soul who happened to be in the wrong place at the wrong time and was jumped by a savage attacker.

When I was a field training officer, I used to tell my new recruits, "There are only five legitimate crimes that occur in Grand Rapids each year out of over 130,000 calls for service that we respond to. Odds are you aren't going to get one of them." Obviously I meant it somewhat tongue-in-cheek, but I used it as a reality check for new recruits to keep things in perspective; a lot of the reports we take are going nowhere and amount to little more than busywork.

All this busywork is draining and also leads to the cynicism and the disgusted sighs one hears in a police squad room. The street cop feels only exasperation, as so many of the day's calls and work generated by them seem meaningless. I came to realize what former Chicago Mayor

Richard P. Daley meant when he once said, "The purpose of the police is not to create disorder, but is to preserve disorder." It often feels like you are beating your head against the wall.

As the afternoon progresses, the types of calls become more diverse. Afternoons are when most mental health petitions make their way from court to the police department. Patrol officers are the ones assigned to attempt to pick up these mentally unstable people and transport them to a designated mental health facility or hospital. I always hated those calls. Subjects in the middle of a mental breakdown are prone to react unpredictably when they learn that their freedom is about to be taken away. When they resist, mentals seem to have superhuman strength. Some of the biggest knockdown-dragout fights I had over the years were with mental subjects. It only adds to the frustration when our failed mental health system lets these people out just a few days later. I can't tell you how many people I transported to mental health facilities who were so deranged and troubled that they were scary to be around. Yet on many occasions I would see these same subjects back on the streets before my report had even been uploaded and reviewed.

Potential unpredictability

All calls have potential unpredictability. An officer eventually gets comfortable on the street, but can never completely let his guard down. One time, Chad and I were trying to make a simple traffic warrant arrest after first responding to a trouble-with-a-person call at an upstairs apartment on Plainfield Avenue. It is common practice for officers to conduct what is known as a "file check" of the parties involved whenever at a call. A file check involves checking for warrants through state and federal computer systems. At this call, one of the females involved had not taken care of a traffic violation ticket she had received in the past and a misdemeanor bench warrant had been issued for her arrest. This is not unusual. These warrants usually involve a trip to jail for booking and only merit a low bond. If the arrestee cannot bond out immediately, they are typically released the next day after arraignment, with another court date set. People know this. No one wants to go to jail, but the relative insignificance of these warrants usually lends itself to compliance rather than attempted flight. But not always.

In this incident, a subject named Rashawn had one of these minor warrants. However, when we informed Rashawn that she had this traffic warrant, she tried to jump out the second story window! She was dangling out the window above busy Plainfield Avenue traffic as Chad and I tried to hang onto her arms. I still clearly remember Chad pleading with her, "C'mon Rashawn. It's just a traffic warrant!" as we clung to each arm and tried to prevent her from falling. Rashawn was a big woman. Chad and I finally pulled her back in through the window and arrested her. It turns out that she was wearing a diaper under her clothes. She tried to jump out the window, nearly killing herself, to avoid the embarrassment of others at the jail seeing she had on a diaper. Nothing can ever be assumed to be routine.

Not everything is all serious business though. Real cops have a lot of light-hearted moments between incidents and while on calls. We have our fun. Back in 1993, when Grand Rapids had the highest number of homicides in its history, it seemed like we had the local news filming us at some shooting scene nearly every night. It got tiresome. It's awkward having news cameras around.

To lighten things up, I made a game out of it. I devised my three tips for how to get on TV. The first thing an officer should do is visibly point something out to a sergeant. Another way to ensure a cameo news appearance is to start shining a flashlight at the ground as if searching for evidence, whether any evidence exists there or not. Lastly, the anguished or concerned gaze at the cameraperson almost always does the trick. The next night I responded to a fatal apartment fire and tested my theory. Sure enough, I was the only officer who made the news!

Another time, I and three other officers were sent on a contentious domestic call involving an older couple. We were all young officers at the time. I was in my late 20s. The male half was completely intoxicated and at the stage of inebriation whereby he was combative and argumentative, which is nothing out of the ordinary on this type of call. The obstinate male half didn't like what we were telling him. He tried to wrestle control of the situation away from us by questioning our ability to police a domestic situation due to our young ages. He didn't think we had the wisdom to understand his situation.

One by one he asked the other officers how old they were. The responses given by the respective officers were truthful: 26, 23, 25. Then he got to me and I responded, "I'm 55." I don't claim to be baby-faced, but there's no way I looked fifty-five years old at that time! This guy was so drunk, though, that he fell for it. He exclaimed, "Now you are old enough to know what I'm talking about! I'll listen to you!" With our credibility restored with the male half of this domestic because of my false claim of advanced age, we quickly quelled the situation. Order was restored at the house to the satisfaction of both parties and we all had a long laugh that kept things light for the rest of the shift.

Street cops also often rely on gallows humor and sarcasm to cope with a lot of the tragedy we see. Some of this may come across as crude or insensitive to the casual citizen, but it is a natural and often needed psychological defense mechanism to decompress. When I was union president, I always opposed in-car video cameras and body cameras. It was not because I was afraid of misdeeds being caught on video. My concerns have always been the intrusion cameras can create that prevents officers from being able to speak freely among the themselves, gallows humor being one example.

By mid-afternoon, patrolmen are drained. Calls are sometimes stressful. We expect that. But just driving around for twelve hours in an urban setting is exhausting by itself. The officer literally makes thousands of driving decisions daily just traveling the city's thoroughfares. This isn't exclusive to police officers, of course. Bus drivers, delivery drivers, cabbies, and ride-share drivers (and sometimes mothers!) also endure the fatigue of long periods of city driving. The difference is that they are not also trying to observe situations and conditions around them while driving. Most other occupations are also not responsible for an emergency response to serious incidents in densely populated areas, which has immense stressors and liabilities of its own. In other professions, drivers aren't bombarded with the constant distraction and stimuli of computer messages, radio traffic, in-car video equipment, and operating lights and sirens.

Among guys who have spent most of their careers on the street, it is rare to find one who does not have some type of chronic back, knee, or joint problem from all the time spent getting in and out of a police cruiser. For once my short, compact build seemed to benefit me. I am one of the few guys I know who never suffered from these problems, while the tall guys often did.

The burden of wearing a 29-pound gun belt around the waist also adds to back and hip problems. The human body was not designed to have that kind of device strapped around the mid-section for twelve hours each day for a quarter of a century.

While the call volume increases as the shift progresses, at the same time the patrol officer naturally gets more tired. I found I was more likely to make mistakes late in the day, especially as I got older. My temper got shorter with the onset of fatigue and sensory overload. When an officer gets tired, he must guard against cutting corners, letting his guard down, and allowing his temper to get the best of him.

Each day a new narrative

One thing that was always on my mind was the possibility that my life could change forever in the matter of a few seconds. A mistake when applying force could end my career and take away my freedom. An impulsive, misspoken word said in anger could wind up on the evening news. A serious at-fault accident or a mishandled call that leads to death, injury, or public outcry could have ruined all I had worked for in a heartbeat.

Frankly, I thought more about these possibilities than I did about the prospect of getting killed in the line of duty. I always figured if I was killed in the line of duty, it would likely be over quickly. The Lord's judgement would then be swift and perfect. I was comfortable with that. However, a huge mistake that left me still among the living would be hell on earth and the public's and media's judgement would probably be far from just. Today's extreme scrutiny requires our police officers to be almost perfect. That's an unachievable standard to uphold and an indescribable pressure cooker to live in and face each day for 27 years.

By 2012, the brief rejuvenation I felt after shedding my union responsibilities was now long over. The responsibilities of patrol, even without union tasks, was really grating on me. I looked back on those years of union activism, combined with full-time police duties, and often asked myself, "How did I ever do that?"

Being away from union responsibilities did, however, afford me the time to live a bit. In 2013, I went on my first Canada bear hunt north of Thunder Bay in western Ontario. For that week, I got to play "mountain man" for real, with days involving a 10- to 20-mile float down river via boat before arriving at my hunting stand. I sat on the stand for 6 to 8 hours while trying to remain completely motionless. The stands were so remote that the nearest hunter (or human of any kind) was 10 or more miles away. I remember the guide telling me that if I walked due north from my stand, the only civilization between me and Hudson Bay was a fur trading camp, which was a couple hundred miles away. I was successful in harvesting a nice bear on the second to last day. Then it was back to reality two days later patrolling the 'hood.

Myriad types of calls clutter the patrolman's log late in the day. They can range from calls related to problem juveniles as schools let out to the predictable rush hour traffic crashes. The street cop could get sent to pick up a found bicycle or respond to a deadly shooting. He could end the day with a shoplifter or a deadly heroin overdose.

What's most stressful for the street cop as he or she ends a shift is not necessarily the type of call. It is usually the daily struggle of wondering if you will get out on time. The patrol officer does not work a job where he is assured of getting out at his prescribed time. Calls come right up to the last minute of his or her shift. An officer can be within a minute of being called out of service and then a serious incident occurs, adding hours to an already long twelve-hour day. This contributes immensely to an officer's stress level, not to mention fatigue. A twelve-hour day can suddenly become fourteen or fifteen hours without any prior notice.

Family life is greatly affected by this. It is difficult for police families to make definite plans on a work day. Late calls make it so that a lot of birthday parties and kids' ballgames are missed, adding to the tension a patrolman's family already endures. Of course, family life is already more complicated by a job that regularly entails working weekends and holidays.

A career of working weekends and holidays has more of an impact on the individual officer than meets the eye. For example, I am Catholic. The career street cop, depending on his department's day-off rotation, may work Sundays for several months in a row. This prevents the officer from attending church for long blocks of time. I found that for me there needs to be a spiritual component to my well-being. When I'm unable to attend Mass regularly, the spiritual part of my life suffers. This can become a real problem for the individual and his family when this goes on for over twenty-five years.

Even when a shift is over, a police officer is never really off-duty. In many instances, our days off are not our own. There are court appearances, overtime assignments (some voluntary, others mandated), and occasional day-off training.

It is also difficult to just "turn off" the intensity of the job and switch over to being a regular person. I usually found that my first day off would be spent decompressing and catching up on lost sleep. My second day off I could get my personal tasks done. If I was fortunate enough to get a third straight day off, I felt rejuvenated and normal again—but then it was back to work the next day and the process played out all over again.

It is difficult to sum up a day in the life of a street cop. If a patrol officer works 156 days in a year, each one will have its own narrative. Some days could fill a whole chapter, perhaps even an entire book. Others barely produce a blip on a daily patrol log. A day in the life of a patrol officer can contain nearly the full gambit of life's emotions and experiences: stress, death, laughter, boredom, pride, fear, and despair.

9

No Experience Necessary

My job basically consists of masking my contempt for the assholes that run this place…while I fantasize of a life that doesn't so closely resemble hell.

—Kevin Spacey's character
Lester Burnham in the movie *American Beauty*

I can't tell you what the most difficult call is for a police officer. Each officer would give a different answer based on his experiences, sensibilities, and background. I *can* tell you, however, that real cops will overwhelmingly point to as causing the most stress and acrimony: it's by far the police administration. Our police chiefs, deputy chiefs, captains, and lieutenants cause us more grief than most criminals ever will. We often feel they are more interested in self-promotion or self-preservation than watching our backs. Most career patrol officers view the majority of them with contempt. We consider them "pretend cops" or "posers," as so many of them have little to no patrol experience.

The classic Vietnam war movie *Platoon* best illustrates the way career street cops view the brass. The character Lt. Wolfe is a new Army officer assigned as platoon leader. He's a young college graduate with no battle experience. He was given his officer rank because he was a college man, not through leadership or actions exhibited on the battlefield. While Lt. Wolfe is technically the platoon leader, none of the grisly combat veterans respect him. He's the leader in rank only. He hasn't paid his dues; he didn't earn his title.

Consequently, the troops all look to the battle-worn sergeants Barnes and Elias for real leadership. Lt. Wolfe takes a backseat to them throughout the film and mostly just gets in the way. In a nutshell, that's the way career street cops view most police chiefs and command officers. This may sound overly harsh, but it's a sentiment prevalent among many first responders. For the most part, the sentiment is justified.

I have often thought the career path taken by a police chief or command officer is one of the least talked about, most shameless promotional routes in American employment today. The public is mistakenly under the impression that police promotion is a meritocracy and based on accomplishment. Unfortunately, it is anything but that. In most urban medium- to large-sized police departments, citizens would be shocked at how little hands-on patrol experience most command personnel possess. Citizens assume officers of rank must be the best and brightest officers or the ones who have excelled in the job. They must be the ones who solved the big cases, made the biggest arrests, or attained the title through decades of toiling in the toughest neighborhoods, right? Not quite. These types only play a cop on the evening news.

The police chief or administrator usually gains his position via a much different route. It typically involves getting out of working patrol as soon as possible and getting noticed by a command officer, who usually used the same tactic to achieve his rank. This is followed by shameless currying for favor within a specialized unit. From there, the command officer wannabe takes the promotional test as soon as eligible.

The promotion seeker places the highest priority on personal career interests. Getting ahead and achieving a title—or at a bare minimum, securing assignments out of harm's way that provide a resume enhancement—is all that matters. Those interests aren't served by working on the front lines.

Self-centered and often narcissistic, the promotion seeker learns early on via the police pecking order which assignments will get noticed by the powers that be in the least amount of time. They recognize quickly that patrol is dangerous and demanding. They also figure out that the street isn't the fast track to achieving their ambitions.

Patrol is viewed as an unfortunate necessity. It doesn't matter to the promotion seeker that he or she never fully learned the most essential aspect of police work. The pretend cop weasels his way off the street as soon as possible, rationalizing that this is necessary for career advancement.

The tragic end result is that this dubious promotional model ensures that a lot of ranking officers have only dabbled in patrol—and usually only at the beginning of their careers when they were trainees. Rarely does the typical command officer's career trajectory involve more than a cup-of-coffee stint as a first responder.

The confluence of having a small patrol point of reference, coupled with an ego high that comes from drinking the company Kool-Aid, usually makes command officers inattentive and unsympathetic to the needs of the street cop.

Delusion of leadership

What I never understood was the process of delusion that must take place to lead these people to believe they have the experience needed to lead. One would think that deep down, in their most private moments, they must realize they are frauds. A normal person would be guilt-ridden by the reality that they didn't deserve or earn the title through street experience. But that would assume humility—a quality not typically in their makeup.

I think a police administrator instead somehow rationalizes through his or her arrogance and selfish ambition that the lack of patrol experience is not an impediment to good leadership. It seems they convince themselves that they are superior employees who excel so much in the job that they did not need to spend significant time on the street. The streets are dirty and mean and for grunts. Anyone can work patrol. Superior employees like them don't need to spend significant time in that crude, rudimentary aspect of police work. Of course, the fact that the promotion seeker went to great ends to avoid an extended stay on patrol would seem to dispel their claim that "anyone can work patrol." But never mind that small detail.

While at GRPD, I worked for four different chiefs. Whenever one left, there were always high hopes that things would improve under the next one. I always cautioned my fellow street cops that these people didn't get where they are by being an advocate for the little guy. They don't come from our world. They aren't going to stand up for the common officer or his interests unless they coincide with their own. Nothing will change, other than a few subtleties associated with different personalities. With each new hiring, I would sing a little bar from *The Who* song "Won't Get Fooled Again:" *"Meet the new boss. Same as the old boss...."*

The problem for the real cops in a practical sense is that those who can't do the job are charged with leading those of us who can. Unfortunately, people who were barely on the street long enough to have their training wheels taken off run patrol operations for an entire shift, service area, or police department. They make all the policy decisions that govern how the real cops do their jobs. The boneheaded decisions that come from those lacking in the basic fundamentals of patrol operations is a regular cause of friction. It creates a huge divide between command and the troops. It is far and away the greatest cause of low morale in any police department.

The career paths taken by a considerable portion of brass also irk the real cop in that it defies the principle that the best and most qualified person should be awarded rank. That ideal is shot to smithereens when we see the spoils of promotion going largely to people who manipulated and schemed their way to primo assignments and corner offices without going through a fraction of what we have. Those promoted in such circumstances may have formal authority, but they have lost their moral authority in our eyes.

A fellow Grand Rapids officer friend of mine summed it up perfectly when he recalled an old army saying regarding military promotion that stated, "Fuck up, and move up." I would amend it to better apply to police work by specifying, "Suck up and move up."

How did we get to this point in American policing? How can a profession that trumpets fair treatment in the community as a core objective cultivate a culture within the department with such a cock-eyed view of what should be considered good leadership qualifications? In addition to selfish ambition, the disparity can best be discerned by looking at the personality qualities of people the profession rewards. I've noticed there are generally three types prevalent in police management today. Unfortunately, none of the traits associated with these three types are considered by most people to be positive ones.

The first type of officer prone to seek promotion is the Schmoozer. In less polite circles, this type of person would be referred to as a "brownnoser" or "ass kisser." The Schmoozer is the type most likely to achieve police chief status. He or she usually rises through the ranks the most quickly of the three personality types. This kind learns to charm his or her way through life. They are quick to compliment those in power or those who can make them look good. The Schmoozer usually becomes a master of public relations and learns how to make everyone they have contact with feel like vital stakeholders in the community. They are white-collar used car salespeople.

In job interviews, Schmoozers make city administrators or community leaders feel like they are the most important persons in the room. They are quick with a disarming pleasantry or anecdotes, even if it is an obvious exercise in pandering condescension. They commit to memory and have at the tip of their tongues buzz words and catch phrases such as "transparency" or "diversity" that the Schmoozer knows will resonate well with the audience he or she faces. They become master B.S. artists, which helps them push an agenda and makes them a popular selection for chief jobs at a time such as now, when police departments are desperately seeking good publicity.

The Schmoozer's shameless pacification skills make him a favorite of city managers and mayors, as these types are usually polished and articulate and rarely make misstatements to the media. They are also typically easy to keep under control. This is because ass kissing is the method they have always relied on to get them to where they are, so they usually have difficulty shifting gears.

The Schmoozer is unlikely to confront bosses. He is like the excited puppy that rolls onto its back and submissively urinates when his master enters the room. The Schmoozer is also the least likely to stand up for rank-and-file officers when they err, or in times of controversy.

An off-shoot of the Schmoozer is the Show Off. The Show Off is a simpler, louder version of the Schmoozer, although every bit as shameless. The Show Off remains within the Schmoozer category and is a slight variant who is just not as smooth. The Show Off is the guy constantly trying to draw attention to himself. He puts in for every assignment that gains him attention. The Show Off is constantly out there figuratively saying, "Look at me! Look at me! See what I did!"

The second police administration personality type, the Dutiful Company Man, is usually less polished than the Schmoozer. The Dutiful Company Man does not have the charisma of the Schmoozer, nor the force of personality of the third type: The Bully Autocrat. The Dutiful Company Man is least likely of the three to achieve police chief status.

The Dutiful Company Man achieves rank through reliable loyalty to the department. He or she never publicly criticizes policy or the department. The Dutiful Company Man is a fence sitter who rarely sticks a neck out, especially if it might jeopardize his or her career. These are the ones who never go to a union meeting. They don't have the cult of personality to compete with the Schmoozer or Bully Autocrat, but he or she earns trust by being loyal toilers the brass knows will always toe the line. Dutiful Company Man may have the same selfish promotional ambitions as the other two types, but the brass usually doesn't consider him or her to be a threat to them due to a lack of charisma.

The Dutiful Company Man promotion seeker often spent considerable time in a specialized unit where enough people got to see him or her never rock the boat. He or she may be very dedicated. They may also come from a support services role at which they proved to be capable task masters or technocrats. Once promoted, the Dutiful Company Man is reliant on the procedures manual for decision making and is rarely pragmatic.

The Bully Autocrat, or Authoritarian, is the third dominant personality type and potentially the worst command type for the average street cop. This type, as the name implies, uses intimidation and a forceful personality to bully his way into positions of authority within the department. He often does this through a domineering personality and imposing presence.

The Bully Autocrat lacks sophistication and often enters the promotional realm through units such as SWAT or vice, where the lack of polish is less visible to the public. Insecure, as bullies always are, these people are apt to alleviate their insecurities by making their own little kingdom within the organization which they try to control unilaterally. They are typically not open to other points of view besides their own. Their aggressive style may lead them to pursue more authority or control within the organization than their rank allows. Their inflated sense of their own value to the department often causes them to be over-invested in their unit and job title. The Bully Autocrat's self-identity is fueled by the perception that they are a mover and a shaker and more important than they really are.

With the march toward better police-community relations, the Bully Autocrat is less likely to become a chief or sheriff nowadays, as their confrontational style doesn't lend itself to good community rapport. However, it does still happen. Arizona's former Maricopa County Sheriff Joseph Arpaio and former Milwaukee County Sheriff David A. Clarke Jr. are examples of the Bully Autocrat who have garnered national attention in recent years.

Critics will contend that the personality traits I outlined can be found in most any workplace. After all, nearly every place of employment has its share of suck-ups, schemers, bullies, and wayward nephews of the boss. Perhaps. The reason it has a greater effect on policing than in the private sector, however, is that the manager or CEO of a business ultimately needs to turn a profit. There is a bottom line that needs to be met. Sooner or later there must be a sufficient degree of competence and if not, the manager loses his job or the company goes out of business. In law enforcement, there is no such clear delineation. People with these less-than-flattering personality qualities and no street experience can thrive unchecked in a police department, sometimes for decades.

Of course, these characterizations of the modern police administrator do not apply to all of them. I met some very good command personnel in my 27 years. I alluded to the great respect I had for Captain Phil Jager in an earlier chapter as one such example. However, the negative personality traits and career tracks I have outlined are pervasive enough that real cops find many promotions to be undeserved and troubling. Whenever Human Resources posted for a promotional exam and listed the qualifications, I always sarcastically muttered to myself that H.R. had left out "No patrol experience necessary" in the job description.

During my time as a union official, I had the opportunity to attend many national police conferences. It was amazing how many times I heard rank-and-file officers from around the country describe the same sad spectacle at their own departments.

It's not just the line officers who suffer from today's poor and inexperienced police leadership. The citizens do too. It's the taxpayer who is forced to pick up the tab for their botched decisions and policy rollouts. On two different occasions at GRPD I saw the implementation of computer-aided dispatch systems that were impractical and fraught with problems. In the first instance, the system was so unworkable that it had to be replaced at a cost of millions of dollars. In both cases, any patrol officer would've noticed within minutes that the systems were flawed and impractical. A career bureaucrat doesn't discern the obvious, however. They are simply unqualified to make such decisions due to a lack of in-the-trenches-experience.

Another example of the taxpayer getting sold a bill of goods by these non-cops comes when the average citizen gets stuck with all the costs associated with meaningless "accreditations" that are currently in vogue. Police accreditation offers the layperson a window into the soul of the police chief's twisted priorities.

"Accreditation" is one of the biggest shams I've ever seen. It came to prominence when a bunch of scheming, retired law enforcement brass dreamed up a list of ideals they concluded a good police department should possess in order to be an "accredited" department—which means absolutely nothing. They fabricated an official-sounding name for their group: The Commission on Accreditation for Law Enforcement Agencies (CALEA). The group of conniving ex-bureaucrats that fabricated "accreditation" has no governmental authority at all. There isn't even a fake college degree in "studies in police accreditation" to at least make a flimsy argument that they have some sort of academic expertise to peddle their line of nonsense. Their accreditation is about as valuable as a degree from Trump University.

That doesn't matter to today's police chiefs, though. "Accreditation" is an awesome bullet point on a resume. It means bragging rights at the next chiefs' convention. It's right up the B.S. artist's alley, not to mention a potential easy retirement job if they can get their current department to subscribe to the scam. Somehow in a time of declining officer numbers, there is still money to pursue the requirements needed for a phony accreditation. That's the way the mind of career police administrators works. Therein lies his twisted priorities.

I was so fed up with the leadership that I tried to be a ghost at GRPD during my last few years there. I had fought my wars through the union for two-thirds of my career. I now just wanted to fulfill my duties and otherwise be left alone. I even put in for an inside job. I was hoping to land a spot in the Property Management Unit to ride out the rest of my time. This is a low-key job involving checking in evidence, issuing equipment, etc.

In the old days, this was considered a sort of pre-retirement job for old street cops who had paid their dues. It was an assignment well-suited for older officers who were nearing retirement and needed a much-deserved break from decades on the street. During the "Jager PD" days when William Hegarty was chief, management recognized that when a career patrolman such as myself put in for a job like property management, it meant he needed a break; it was time to get him off the street. Not anymore. I requested consideration for the job on two separate occasions.

In the first instance, I spoke personally to then-Chief Kevin Belk about the position. I knew I was in trouble when he quickly changed the subject and nervously referred me to the captain who would be making recommendations for the assignment. Anyone who knew Kevin Belk knew he never deferred to his captains for anything. He was the ultimate control freak. It was Belk's polite way of telling me to drop dead.

In the second go-round, I was the only person who put in for the job who was not afforded an interview. Apparently, my captain at the time thought so little of me that he didn't even pass my name along for consideration. I had never had a single run-in with this guy. It was apparently a petty torment for some perceived past slight. I had been a guy with the organizational skills to run the second largest municipal police union in Michigan for nearly six years, yet I wasn't given any consideration for the job. After all I had accomplished, it was difficult to believe I would've been incapable of checking in found bicycles and handing out tie clips.

The treatment I received was disappointing, but not surprising. It reaffirmed what I had already known about the administration. They weren't going to let me ride off into the sunset. Things would be difficult right up to the end. In some ways, the rejection came as a relief. By now I was what I would term "an institutional man," comparable to a prison inmate who had been in prison for so long that he could no longer assimilate into the outside world. Patrol was all I knew.

The kind of poor management described above is not exclusive to Grand Rapids, of course. I've noticed the trend play out over and over throughout the country during times of controversy, especially if there is a racial component. You see, the scariest thing in the world for a police chief is the possibility of racial unrest. If the minority community is upset about a police action, today's chiefs will always acquiesce—whether it is justified or not.

For example, in the summer of 2017 there was an incident in Cobb County, Georgia, involving a police lieutenant and a traffic stop. The officer, Greg Abbott, had stopped a person who appeared to have emotional issues. The woman he pulled over refused to cooperate with the officer and refused even the most basic of lawful commands. The disturbed person apparently refused to comply out of an irrational fear that she would be shot by police. The police officer is captured on dashcam video saying to the white female driver, "We only shoot black people," which appeared to be a sarcastic reference to slanted media coverage regarding police shootings. The officer also appears to recognize that the person has possible mental issues and is trying to de-escalate the situation by trying to reason with the person, however awkward his attempt may have been.

The words chosen by the officer are unquestionably misguided and cringeworthy in this era of racial sensitivity. However, it did not appear to be a statement delivered with a threat of any type, nor with malice toward the driver or black people in general. He's clearly being facetious and sarcastic when he claims police only shoot black people.

As a street cop who has encountered several similar situations, I recognized immediately what the officer was trying to do. He was trying to avoid using force by speaking to the person in a manner he felt she might understand. It was an obvious attempt at de-escalation, all unnecessary sarcasm aside. His approach was an effort to avoid dragging the person out of the car kicking and screaming, which would've been an even more controversial situation. He obviously should've used different words and the sarcasm should have been shelved, but there was nothing sinister there.

However, the media quickly seized on the statements of the officer as another "Gotcha!" moment to make the police look like brutal racists. The full context of the incident was not presented, at least not in the national coverage I was privy too.

The situation was further complicated by the fact that the incident had occurred a year prior to the video coming to light. In that ensuing year, no mention was made of the officer making other racially insensitive statements before or after this incident. Nothing presented in the media indicated he had been disciplined for inappropriate conduct of any kind during that time.

It appeared to be an isolated incident; a teachable moment. However, a new Director of Public Safety in Cobb County, Samuel Heaton, recommended terminating the 27-year veteran officer. Heaton made this recommendation even after making media statements where he claimed he knew Abbot to be "an honorable man."

Rather than explain to the media the full context of the officer's comments, using the opportunity to train the lieutenant in alternative de-escalation methods and educating the public as to why the incident happened, the new chief took the cowardly way out. When faced with the choice of being a leader or bowing to the custodians of political correctness, the new chief not only bowed, he dropped to his knees. The chief showed no loyalty to a veteran officer who had devoted the best years of his life to that community.

Officers in a situation like this need a strong leader to have their backs. This chief completely failed his men. Ultimately the officer involved chose to retire, clearly earlier than he had intended, to avoid being fired.

Closer to home in nearby Kalamazoo, Michigan, there was a similar example of terrible leadership at around the same time. In August 2017, the Kalamazoo Department of Public Safety inexplicably issued a press release hanging a street sergeant out to dry. KDPS released police video camera footage that showed an angry and belligerent black male suspect getting into the face of a patrol sergeant. The hostile suspect appears aggravated and poised to initiate a physical confrontation until the sergeant backs him off in the only manner that appeared to be available at that moment. He put his arm out and held the subject's neck—for less than two seconds! There was no choke hold and no strikes, just a move by a police officer to thwart an angry subject coming at him in an aggressive way.

Furthermore, there was no public outcry, no controversy stemming from the incident, and no report of injury or harm to the subject whose neck was grabbed. What was KDPS Chief Jeff Hadley's response? His department released a statement announcing to the world that the officer had been reprimanded. It was obvious what he was doing. Hadley was trying to show the community what a great guy he was. It was like he was saying, "See how we embrace transparency?! Do you like me now? Please tell me you like me."

I believe a good argument could be made that the sergeant did nothing wrong to begin with, considering all the dynamics of the situation. But even if one wants to accept the premise that he did act improperly, to publicly disgrace your officer in such a way to earn brownie points with the public is a shameless act. Sure, Chief Hadley showed his transparency, but at what cost? How will his actions impact officer morale when Hadley demonstrates to his troops that he will publicly embarrass them if it benefits his image?

I completely agree that Kalamazoo DPS had a duty to investigate the complaint against its officer. They also had an obligation to sustain a complaint that violated their procedure. But unless there is some back story here that was never revealed in media coverage, the ensuing corrective action should not have involved public humiliation of one of the men in Hadley's charge.

Hadley, an obvious disciple of the Schmoozer command model, curiously high-tailed it out of Kalamazoo in November 2017 for a job in Savannah, Georgia. I'm sure he wouldn't have hesitated in an interview to use the public shaming of one of his men was an example to prove his unwavering commitment to transparency, however.

On the east side of Michigan, in Ferndale, the police department posted a photo on its own Twitter account of one of its police cars parked in a handicap zone at a McDonald's restaurant. The caption read something to the effect of, "This is not how we roll." The Twitter entry goes on to point out how the officer who illegally parked there has been "dealt with." I'm not defending the officer's decision to park in a handicap space. The poor decision may in fact warrant a reprimand. However, it should have been handled internally and in a way that didn't belittle the officer via a social media post just so the administration can prove how righteous it is.

If I had been the officer in either the Kalamazoo case or the Ferndale incident, I would've felt like a citizen back in colonial times placed in stocks to be humiliated in the town square. How can this make people want to work for these employers or in the police profession?

Disconnect between command and cops

The disconnect between command and real cops goes even further when it comes to internal employee evaluations. Management typically has a misguided approach in determining a street officer's performance and value. In Grand Rapids, this was complicated further in the late 1990s when the chief at the time, Harry Dolan, reorganized the department and eliminated the long-standing practice of having shift captains.

Captains from that point on worked essentially banker's hours. They were not working when most of the personnel under their command—nightshift patrol—was on duty. They also were no longer at patrol lineups. Rather than seeing their troops in action, the brass was limited to the review of monthly patrol statistics as the primary method of determining job performance. Instead of knowing Officer X-Y-Z from working with him or her, the captains were limited to viewing monthly totals of arrests and traffic stops when evaluating the officer.

Judging performance via an individual officer's numbers is a blunt and obtuse tool. It is very misleading. Officer arrest and ticket totals vary based on a plethora of factors. The shift hours, geographical area, traffic volume, crime rates, call numbers, and staffing levels are just a few. Some of the best officers I ever had the privilege of working with were not necessarily big numbers guys. The big-picture, well-rounded officers learn that problems aren't only solved by an arrest. The community isn't always best served when a citation is issued or a person is taken to jail. In fact, some of the most impactful resolutions and lasting bridges made with the community come when the officer doesn't use his ticket book or handcuffs. These resolutions don't show up on monthly totals, however. They can't be quantified.

Unfortunately, in the first decade of the 2000s there was a national push toward using numbers as the best indicator of officer performance. Quantity of arrests replaced quality. The end result was disastrous, as officers were forced to rack up big numbers of arrests and tickets, which fractured police-community relations. As is so often the case, some career administrator dreams up one of these theories. They then present it at some national chief's conference, seminar, or in a trade magazine, and all the other pretend cops and their giant egos rush to jump onboard.

There was even an idea floated in Grand Rapids that would have done an end run around ticket quota laws. The city brought in a career technocrat named D.J. Van Meter, who supposedly had been a sworn officer in Ohio, to present a system he termed "Quota Free Policing." I could tell the moment I met this guy that he was so far removed from being in a police car that he wouldn't be able to find the lights and siren. His system was "quota free" in name only.

The methodology peddled by Van Meter essentially pitted fellow officers against each other. It created a model whereby each officer competed to stay above a monthly median statistical number established by patrolmen themselves with regard to tickets, arrests, or whatever statistic command deemed important. He contended that since the officers themselves were establishing the average—not management—it technically wasn't a quota.

It was a ridiculous play on semantics to claim that Van Meter's system was not quota-based when an officer's evaluation depended on out-dueling his fellow officers in a system put in place by managerial decree. It was like the leader of a dog-fighting ring claiming no culpability in the killing of animals because, technically, the dogs did it to themselves! How can any community be well served by patrol officers engaging in cutthroat competition against their coworkers to see who can stop Granny on her way to church the most times every month? And if an officer doesn't outperform his or her partners, his job status hangs in the balance.

I spent the first few years as union president battling these kinds of evaluation proposals that did not accurately reflect officer performance and quickly sapped morale. Luckily, we squelched the Van Meter system before it could be implemented. But this is the kind of nonsense the pretend cops are constantly dreaming up.

GRPD management was also hung up on a fake stat known as "field interrogations," or "F.I.s." The F.I. was an investigative tool that had been around long before I started. It was designed as an instrument to obtain information on suspicious persons when there was not enough probable cause to make an arrest. For example, if there was a serial rapist terrorizing a certain neighborhood, officers would attempt to stop and ID subjects who matched a suspect description or who otherwise appeared suspicious. If no crime or probable cause could be established, the subject was released and a field interrogation report was written. The hope was that information gathered would be used by investigators in solving the case.

Instead of being an investigative tool used sparingly and only in appropriate circumstances, management perverted the field interrogation into being a means to assess officer productivity. It became Grand Rapids' version of a watered-down "stop and frisk." Some captains even told their officers how many F.I.s they expected of them each month. The unfortunate result was that a legitimate investigative tool, only appropriate in specific circumstances, was relegated to a mass-produced harassment action that bordered on being a civil rights violation. I know officers who "F.I.'d" the same homeless guy, prostitute, or dumpster diver numerous times just to comply with the ill-advised directive. But how would command know the idea was unwise? They never worked the street, so practical application was foreign to them.

The misguided performance evaluation schemes and the field interrogation numbers game would just be more laughable examples of police managerial folly if they did not have such negative consequences in the community. The stat-based models the non-cops came up with throughout the country in the first decade of the 2000s are, in my opinion, largely responsible for the current friction between the police and the community.

Officers were driven by management to emphasize quantity over quality in ticket numbers, arrests, and citizen contacts. A tone-deaf generation of street-ignorant police commanders pushed officers into what amounted to piece-rate policing. Eventually the citizens pushed back, especially in the inner cities where police patrol was the most heavily concentrated. As usual, when I voiced my concerns I was quickly derided as the typical "union boss" trying to protect the low producers. Finally and fortunately, Chief David Rahinsky wisely reigned in the field interrogation practice as an officer evaluation tool shortly after assuming the helm of GRPD in 2014.

While the pretend cops placed an inordinate emphasis on patrol-generated numbers, they all but dismissed other attributes that most employers value dearly. Virtues like reliability and dependability often go unnoticed. For example, I had a twelve-and-a-half year span in which I never called in sick for a day of work. That is rare in a job with long hours, court appearances on days off, and exposure to extreme weather conditions and citizens with every communicable disease known to mankind. It was even more remarkable considering that my tenure as union president and the additional responsibilities that came with that position coincided with the twelve-year span. However, no one from command ever noticed. I never once had anyone mention my reliability or dedication to work attendance. They sure noticed, though, when I didn't play along with the field interrogation harassment game!

The disconnect between administrators and street cops doesn't end with disagreements over performance evaluations or the fast-track used by command to achieve their ranks. It affects us each day throughout our shifts. There is often a feeling of being forgotten when management repeatedly robs patrol to fill whatever new-fangled job position they create without replacing the open patrol slot. This not only kills morale, but it creates legitimate officer safety concerns when huge swaths of the city are patrolled with a skeleton crew.

Moreover, a simple policy decision to re-classify call-for-service types can immediately turn the street cop's world upside down. A few years before I retired, we endured this in Grand Rapids. GRPD joined a coordinated, county-wide, computer-aided dispatch system and 9-1-1 cellular call system. This prompted a group of administrators from the involved departments to form a committee to implement this. No GRPD patrol officers were included, of course.

What came out of this was a complicated and subjective protocol for prioritizing calls for service. Civilian call takers were asked to rate the priority or severity of the incoming calls in a matter of seconds. The degrees of urgency went from a scale of 1 to 4, to something like 1 to 9. The nine different call priorities were way too many to sift through and accurately assign on the fly. As a result, they were often improperly prioritized.

Suddenly calls, which in the past would merit a delayed response, now required officers to be sent immediately from any corner of the city. It was pure insanity. We went from being responsible for our assigned beat to being constantly bounced around the city like balls in a pinball machine. This created a variety of problems, not least of which was that our back-up was often routed to far-away regions of the city on calls of piddling significance.

Once again, when we brought these concerns to management, we were basically told that this was the way it was going to be so deal with it. Command continued on in their lives of air-conditioned offices, free take-home cars, and relative assurance that they would go home every day on time. They remained oblivious and apathetic to the strife they had caused. The real cop was again left to sift through the rubble of policy decisions formulated out of theoretical aspirations, but which were impractical in their implementation.

I expect any police chief or command person will be completely dismissive of this chapter. They won't easily take such pointed criticism from some lowly career patrolman. They also don't want the jig to be up. They are scared to death that the public will finally realize the emperor has no clothes. They don't want the truth known about their shameless, self-serving career paths or their cushy fake jobs.

This author has enough history dealing with their ilk to know the tactics that will be used. They will likely attempt to discredit me by asserting that I am merely a "disgruntled ex-employee," or refer to me as "someone who is unhappy with his own lack of career advancement and is thereby taking it out on others who were more successful." This is nonsense. The fact of the matter is that I never sought promotion. I not only did not seek promotion, I never took a promotional test. I consider this to be a badge of honor. The only disgruntlement I felt stemmed from their poor leadership.

In all fairness to police chiefs and command officers, they hold the reigns of leadership at a tough time. I recognize this. There are some very good leaders at GRPD and nationally. I do not intend to paint all of them with too broad a brush. I was impressed with Clark County Sheriff Joe Lombardo in the wake of the Las Vegas mass shooting. Similarly, retired Dallas Chief David Brown handled the tragedy of the gunning down of his officers in June 2016 with candor and frankness that was refreshing and right on the mark.

Today's leaders are also making important strides in improving police/community relations. Things like citizen police academies and youth Explorer programs that initially received a lukewarm response from the rank-and-file have turned out to be beneficial programs. If today's police leaders could only better blend their desire for community support with the needs of their first responders, policing in America would be much better served.

Just as departments strive for ethnic and gender diversity, police management needs to create a command staff that is more inclusive of the majority of officers who patrol the streets. The "no patrol experience necessary" practice of promotion needs to be re-examined and eliminated. If that happens, the community will find police departments more attentive to their needs and there will be better policy formulation that gains not only the first responders' buy-in, but also respect for his or her bosses. In the meantime, the pretend cops reign supreme.

10

The Street Cop, Race, and Politics

Observations from a Blue-eyed Devil and Overpaid Government Employee

Nothing in the world is more dangerous than sincere ignorance and conscientious stupidity.

—Martin Luther King, Jr.

Police officers in this time of divided politics and strained race relations are forced to navigate through a labyrinth of political extremism and misdirected anger. During my nearly twenty years working patrol in the inner city of Grand Rapids, I'm sure I set foot in over a thousand different homes, businesses, schools, and churches in the core city. I spent more of my waking hours in what some refer to as "the ghetto" than I did in my suburban neighborhood.

This gave me first-hand exposure to a wide array of ethnic cultures, vastly different income levels, and varieties of religions, creeds, and political ideologies. While spending so many shifts in the heart of the inner city, I became familiar with the plight of the impoverished core city.

I spent the majority of my off time at my cabin in a rural northern Michigan county and in a section of that county with a very high poverty rate. While there, I became acquainted with the rural way of life and its cultural beliefs. I moved there full-time upon my retirement.

The experiences of working in the predominantly black urban core and then living in a mostly poor, white rural area has given me a unique perspective on race relations. I have concluded that we do not have a race problem in this country. We have an access-to-economic-upward-mobility problem. We have a 1% problem. By this I mean that wealth accumulation in the hands of the top-tier 1% of earners has, at least in part, resulted in a shrinking middle class. It has stifled access to the economic upward mobility of previous generations. I saw the gap between the ultra-rich and the working poor widen during my time as a police officer. Hopelessness and long-term economic despair are found in those left behind. This sometimes gets mistaken for racial discrimination rather than the more complex socio-economic problem that it actually is.

While it is true that people in this economic reality become more tribal, it should not be confused with racism. It is, more accurately, the reality of similarly hopeless people in a state of stagnant opportunity.

For those in the inner city and rural areas who can't compete, there is a feeling of malaise and a belief that there is little opportunity. There is a sense that America has become a caste-based society in which the economic class one is born into is where one remains—or occasionally move backward. The American dream of working hard and assimilating into the middle class has left the inner city, along with many high-paying manufacturing jobs.

In rural America, the family farm no longer offers a viable living. Mobile homes dot small land parcels carved out of what were once sprawling, multi-generational family farms. In many ways, it felt like I was going back in time when I made my cabin my home. There is no broad-band internet. Cell phone coverage is spotty. No cable TV is available (satellite dishes are as ubiquitous as the mobile homes) and

Main Street has more cars from the 1990s than ones manufactured in the 21st century.

On my daily walks down the little-traveled dirt road in front of my home, discarded beer cans, crumpled losing lottery tickets, and even the occasional hypodermic needle serve as sad reminders of desperate lives in an area where long-term hope has been replaced by insidious coping mechanisms intended only to get users through another day.

While working the inner city, I came across classmates from my school days in suburban Wyoming whose families had descended back into urban poverty after being on the cusp of the middle class in the 1970s and '80s, when good-paying manufacturing jobs made that possible for those without a college degree. One of the star quarterbacks from my high school football days was found dead in a downtown dumpster after succumbing to a heroin overdose.

Consequently, there is a huge swath of poor and working-class people in urban and rural areas that are frustrated and angry. They are lashing out. The problem this creates for police is that the disenfranchised sometimes misdirect their angst at us. The economic complexities that created the situation are many and not always easy to discern, especially for people who may lack education. People in these situations instead tend to project their ire onto something tangible. They need a boogeyman to blame. For the disgruntled minority it can be the agent of the establishment seen most frequently in their neighborhoods—the police.

In poor areas of rural America, the disenfranchised misdirect their anger toward the government or the establishment, which they often incorrectly believe to be the cause of their plight either due to its perceived intrusiveness or lack of concern for their needs. As a result, they often look at government employees with stark cynicism. This includes those of us who serve in law enforcement. The rural white poor and suburban working class may not have animosity for what the police represent—in fact they often support law enforcement in our mission. But this usually ends with the job description and respect for the badge. When any government employee's pay or benefits are in dispute, they return to the "overpaid civil servant" anti-government mantra, either directly in their rhetoric or implicitly with their votes.

The more fanatical elements of these socio-economic classes organize into grassroots populist movements they believe stand up to the forces that, in their minds, created their predicament. They are "mad as hell and are not going to take it anymore." Unfortunately, in most instances the movements they choose to rally around only work against their intended purpose.

I have often felt that both the Tea Party Movement of 2010 and the Black Lives Matter movement of today have much in common in that both misdirected their anger. Both groups were also highjacked by political ideologues from both extremes of the political spectrum who ruined whatever populist purity of mission originally existed within them. This is not to say that each movement is not largely comprised of decent, salt-of-the-earth people who really want change for the better. However, somewhere there is a disconnect with the true root cause of their concerns. The real reason for the black person's plight is not abusive, out-of-control police officers shooting innocent black people in the inner cities. Similarly, "big government" and my defined-benefit pension aren't the reasons why working-class whites had their jobs sent to China.

Politics and hurting themselves

Both movements in the end hurt their own objectives. The Tea Partyers produced a conservative wave of legislators who played right into the hands of the very establishment they despise. The huge conservative majorities ushered in in 2010 empowered the interests of an almost libertarian juggernaut of legislators with the policy agendas of billionaire oligarchs. They took office with an ideology that would dismantle much of the social safety net the working class who voted for them is dependent on.

I find it ironic that whenever I talk public policy with friends near my cabin, they believe all the government's financial shortfalls would end if only we eliminated the "bums on welfare." Yet almost every one of them is nearly completely dependent on either Social Security, Medicare, or veteran's benefits for their survival—apparently unaware that these too are government programs. Farm subsidies are prevalent for the few who still dabble in some form of agriculture. The recipients of these subsidies rail against welfare recipients with a fervent hatred as they lean on the hood of a pickup overlooking an idle farm field that the government pays them not to plant. The hypocrisy is completely lost on them.

With few private or parochial schools available and even fewer of these people able to afford the ones that are, rural working-class whites are heavily reliant on public schools for their children's education. Yet they elect legislators who will protect low tax rates for millionaires and billionaires at the expense of adequately funding struggling schools. Their community's under-funded schools' inability to compete with wealthier districts only makes it that much more difficult for the rural poor to get the education they need to compete in a high-tech world. The vicious cycle not only continues—it worsens.

Meanwhile, the Black Lives Matter folks, along with their progressive allies, hurt their own cause with their tactics. They have little credibility with mainstream America due to the way they gin-up police brutality accusations before all the facts are known. Their "protest first, ask questions later" knee-jerk method of reacting to controversial police uses of force makes them appear as a fringe element. Most citizens want to reserve judgement on police actions until all facts come to light—but not the Black Lives Matter leadership.

Even the very name of their movement, Black Lives Matter, has an antagonistic quality to it. It's offensive, as it implies black lives never mattered to begin with. It's the kind of leading, poorly-premised slogan that offends people—sort of like the trial attorney who asks the loaded question, "Have you stopped beating your wife?" to the man with no history of domestic violence.

The movement then further alienates mainstream citizens when participants continue to promote destructive "identity politics" whereby people are labeled by their race, gender, or sexual orientation. They seem to find a racial component to almost *everything*.

159

As I was putting the finishing touches on this chapter, I saw another disgusting example of this. Two black men at a downtown Philadelphia Starbucks loitered at the business without purchasing anything in April 2018. They lingered at a table, claiming to be waiting for a friend after first wanting to use the restroom, which is against Starbuck's policy.

I'm familiar with these kinds of calls. Table space is at a premium in high-rent, downtown business districts, prompting businesses to call the police when subjects refuse to leave and are not paying customers. Businesses with a high-rent overhead and limited square footage simply can't relinquish valuable table space to nonpaying people. As nonpaying loiterers, the men were also denied their request to use the restroom. This too is common policy in core urban areas, as it is typical for homeless transients to enter these businesses and monopolize bathrooms as they try to give themselves sponge baths, discard soiled undergarments, or attempt to escape the elements. Heroin addicts use rest rooms as a safe haven to shoot up. Clearly, none of these scenarios is good for business.

In the Starbuck's case, the two men were eventually arrested by police for trespassing upon the request of the business. Whether the Starbuck's employees were discriminating against the men due to their race or simply following policy is questionable and not what I'm trying to debate here.

What got my attention was the way the police officers, who were doing their jobs by responding to a complaint, were wrongly thrust into the controversy. The adherents of identity politics quickly turned the conversation away from the discussion of a possibly flawed Starbuck's policy into another unfair insinuation of police bias. They contended the incident was yet another example of innocent black men being discriminated against and wrongly arrested. They argued the police would not have arrested the subjects had they not been black. Not a single cable news pundit I watched placed any responsibility on the two men who decided to loiter at a business after being asked by management to leave.

The controversy then took a turn toward the absurd when progressive Sirius Radio host Mark Thompson, a regular supporter of Black Lives

Matter, made the ridiculous statement in an interview on MSNBC in which he asserted the two black men were fortunate to not have been shot by the responding officers during the arrest. Really? How can any reasonable person claim police shoot non-resistant trespassers? Has there been a single incident of that happening anywhere in America?

Objective thinkers who hear a ludicrous statement such as the one made by a left-wing pundit like Thompson view him as outrageous. He then becomes as much of a millstone around the neck of the Black Lives Matter and progressive movements in general as white supremacist Richard Spencer is to the conservative movement. He destroys the movement's credibility with anyone outside of that small circle of people with similar radical views. The cause the movement champions is then relegated to being a conglomerate of kooks and cranks in the eyes of fair-minded people. The argument is immediately lost within the mainstream.

A similar response is elicited by the actions of NFL players who take a knee during the national anthem. As a former police officer, I realize the premise of their protest is flawed to begin with. But setting my knowledge aside, even if there was merit to their concerns, entering into an act of protest that most mainstream Americans view as disrespectful ruins the point they are trying to make. To disparage the national anthem makes these guys look like unpatriotic, spoiled brats who don't appreciate a great country that provided them with the opportunity to make more money during the two-minute playing of that anthem than many people watching the game will make in a week or longer. Everyday Americans view these guys as one tiny step above a flag burner and not as social crusaders.

Not surprisingly, progressives such as those in the Black Lives Matter movement support these ill-conceived protests and consider them to be the modern extension of Dr. Martin Luther King Jr.'s Civil Rights crusade. But the resulting identity politics that go along with these protests appears to be completely inconsistent with the teachings of Dr. King. It is difficult to believe Dr. King, who promoted his dream of a "color blind society," would embrace identity politics and its constant references to race and gender in labeling people. Dr. King instead believed in viewing individuals by the content of their character. However, this appears to be lost on the purveyors of the divisive, identity politics ideology.

While it is valiant to point out legitimate inequalities, modern progressives overplay the race card. It is fostering a culture of victimhood at the expense of personal responsibility. This turns off hardworking people not associated with the cause. People become disgusted whenever they turn on a cable news show and see someone bringing up institutional racism and some promoter of identity politics blaming "whitey" once again for every societal ill. Many working-class and poor whites are struggling themselves, and take great issue with being blamed for the disgruntlement of others when they typically had no individual culpability in the cause of the grievance.

Black Lives Matters advocates can't simply rely on the broad umbrella of "institutional racism" to make their case. Thoughtful people want specifics, and to win them over you better be able to deliver the goods. You need to prove the allegations. Any time you make accusations of racism when it's not warranted, people get angry. This is especially true with cops. A lot of hard-working, honest police officers who may lean toward progressive economic policy will vote against progressive candidates solely because they are tired of being villainized by anti-white identity political rhetoric. The sycophants for Black Lives Matter not only lose the argument, they lose the opportunity to control the levers of elected power to make the changes they seek.

When I sat on the union's political action committee, we interviewed a mayoral candidate who claimed minorities could not be racists themselves, because they are victims of institutional racism and do not hold the power in society. That's the equivalent of saying the victim of a robbery can't also be a thief. It's an outlandish assertion and creates a strong negative, emotional response from working-class white people, who often vote against the progressive cause in response—even if it hurts them financially.

In the aftermath of Ferguson, it was common for black people in the inner city of Grand Rapids to raise their arms in the "hands up, don't shoot" gesture every time I drove by them in my police cruiser.

Others spit on the ground in a sign of disrespect. It didn't matter that I had dealt with many of these individuals on several occasions and had treated them with nothing but respect. They knew me. They knew I had always been fair with them. It also didn't matter to them that Grand Rapids was 460 miles away from Ferguson, Missouri, and Grand Rapids had no incidents of unarmed black men being shot by police officers.

Some black people were so fired up that they approached every contact as a confrontation. Logic was distorted by irrational animosity. Some wished to use race as a way to manipulate the situation and distract from the violation of the law at hand. The tired old excuse of, "You are only arresting me because I'm black" became prevalent again. The reality is, "I arrested you, sir, because you just beat the hell out of your wife."

One guy told me that whatever I said didn't matter because, "You don't know what it is like to be black." I responded by saying, "True. But you don't know what it is like to be a police officer, so that makes us even. Now let's find some common ground." That seemed to strike a positive chord and put things in perspective for him. It turned things down a notch. He could relate to me after that and the hostility disappeared.

In the wake of Ferguson, there was a wave of policy overreaction. Suddenly, without provocation, the Grand Rapids City Commission passed a resolution requiring all patrol officers to wear body cameras. This cost Grand Rapids taxpayers well over $1 million. That was just for the initial purchase. Maintenance costs and additional cash outlays for replacements and data storage created a permanent budgetary line item that will cost citizens money from this time forward—all due to a knee-jerk reaction.

Body cameras were offensive to us for a variety of reasons. We weren't afraid of what body cameras would reveal; we objected to the guilt-by-association when we had no problem in our own community. We were down scores of sworn officers from our pre-9/11 peak and we were still trying to recover from the personnel losses of the Great

Recession. Money spent on body cameras was only going to detract from restaffing.

We had also suffered through several concessionary contracts over the past decade and longer. It was a punch in the gut for hard-working cops to be told time after time at the bargaining table that the city had no money for wages and benefits that were critical to our families. But the city could now, on a whim, produce a large outlay of cash for body cameras. More money was then suddenly found for Implicit Bias Training—again with the city administration apparently unaware that this was Grand Rapids and the alleged problem was in Ferguson.

The rush to equip police with body cameras all around the country didn't achieve the results cop haters were looking for. In 2017, a study of 2,000 officers in the state of Washington found that a review of body camera footage showed no reduction in incidents of use of force. Of course it didn't! That shouldn't have been unexpected. With the exception of a few anomalies, police use force only out of necessity in a rising use-of-force continuum—and this necessity is dictated by the actions of the citizen, not the officer. Officers are going to defend themselves or citizens in danger whether a camera is on them or not! Strict use-of-force guidelines and training existed long before the implementation of body cameras and officers are going to react as they are trained, and rightfully so.

The lie of wide-spread police brutality has become so entrenched by the disenfranchised, however, that pundits did not spin the study's findings as an exoneration of police conduct. They instead concluded that the police are so out of control, they are going to use excessive force and abuse citizens no matter what is done. Police just can't win.

The myth of the abusive police officer has been swallowed whole by so many liberal activists and poor people in the inner city that they remind me of the "birther" conspiracy theorists in poor, white conservative circles who believe Barack Obama was born in Kenya. It doesn't matter how much evidence is presented to the contrary, they are going to believe what they want to believe. Period.

The same phenomenon exists whenever police officers are acquitted around the country in deadly-force incidents. Black Lives Matter and their identity politics apologists don't come to the reasonable conclusion that officers were acquitted for the simple reason that they should have been; their actions were justified. No way. Instead, they impugn the courts, the juries, and the whole criminal justice system. They don't realize how silly they sound. They seem to believe that all facets of the criminal justice system are rigged to protect officers who kill black men. To honestly conclude that, one would have to believe that in case after case throughout the country, pro-police/anti-minority forces have somehow conspired to rig juries, cajole judges, and intimidate witnesses via some nationwide, invisible secret network that is apparently so extensive it would make even the most powerful mafia godfather envious.

Probably a more accurate takeaway is that the cases were much different when factually presented to a jury in court than they appeared in the sensationalized tidbits shown in distorted media coverage. Perhaps there is a lesson to be gleaned about not jumping to conclusions without knowing all the facts. Of course, these obvious conclusions are too painful to arrive at for people so convinced of a false reality.

During the years since Ferguson, the criminal element has quickly seized upon the opportunity to exploit racial acrimony. I was once sent to arrest an African American male who had been making threats about blowing up a daycare center where an estranged love interest worked. I responded to the address, along with other officers, and we located the suspect at his home. We took the suspect into custody without incident and no force was used.

But once outside his home in a predominately black neighborhood, the suspect began screaming at the top of his lungs about how police were wrongly arresting "just another poor black man in their neighborhood." His shouts and rants were loud and prolonged enough that a few neighbors came outside to investigate. This is precisely what the suspect wanted, as he was trying to persuade his neighbors to turn on us. Fortunately for us, his neighbors seemed to recognize his attempted ruse, perhaps due to being familiar with this miscreant. They never took the bait.

This coincides with another unreported reality: most black residents in Grand Rapids and throughout the U.S. know the truth. After the events in Ferguson and the ensuing relentless bashing of the police, I had more African-American citizens approach me out of nowhere and thank me for my service than at any other time in my career. This was their way of saying, "We know that what's being said about you is crap, so please don't think all black people feel like the people you see on TV." It took courage for these citizens to say what they did and I always took time to express my sincere appreciation.

Back in poor, rural white areas of Michigan, their Tea Party elected representatives went to Michigan's state capitol in Lansing and continued to slash state revenue sharing and passed legislation and budgets that continued to reduce our staffing. These right-wing extremists passed, in rapid succession, legislation that taxed our pensions and doubled what we contributed to our health insurance premiums. They made Michigan, the once-proud home of the labor movement, a Right-To-Work state. Republican Governor Rick Snyder was too weak to stand up to any of the extremists and will go down as the most anti-police/anti-labor governor in Michigan's history.

One GRPD officer did the math and found that, considering a normal life expectancy, the pension tax and health insurance changes alone would cost him over $100,000. For me personally, it reduced my net pension by 4.35% each year. This is a significant blow because the rules were changed when I was already 80% through my career and at a point where I did not have time to adjust for the significant loss of retirement income. I was told by a state representative at the time that the tax on police pensions helped pay for tax credits for big business, as well as actual state *payouts* to some of these corporations in the form of subsidies and incentives. In other words, these companies not only paid zero state taxes, but were actually being paid by the State of Michigan. A portion of these subsidies were funded by fixed-income retirees living on pensions.

Most of the agenda was pushed by the interests of the 1% of billionaires, including Grand Rapids' own Devos family, and harmed not only police officers, firefighters, and teachers, but the very poor and working class rural and suburban voters who elected these politicians. The rural Montcalm County Sheriff's Department, my first police job, was reduced for a time to not having a night shift road patrol. Imagine living in a 720-square-mile county with no police protection for a significant portion of the day!

By Fall 2017, the county had been stripped of revenues to the extent that the county's district court judge threatened to sue the Montcalm County Board of Commissioners if they proceeded with a mandate to force the court to cut any more from its budget. The judge contended that further reductions would prevent the court from being able to perform its legal obligations. I suppose that this was a component of small government that Fox News or Rush Limbaugh forgot to mention when they duped naïve voters who elected the politicians who orchestrated this unconscionable betrayal of public safety.

Buyers' remorse?

I'm sure many working-class white voters will deny having any buyer's remorse for choosing the legislators they elected. They will still conclude that all these troubles would be solved if we just got rid of "the bums on welfare." The propagandists from whom they get their daily political affirmation will continue promoting these ignorant views, and will also tell them another tax cut for the rich will stimulate local economies and get them back their jobs at the mill. After all, tax cuts, coupled with privatization, are the solutions for everything.

Another one of the effects of an economy so lacking in upward mobility is that people become stuck in a homogenous, stagnant culture with those kinds of provincial views. The views fester and often get more extreme. With it comes acceptance of far-fetched conspiracy theories, urban legend, folklore, and the solidification of pre-existing prejudices. People often show their ugly sides. Many have never had exposure to people outside of their socioeconomic class, race, or religious creed and have no experience with any other point of view. They become cynical and close-minded, distrusting and often fearing others not like them. They usually have limited means to obtain information and even less

167

contact with policy makers—often leading them to form their views solely from propagandist talk radio, slanted cable news shows, or fabricated stories from internet trolls.

People in these situations have less exposure to the wide-ranging life experiences of the middle class from which to draw their opinions. This can create gullibility to accepting false narratives. They typically adhere to simple, hot-button social issues they can understand and make those issues their line in the sand. They cling to them with an almost white-knuckled, cult-like and rabid fanaticism. With the internet and social media, there is also always an outlet available to solidify their fears or ideology, no matter how outrageous. It may be fear of gun confiscation; animosity toward the police; nationalism inspired by conspiracy theories promoting fears of one world government domination; the "deep state;" abortion. These can cut across racial and ideological lines.

Victimhood reigns supreme with both groups. Impoverished blacks regularly play the race card. Poor or underemployed whites do as well, in a subtler way, by blaming his or her situation on affirmative action, "welfare queens," "The Establishment," or any number of conspiracy theories.

When I worked Grand Rapids' inner city, there was a white male, open-carry gun advocate who left his home in northern, rural Kent County and went to a black neighborhood in the inner city. He would strut around, marching back and forth in a residential neighborhood with a handgun holstered to his side. It was an act of antagonism. He was hoping to be confronted by either a black person or a police officer, hiding behind exercising his 2nd Amendment rights to justify the chip on his shoulder.

While I don't claim to know this guy's economic background, he did not appear overly prosperous. He wasn't lobbying to get high-paying manufacturing jobs returned to Michigan. He wasn't protesting the new Right to Work Law that hurt his ability to organize. He wasn't decrying Wall Street greed or financial market deregulation that likely crushed his fledgling 401k. Nope. This guy's reality had digressed to the point where wearing a gun on his hip in a black neighborhood was his rebel yell.

Mr. Open Carry Guy made his little sojourns to the city on several occasions. Understandably alarmed by a stranger armed with a gun walking in front of their homes, area residents called the police. I responded. I tried to reason with him and explained that I, too, supported gun rights. However, a person marching in front of houses in a highly-populated residential neighborhood armed with a gun was unnerving residents and hurting his cause. He couldn't care less.

With logic not working, I downshifted to a more simplistic line of reasoning he could understand. I informed him that in response to his 2nd Amendment display, I was going to orchestrate a similar demonstration. I told him that I, along with several of my black officer friends, was going to show up in his neighborhood and do the same thing in front of his house. I put an exclamation point on the conversation by reminding him his gun toting wasn't going to make his penis any larger. Apparently having had his self-deluded alpha-male facade shattered, Open Carry Guy didn't show up much after that. Hopefully this gentleman now limits his weapon carrying to his militia maneuvers—between listening to episodes of Alex Jones.

Late in my career, after seeing people like Open Carry Guy and so many of my fellow white, working-class brethren go off the rails, I lamented that far too many working-class whites had replaced tempered reason with extremism. Many ended up in one of three distinct categories: (a) fanatical attendees of huge, cult-like entertainment churches; (b) right wing anti-government extremist conspiracy kooks; or (c) heroin addicts. Obviously, none of these extremes lend themselves to open-minded intellectual curiosity or a break from rigid focus.

In low income black neighborhoods, I was sometimes called a "blue-eyed devil" or a "peckerwood," in addition to the old standbys "honkey," "cracker," and "The Man." I met several African-Americans who insisted the crack cocaine epidemic was a white man's covert operation orchestrated by the CIA to exterminate the black race. Another conspiracy theory I heard bandied about to explain the huge upswing in gang killings in Chicago was the notion that the FBI was sponsoring Chicago street gangs as hit squads to kill off black people. In the late '90s I heard a conspiracy theory claiming rappers Tupac Shakur and Biggy Smalls were killed by government-hired assassins because they were becoming too powerful and were a threat to the federal government. I even read about an urban neighborhood newspaper in Philadelphia warning blacks to flee the city before the 2004 election because George W. Bush was going to use nuclear weapons on them to suppress their vote.

I believe these examples relate more to ignorance, gullibility, and frustration than to racism. It seems to me that the best cure for this is a large and attainable middle class that reduces this economic stagnation and produces educational opportunities. What spared me from this ignorance can spare others as well. When desperation is replaced by hope, the cynicism, misdirected outrage, and stunted ideological maturity will begin to wane. So will taking pot shots at perceived scapegoats—the police being just one of them.

Much of society's stereotyping surrounding police and race will go away with knowledge and experiences only economic upward mobility can bring. The many contradictions associated with these negative stereotypes may also disappear.

One such contradiction not often recognized by police critics and race baiters is that within our ranks, there is little racial division in America's police departments. We don't identify each other by race. We see only blue—not black, white, brown, or yellow. We entrust our lives to our partners and don't have any interest in classifying each other along racial lines. Yes, there are times when there is grumbling about a particular promotion or job assignment that some may feel was given to an individual based on race or gender, but that does not taint the way we feel about him or her personally. Most of the time it is remarkable just how color-blind the police culture really is. With this in mind, does it seem likely that men and women, who work in close racial harmony with each other, would suddenly turn on a switch and begin treating the citizenry with bigotry once we hit the street? That's another inconsistency in the stereotyping of police that hasn't been rationally resolved by the cop haters.

I think another thing that gets lost when discussing police and race relations is the long-term consequences from sustained attacks on public employees. Conservatives, who claim to support the police and law and order, are systematically targeting public employee benefits, pensions, and collective bargaining rights. This sustained attack on police compensation has the profession on the cusp of being knocked out of the middle class.

Meanwhile progressives, who normally claim to be champions of labor and bargaining rights, often spend more time playing footsy with the Black Lives Matter crowd and promoting identity politics than in defending the attack on unions, police officer pay, benefits, and staffing levels.

False narrative

As I have demonstrated throughout this book, assertions that the police are out-of-control racists hellbent on killing unarmed black men are complete nonsense. However, America runs a real risk of seeing this false narrative become reality if the attack on police compensation and the profession in general does not relent. I cannot emphasize this enough. We are already seeing a nationwide drop in police applicants. Good, quality people are no longer entering careers in law enforcement. The result will be the nightmare the Black Lives Matter supporters incorrectly assert is happening now: police forces really *will* be comprised of the poorly educated, big bully cop.

The considerate, empathetic, and deliberative college graduate will be replaced by the provincial, uneducated "prick cop" wielding a big night stick and hair trigger. If one thinks police-community relations are bad now, wait until society sees what occurs when the strides toward professionalism in law enforcement made in the 1980s and 1990s are replaced by simple-minded authoritarianism.

Both political parties are complicit in promoting these ends. Republicans are determined to let us wither on the vine by not providing us with necessary funding and by reducing our standard of living. They continue to promote historically low tax rates for the ultra-rich at the expense of securing public safety. They are held hostage by billionaire interests that want to destroy unions—especially public employee unions—which they deem to be the last bastion of labor strength in the country. Republican governors such as Michigan's Rick Snyder, Wisconsin's Scott Walker, and Kansas' Sam Brownback have erased a generation of forward strides and did so unnecessarily and punitively. During the last third of my career, I did more fighting with conservative legislators attempting to destroy my standard of living than I did fighting with criminals in the streets.

Democrats have done a good job standing up to efforts toward privatization and attacks on police benefits and collective bargaining rights. However, their insistence on placating anti-police organizers instead of educating them has given credibility to their exaggerated claims of police brutality. Progressive, knee-jerk government solutions have also led to costly, ill-conceived policies and expenditures, rather than adding police officers who could actually make a difference in troubled communities.

They have also placed far too much emphasis on controversial social issues over common folks' everyday concerns. Cops don't want their elected officials arguing about access to transgender bathrooms. We don't want our leaders promoting even more dopers in an already stoned and over-medicated generation with marijuana legalization proposals. Police officers want to know our leaders have our backs as we do our jobs and at the bargaining table.

Both political parties need to hang a sign outside of their respective headquarters that reads, "Closed for remodeling." They need to rethink their priorities when it comes to policing and its needs. There is a large group of police officers and police families who feel ignored and often under attack by our elected officials from both sides.

Any discussion of police and race should also include recognition of where our country's police officers come from. Most police officers come from backgrounds similar to mine. We are predominately white, but usually don't come from money. Police work has traditionally been—and still remains—a gateway career from the working class to the middle class for primarily first and second-generation immigrants.

Consequently, few of us come from privilege. Most of our families came to America after the turn of the 20th century. We do not come from Ivy league families or from a network of establishment connections.

Few of us come from backgrounds where it could be argued that we are recipients of what is typically termed "white privilege." Sure, there are some legacy cases of nepotism where a father or grandfather uses connections to forward the careers of his children, but none of us come from the Bush or Kennedy families. If there really is white privilege in this country, I can assure the reader that this working-class white man was never let in on the super-secret handshake.

It is because most of us have forged our own paths in a difficult job that the subject of affirmative action and diversity in hiring and promotion is a touchy subject in law enforcement. I got my first taste of this the first time I applied to GRPD. Two guys who were my friends from the police academy at Grand Valley State were hired before me. One was of Asian background, the other had Native American lineage. I outscored both of them on the civil service test. All three of us graduated in the same police academy class. We all had the same bachelor's degree from Grand Valley State. I was passed over simply because of the color of my skin. Ultimately, things still worked out for me. I was hired at GRPD in the next recruit class. However, my two friends had more seniority than me for the rest of our careers. This translated into them having vacation and shift bid rights over me, as well as a bigger pension which affects me even now.

As I grew older, racial and gender favoritism became harder to swallow. It was difficult to see, year after year, a contingent of minority and female officers awarded promotions and choice assignments mostly on the basis of gender or minority status. Many were given much easier career paths whereby they were allowed to waltz along mostly out of harm's way. This was accomplished by giving these officers inside investigative desk jobs or public relations assignments in community liaison roles, from which the brass could show off to the community their dedication to "diversity." Meanwhile, I was still shagging dangerous calls in my late 40s.

This is the elephant in the room few want to talk about. Diversity goals are great, but people also need to know that someone loses, too. In many cases, those who lose are far from privileged and are just trying to achieve middle-class opportunity themselves.

I have been brutally honest throughout this book. I have divulged my personal trials with depression and the struggles from my working-class, Irish-Lithuanian familial roots and broken home. The last thing I want to do is claim victimhood. That being said, it's easy to see that I am not someone who can trace his family history back to the Mayflower or old money privilege. However, many of the minorities and females who were given deference over me had advantaged backgrounds considerably greater than mine. This is why white male officers are so sensitive on the topic of race. It can make a white officer bitter to see what goes on in all of the internal machinations of the department, only to be called the root of all societal evils by pundits and talking heads on TV news once we go home at night.

Privately, minority officers often complain about racial and gender-based promotions as well. Qualified minorities don't want there to be an asterisk by their rank or to be whispered about as a "token" around the police department water cooler. Qualified officers want to know they got where they are based on merit, not because of race or gender.

I do not want to leave the impression that I am against diversity in policing. While in a perfect world race and gender should not matter, I recognize that we are not yet there as a society. People in difficult situations want to see at least some representation of backgrounds and ethnicities similar to their own among the civil servants in their neighborhoods. I understand this. There needs to be some recognition, though, that it comes with a price for those left behind. As long as race is involved in hiring and promotions, there will be racial divisions in this country.

Racial Profiling

No chapter on police and race would be complete without addressing implicit bias and what has become known as racial profiling. Certainly, we all have preconceived notions based on personal experience as well as societal norms. What I noticed in my police career is that many of these biases are based more on personal conduct and appearance than skin color. There is a personal responsibility element that does not get touched on in most discussions about biases.

When black youths walk down the street wearing a Scarface t-shirt and pants hanging down below their ass crack, most people are going to lock their car doors when they go by. Is it because of their race? Maybe. More likely it is because that individual made the decision to don attire that emulates gang culture. People of all races view street gangs as potential threats to their safety. The act of locking a car door or crossing the street is in response to the negative image the person created for themselves, not necessarily as an act of racism.

The same thing happens with individuals opt to present themselves in manners that do not comply with societal norms or mores. An example of this is the biker culture. Many whites in motorcycle clubs wear biker gang patches and jackets, wear their hair long and look unkempt. People associate this look with outlaw biker gangs such as Hell's Angels. I have no doubt that most of these bikers are law-abiding citizens, but the way they choose to comport themselves conjures up negative images in the minds of people not familiar with their culture. They too see stereotyping and nervous passersby. Most of these bikers are white, so it demonstrates that negative stereotypes aren't necessarily racial in nature.

I had personal experience with this. As a career patrol officer, I kept myself well-groomed with short cropped, and later shaved, hair. My brother Jeff is also a police officer. However, he worked many years undercover in vice and special investigation units. Consequently, he often tried to look like the criminal element he was trying to infiltrate. He often had long hair, was unshaven, wore gaudy earrings and tattered clothes complete with heavy metal band logos consistent with the stereotypical "head banger" drug culture. We both had savings accounts at the same bank. We are both white males and only two years apart in age. But when I went to the bank, I made my transaction without incident and usually without ID. My brother, on the other hand, would often go to the same bank branch, sometimes even the same teller, and would be asked to provide three pieces of identification just to cash his paycheck.

The bias shown him was obviously not racial. It was due to his appearance. My brother Jeff didn't have much choice in how he presented himself because of his work assignment. However, most individuals do have a choice in how they appear, speak, and conduct themselves. It's not institutional racism when the choice an individual makes in presenting in himself or herself has a negative connotation when compared to the rest of society.

Race and politics and how they relate to the police are difficult subjects on which to find consensus. My goal is to give a working cop's view of racial tensions and political impacts on cops from someone who has spent his career in the crosshairs. I hope to leave the impression that much of today's rage directed at the police is borne more out of hopelessness for a considerable portion of Americans trapped generationally in the lower and working classes rather than substantiated racist police brutality or implicit bias.

Unfortunately, neither political party goes to bat for the police and both share responsibility for banishing today's police to the edge of being a job that the best potential candidates no longer want to do. This makes the dedicated police officer feel not only unappreciated, but unjustly under siege politically and by media sensationalism. It is difficult to see a happy ending if things don't change soon. Let's pray that God still loves the infantry.

11

Better to Burn Out than Fade Away

The mass of men lead lives of quiet desperation.

—Henry David Thoreau

Post-Traumatic Stress Disorder (PTSD) is a condition most often associated with combat veterans and military personnel. However, some studies show that up to 34% of frontline police officers show symptoms of PTSD due to the cumulative effects of experiencing traumatic death, serious injury, internal politics, officer-involved shootings, and unrelenting job stressors. While not every officer will experience PTSD, nearly every line officer will become burned out at various points of his or her career.

I have made references to being burned out several times in previous chapters, but I have until now only mentioned it in passing. To understand the true experience of a career patrol officer, the subject warrants a more detailed description because burnout is a frequent phenomenon among street cops—but it gets little attention. It is the dirty little secret that cheerleaders in the administration never admit publicly. Everything is a public relations mission where all that's said is how dedicated officers are to the community. They may be dedicated,

177

but the truth is that a large percentage of veteran police officers on the street are completely burned out. Many spend as much as half of their street career feeling hopelessly trapped.

My last few years at GRPD were a textbook example of burnout. I no longer wanted to be a cop. I would sometimes have almost a road rage reaction to the calls I was dispatched to. Everything was pure drudgery. I felt a nearly maniacal hatred at times for my fellow officers who I felt did not pull their weight. I often muttered to myself, "God, how I hate this shitty, dead-end job!"

I tuned out all but the most important information put out by an administration I despised. I took pride in the fact that I never read a single email from the pretend cops of the command staff the last two years I was there. Command-generated emails got an automatic "delete" without ever being opened. I suppose this was my passive-aggressive way of giving them the middle finger. This sometimes meant I was in the dark about certain new policies that were put out via email, but I was so used to the job by this point that I could fake my way through it.

Just walking into police headquarters in the morning was enough to get me in a bad mood. There was almost a depressing pall in the air.

I once read a biography about Rocky Marciano, the only undefeated heavyweight champion in boxing history. Marciano was known for being an extremely hard worker and fanatical trainer. Despite this, toward the end of his career Marciano complained he could no longer stand the smell of the gym. He knew it was time to retire.

It was like that for me just going into the headquarters building. Getting on the elevator to go down from the main level to the squad room felt like a metaphor for descending into Hell. If other guys were on the elevator with me, I would sometimes sarcastically blurt, "Dead men walking!" as the elevator door opened and we made the trek down the long hallway to the locker room. It felt as if we were going to our execution and were walking the green mile! Other times when around my buddy Tim Orent, one of us would mimic Sgt. Barnes in *Platoon* and say, "Take the pain!"

Even little things would get to me, such as the smell of a sweat-drenched bulletproof vest at the end of a long shift or the annoying voice inflections of certain dispatchers. All I would think about between calls was retirement—often running the numbers over and over again to arrive at the most advantageous pension formula.

I wasn't alone. By now everyone on day shift was a veteran officer. Virtually all of us felt the same way, only in varying degrees. I still recall two colleagues who would sit on the ledge in front of their lockers every morning with a look of total defeat on their faces. They were pondering the upcoming day and almost psyching themselves up before getting their uniforms on. They seemed to be asking themselves how they could get out of the doom of a new shift, before giving an audible sigh indicating they had resigned themselves to their fate.

Almost nothing the command staff did made sense to me anymore. It was abundantly clear that there was no room in this guy's police department for a foot soldier like me anymore. I was now the crusty old guy, just like the ones I saw when I started over a quarter century earlier. A dispatcher friend told me that the other dispatchers were intimidated by me, apparently due to the tongue-lashings I gave them at one time or another when they sent me on calls I felt I shouldn't have gotten.

I knew my retirement date was five years out. I found a phone app that counted down to that date second-by-second. Among cops close to retirement, it is common practice to ask each other how much time he has left—similar to a soldier nearing the end of his tour of duty. It's almost a greeting among older officers. Whenever a colleague asked, "Dave, when are you going?" I had the phone app handy to immediately quote an exact number of days and minutes. It was a cool little prop that usually provoked a laugh. High fives and hoots and howls would abound when bench marks were reached, like having fewer than 1,000 days left.

People in more prim and proper professions will likely refer to job burnout in a more formal way, such as "plateauing" or "career stagnation." In law enforcement we have a cruder way of describing it. In police jargon, we call burnout "having your shit tank full." This refers to the reality that every cop can only handle so much crap. Finally, it gets to the point where he or she can take no more. Hence, his or her "shit tank is full." I was at that point. A person can only deal with so much tragedy, confrontation, bureaucracy, and conflict. Eventually, the mind and body cry out. There were certain types of calls I just couldn't take anymore. Some calls would elicit a negative psychological response before I even responded.

Probably the thing that got to me most when I neared the end of my career was the smell of dead bodies. If you have never smelled a decaying body, I hope you never have to. A decaying human body smells like nothing else. It is a horrible, putrid sweet odor that is so intense you never forget it. When I was younger, I could handle that horrible smell as just an unpleasant reality of the job. After all, I had that penchant for drawing the nasty death calls. However, by the end of my career I had experienced it so many times that I could barely tolerate walking into a house with a dead body in it. Olfactory stimuli can produce a powerful psychological response. Rotting human flesh had that effect on me by now.

Bad calls, bad memories

I think the call that pushed me over the edge came when I was four or five years away from retirement. I was sent to a welfare check on the city's southeast side. It was late summer and a hot day. I met the caller in front of the house. He was the father of the resident there. He indicated that he had not heard from his son in over a month. The father was concerned about his son's welfare and requested I check the house for him. The house was locked up tighter than a drum, with doors and windows locked and shades drawn so that it was impossible to see inside.

The complainant had a key that I used to unlock the front door. I told the caller to wait outside. The second I swung open the door, I was hit by a wall of death stench like I had never encountered before. The combination of summer heat, a body that had been rotting for weeks, and no ventilation had contained the putrid, stagnant air completely within the house. I knew exactly what I was going to find. I kept my composure and asked the father to remain outside and to prepare for the worst.

Once inside, I could not immediately find the deceased. Usually the odor is more intense as you approach the room where the body is located. In this particular case, the house had been so buttoned up that the entire house was permeated with dead body redolence. I saw a concentration of flies in a stairwell leading to the upstairs. This prompted me to proceed to the second floor, where I found the dead body in a state of horrific decay.

The body lay in a bath tub filled with water. The deceased had been in the tub of bath water for at least three weeks. The body was in such a state of decay, with blackened flesh covered with maggots and flies, that it was unrecognizable. It had partially melded into the bath water at the water line, creating a gruesome, soupy semi-liquid that looked something like melted candle wax.

The smell was so horrific that I had to hold my breath to keep from throwing up. It was so bad, I toyed with calling the fire department to the scene so I could use one of their respirator air tanks. I decided against making it that big of production, however. Instead, I improvised a more simplistic and primitive system to cope with the stench as I tried to determine cause of death. I would go outside for fresh air for several minutes, hold my breath before I reentered the house, and inspect the death scene for as long as I could hold my breath. This gave me a minute or two before I would run outside for more fresh air. This scenario played out several times before I determined that the deceased had died by his own hand after he fatally stabbed himself in the tub.

I discouraged the father of the deceased from entering the house, instead convincing him to remember his son the way he used to be. I sent the father on his way and informed him the medical examiner's office would contact him.

I had handled many unpleasant death investigations in my time as a police officer, some that were perhaps even more gruesome than this one. However, the intensity of the odor of this one was so bad that I still had the awful smell in my nostrils and sinuses well after the end of my shift. It permeated my uniform and everything needed to be washed afterward. I even had to wipe down my gun belt and holster. After that call, I shuddered and cringed whenever I had to respond to a death.

Even a guy like me, who possessed mental fortitude and an ability to compartmentalize tragic events, has a few chinks in his mental armor by this point in a career. Many officers will tell you that a death involving a child is the hardest call for them to face. Dealing with the tragedy of dead children for a quarter century finally gets to even the most hardened soul.

On one of the last Christmases I worked, I came across a fatal traffic crash at Hall Street and Buchanan Avenue on the southwest side. A four-year-old girl was killed when a drunk driver ran a red light, causing the multi-vehicle crash. I rolled up on the crash within a minute or two of impact, and before 9-1-1 call takers had had time to dispatch the call.

As I walked up to the crash, several frantic witnesses informed me that the drunk driver who had caused the crash had fled the scene on foot. The scene was complete chaos, with people running around yelling and screaming and injured parties trapped in heavily-damaged vehicles. A first responder's first duty is always to render aid to any injured, so I could not yet pursue the suspect. I did not immediately know the extent of injuries, but one witness told me that a four-year old girl from one of the crash vehicles did not appear to be breathing.

I quickly ran to her aid. When I checked on her, I saw the steam from her breath rising into the freezing air. This led me to believe that the little girl was still breathing. I had already requested an emergency response from medical units. I was still the only first responder on scene, so with medical on its way and believing the child was still breathing, I moved on to check other victims. Time was of the essence. Things were chaotic and moving fast. It was imperative that I also put out a broadcast with the hit-and-run suspect's description and his direction of flight to optimize our chances of catching him.

By the time medical units arrived, the four-year old child had stopped breathing. GR firefighters commenced CPR immediately, but to no avail. The child died at the scene. It occurred to me later that the breath

I initially saw coming from the child's mouth may not have been from breathing, but was merely steam escaping from her warm open mouth exposed to the frigid December air. I wondered if I mistook this for breathing and should have started CPR right then. Maybe the couple minutes between my initial assessment and the time GR fire personnel arrived would've made a difference. Later, doctors told me that her internal injuries were so extensive that no action at the scene could have saved her. However, it's still a call about which I second guess myself. It's a call that causes more than a tinge of guilt and regret, especially since the child essentially died in my arms. Some days, I still see that little girl's lifeless face with breath drifting up from her mouth.

The entire call was tragic. The deceased girl's family was from the Detroit area, and was in Grand Rapids for a Christmas event for their church. In addition to the child who died, several other members of the family were seriously injured. The entire family needed medical treatment at the hospital and were all transported there via ambulance. No one in the family spoke fluent English, making communication more difficult. It was the only time in my career I needed to tell a mother her child had been killed through an interpreter.

The only good news was that Officer Brian Grooms, as he so often did, located the hit-and-run suspect several blocks away. The driver was later convicted in the girl's death and received a considerable prison sentence.

Just because a street cop is tired and at the end of his career, doesn't mean that the intensity and demands of the job wane, as the aforementioned calls suggest. Every now and then, a new wrinkle is thrown into the works. During the last five years of my career, I responded to more heroin overdoses than I had in the first twenty-one years combined. What has now been labeled "The Opioid Crisis" led to a new way of responding to drug and medical calls, with officers now trained in administering the overdose drug Narcan. We also had to worry about exposure to fentanyl-laced substances, which had never been a big risk before.

My long tenure on the street was perhaps best exemplified by a call I had on Bemis Street on the southeast side. I responded to a call with a sergeant who had started around the same time I had. We both were momentarily stunned when one of the subjects of the call was a well-known doper and gang member who both of us had dealt with on several occasions in the 1990s. He had been convicted of numerous drug charges and was suspected in several gang-related shootings when we were young officers. We both thought he was still locked away in prison. Not only was he at the scene, but he looked exactly as he did in the early '90s. He seemingly hadn't aged at all. It wasn't until we investigated further that we learned this guy was actually the *son* of our long-time 1990s drug-dealing adversary. He had an uncanny resemblance to his father, who was still (thankfully) shuttered away in prison. It reminded me how by now I had dealt with two and sometimes three generations of miscreants from the city's troublesome families.

I was ready to be done with police work, but I was determined not to shirk my responsibilities. I made sure I fulfilled my duties with professionalism. I did not try to pawn off my calls on co-workers and I remained diligent in my investigation of incidents I responded to.

It may sound strange to some outside law enforcement, but as I have mentioned previously, a patrol officer does eventually reach a point where he is comfortable, almost relaxed, on the street. It can become easy to let one's guard down when this occurs. This is especially true as a patrol officer ages. It can become easy to put too much trust in your experience. Things can still happen very fast and without warning. The criminal element does not care that an old officer is a year away from retirement. No mercy is afforded them. I had that point driven home on several occasions.

I remember a quiet Sunday afternoon when I was winding down from a long weekend of work. On the twelve-hour shift rotation we worked at GRPD, we worked 36 hours in a three-day stretch every other weekend. By the end of the weekend, officers are tired and hoping for an uneventful Sunday afternoon. I had parked my cruiser in a shaded area of MLK Park on Fuller Avenue on this unseasonably warm day. The goal was to get through the next few hours and go home. This was chill time.

While I was parked, a woman pulled up in her vehicle and informed me that a disorderly female was walking up and down Fuller Avenue knocking over trash cans and dumping trash in the street a few blocks north of where I was parked. I informed the woman I would check it out and left to investigate.

I located the female in question, still walking along and knocking over trash cans. I recognized her as a woman with mental problems who I had dealt with before. I had recently responded to call where she was sleeping on a stranger's front porch. Before taking her nap at a random home, she had dismantled a decorative plastic owl at the fire station across the street because she thought the plastic owl was staring at her. She clearly had her issues.

In this latest incident, I immediately noticed that she was highly agitated. It was my hope to simply calm her and convince her to pick up the overturned trash cans and order her to cease and desist any further such activity. I wasn't looking to turn this into the crime of the century. I just wanted her to knock it off so I could return to my quiet shaded spot in the park.

As I exited my cruiser to initiate contact, she freaked. Her eyes became as large as saucers and she let out an unintelligible, primal scream. It was obvious that she was not going to go gently into that good night. The woman was on a mental bender and would need what Sgt. Barry Bryant used to refer to as "a time out" at the county jail—not to mention a mental health referral.

I informed her that she was under arrest for creating a disturbance. She would not comply with orders to put her hands behind her back. Instead, she began walking away from me. I grabbed her arm and used a takedown maneuver to bring her to the ground as she tried to break free. Once I had her on the ground, her agitation turned to psychotic rage. She bit my arm as I tried to get her arm out from underneath her to allow for handcuffing. In between bites, she was screaming with a guttural intensity that appeared to be something out of a bad horror movie.

The woman was wiry enough that she managed to spin her body around and got on her back, while I remained on top of her trying to control her frantic, psychotic fight-or-flight adrenaline dump. She began spitting in my face. Still wide-eyed, she began cursing my badge and screaming for me to take it off. She claimed the badge was staring at her. She grabbed my badge and tried to rip it off my uniform shirt. When that was unsuccessful, she released the badge and took her free hand and grabbed my taser, which was in a holster on my gun belt. I don't know for sure, but I think she thought the taser was my firearm and she was trying to disarm me.

The irony was that I was carrying a replacement taser and holster that day. My issued taser was being repaired, and I had to take out a loaner at the beginning of my shift. The loaner holster was not attached to my belt in the same secure fashion as my assigned one. This allowed it to be released from my gun belt with less difficulty. As the woman began tugging on the taser, I let go of her and immediately clutched the taser with both hands to prevent its removal. While a taser is not typically a weapon that causes death, if she had been able to get it away from me, she could have used it and incapacitated me and subsequently taken my firearm.

I tried to spin away from the woman, with my hands firmly clinging to the taser. I successfully broke her grasp on the taser. The force of this pulled the entire holster off and it detached from my gun belt. The still-holstered taser lay on the ground a few feet away from her as I finally rolled her over and forced her to the ground face first. I now had control of both of her arms. She was still squirming, screaming, and trying to break free with all of her psychotic might. However, I could tell that I was considerably stronger than her and she could not get away. I immobilized her head to neutralize her biting. The taser was far enough away from the struggle that it was no longer in play. I had already called for backup, so I just hung on to the woman until a second officer arrived on scene. We then handcuffed her and took her into custody. The confrontation had begun on the sidewalk and ended up in the street when all was said and done.

It was another one of those incidents where a simple, misdemeanor disorderly conduct arrest could have led to tragedy. If the woman had successfully disarmed me, I could have been killed or I may have had to preemptively use deadly force on her.

Incredibly, in the aftermath of this near tragedy, a do-gooder passerby approached me and officers on the scene and complained about how rough I had been with this poor woman when taking her to the ground! Here I was, the victim of an attempted disarming. I had been bitten and spat on. Now I had a citizen crusader questioning my actions in a situation where I could have been killed or incapacitated. Thankfully, Sgt. Elliot Bargas was on scene and ran interference for me and smoothed things over.

I saw the woman a few weeks later at a preliminary hearing. She now appeared properly medicated and was a completely different person. It could have been an act, I suppose, but she now seemed completely docile, almost meek. She said hello to me in a quiet, almost timid manner—as if she didn't even remember the incident. Maybe she didn't.

I do not know what happened in the case; I was never subpoenaed for a trial. I recognized that she was a victim of mental illness and I informed the prosecutor that, while I felt she should still face some consequences for her actions, I was more interested in her getting the mental health help she needed. I was not looking to have the book thrown at her. I never took her actions personally.

I saw that same woman one more time before I retired. She was again walking down the street, but this time in an orderly manner. Grateful that she was not knocking over trash cans, I eagerly drove right on by. Rest assured that I did not make contact with her this time!

Shortly after this incident, a friend from my union president days, Captain Mike Maycroft, had mercy on me and moved me to the North Service Area. My long tour of duty in the inner city was now over. Mike and I had fought many union battles together in the old days when I was president of the union and he was president of our F.O.P. lodge. Our careers took different paths, with Mike seeking promotion. He was now the captain in charge of the northeast end. Despite achieving high rank, Mike was one of the few command guys who had appreciation for what I had done over the years. He let me work for him.

I really wanted to finish my last year and a half on the northeast end because it was where I began my career. It was the patrol area formerly known as "Baker Sector," and was where I had the most fun working as a young officer. It was the old stomping grounds for Stinky and a lot of the veteran guys I revered in the old days. It was befitting that I end my career there.

By this time in my career, I was simply marking time. Like most older officers, self-initiated activity was not a high priority. I was still trying to do a good job, but I concentrated more on diligent disposition of my calls for service than on proactive policing.

I recognized that I was not the officer I used to be. I think most of us are in denial when it comes to our own decline. I was not. I could tell I wasn't the officer I was ten years earlier, or even five years before. I couldn't quickly assess situations like I used to. When I was younger, Chad Kooyer used to tell me I was like Tom Brady sizing up an opponent's defense in my ability to read a scene. However, now it took me longer to figure out the angle someone was using to put one over on me. I would miss things sometimes. It wasn't that I had a loss of cognitive ability or mental acuity. I wasn't unfit. I was now two and three decades older than the typical perpetrator on the street. I couldn't relate to the younger generation anymore and society had sped up while I was slowing down.

Also, I started questioning myself more. I had always been extremely confident in my ability to resolve situations, but I wasn't as confident anymore. Policies had changed. Attitudes had changed. The command and supervision were dramatically different. I wasn't as nimble or quick to adapt as I had been before. I sometimes left calls that I used to sleepwalk through now thinking to myself, "Did I do that right?"

Physically, I could see my reaction time was slower. I was nearing 50 years old. I did not have the reflexes I once had. It would be easier for the bad guys to get the drop on me and I realized it. I had to be more strategic in the way I responded to things. The old police adage "Don't be a badass until your backup arrives" was always in the back of my mind. In the old days, I wasn't afraid of anyone.

Younger officers were light years ahead of me in the use of technology. They could access information on in-car computers that I had no idea even existed. I had almost become like Stinky and the Breathalyzer machine he never learned how to use.

Benefits of an aging officer

I still had some positive attributes as a police officer, however. I became more patient with citizens. I tried to be the humble servant, rather than the stern tough guy. At a time when criticism of police-community relations was rampant, I did my best to always be pleasant and respectful. I felt I could still be an asset to the department if the citizens I had contact with came away with a good feeling about the police. My experience helped me in this regard. I was able to handle the strained community relations without too much frustration. I had been through it all before after the Rodney King incident. I came to realize that tensions between the police and some group of citizens flares up once a generation, whether warranted or not. I tried to convey that to the younger officers. Even this will pass, I told them.

Similar to what I had done at the 28th Street McDonald's years before, I made friends with an eclectic group of locals at the Leonard Street McDonald's on the northeast end, which became my new "10-7" spot. I never looked down on people, nor felt I was better than them. I never forgot my working-class roots.

A lot of burned-out officers have a much different attitude, however. This is the time in an officer's career when they sometimes become the rude cop who is short with or crass to citizens. Many burned-out cops are also much less inclined to handle their responsibilities as dutifully as I attempted to do. They respond to this state of mind by "milking" their calls, meaning they remain logged on them for much longer than they need to in order to avoid additional work. This is also called "pimping" your fellow officers, as you are selling them out. This kind of officer regularly sticks his co-workers with what should be his assignments.

As I learned early in my career, you get a window into a person's true character not when things are going well, but instead when things are going poorly. That's when you see what they are really made of. Unfortunately, there is a significant number of burned-out officers who have no problem cutting corners at the expense of the same co-workers who have watched their backs for decades. Of course, this adds to the bitterness and mental fatigue already felt by those forced to pick up the slack.

Other officers deal with burnout by never being at work. They are constantly angling to get the day off. Their names are constantly in the vacation book and they carry a minimal sick time balance. I knew several officers who frittered away tens of thousands of dollars over the course of a career by taking overtime as "comp time" that was converted to time off instead of pay—all because they couldn't stand being on the job.

I had to challenge myself mentally the last couple of years before retirement. I was so tired and remained frustrated beyond belief. It seemed like time stood still when I was at work. The twelve-hour days now left me completely emotionally exhausted. I really had to grind it out.

Younger guys told me how lucky I was compared to them, as I only had another year to go. I explained that it may seem that way to them, but it was like running a marathon. Any runner will tell you that the last couple of miles are the most difficult to get through. In the first half of the marathon, the runner is fresh and strong and the miles go by quickly. By the last mile, the runner labors through every stride. The last mile seems harder than the first 25 combined. It's the same for the career street cop.

I came to loathe mandatory training. This is also a common trait among veteran officers. I knew of an older officer in the early 1990s who hated training so much that he retired instead of going through a demanding field force training about to take place. This is not to say training is unimportant. It is important. But after a quarter century of doing it, the burned-out cop views training with the same disdain that a veteran football player dreads two-a-day July practices.

Even my stellar health began to wane a bit. For many years I was never afflicted by much more than an annual cold. I already alluded to the more than twelve-year stint in which I never called in sick. Now, though, I was riddled by nagging colds and viruses that would take forever to shake. I chalked it up to the toll decades of 4 AM wakeup calls have on the body, along with constant exposure to the outdoor elements and constant contact with an often chronically ill homeless population.

While I tried to be more easygoing and less confrontational with citizens, occasionally my Irish temper and full shit tank boiled over and I would lose my patience. The subject who pushed me would then get both barrels of a verbal shaming that was too politically incorrect for today's hypersensitivities. I was grateful when my partners intervened and did damage control.

I'm far from being an isolated case. The problem of burned-out police officers is likely only to get worse in this country due to two recent developments. To begin with, officers are tending to start the job when they are older. While people in the private sector may not view a guy in his early 30s as old, it creates many potential obstacles in law enforcement. Starting a police career at say, 32, means the officer will not reach 25 years of service until he is 57 years old. He'll reach 30 years at age 62. With any retirement that comes before 25 years on the job, most officers will end up struggling financially. People can fool themselves all they want, but very few people in their late 50s or 60s have any business working the street. This is a young person's game and there are not enough desk jobs to accommodate a police department with a large number of older officers.

Secondly, the political climate in this country has led many police agencies to adopt defined contribution (or 401k-style) retirement plans, scrapping their traditional defined-benefit pensions. This has the likely effect of requiring officers who begin the job, even at a young age, to toil in the profession well into their 50s, 60s, or maybe longer. The modest contributions employees can afford to put into these 401(k)-style plans on a cop's income does not allow for enough capital accumulation to provide a livable retirement income over a typical 25- or 30-year career.

191

This will translate into much older police departments in the coming decades. The next generation of police officers simply will not be able to afford to retire. I can only shudder at the thought of how geriatric police departments will exacerbate the problem of police burnout. I was emotionally shot at age 50 after 27 years. God help the poor souls forced to do that job for 35 or 40 years, or however long it takes to get to Social Security age by then.

This is no small thing. A street cop needs to be done much sooner than this. I have always told people that you can easily tell a retired real cop from a retired pretender. The real cop will give you a number such as "25 years," "20 years," or maybe "28 years" when asked about his number of years on the job. The retired cop who tells you he worked 35 years either worked as an administrator or had a cushy job inside. He certainly didn't work the street. Not these days, anyway.

No one talks about it, but the profession is going to face a huge crisis in another twenty years or so when all of these 401(k) officers are mental and physical wrecks and are nowhere near able to afford to retire. Obviously, the perils of burnout will be just one of myriad issues resulting from these pending senior-citizen police forces.

Job burnout is prevalent in many jobs today as employers demand more and more from employees. Nowhere is this truer than in police work. In many cases, rank-and-file police officers spend a significant portion of their careers laboring in a state of quiet desperation. I am a prime example. As a young man I achieved my dream of becoming a police officer in my hometown and in the department I always wanted to join. By the time I was a middle-aged man, I could hardly stand entering the building.

12

Josiah Ward: Part 2

It is his capacity for self-improvement and self-redemption which most distinguishes man from the mere brute.

—Aung San Suu Kyi, Nobel Peace Prize laureate, 1991

A person facing retirement is beset by a wide array of emotions. I was no different. I was a few months away in December 2016. It appeared that my final days on the street would end even sooner because earlier in the autumn I was diagnosed with a torn rotator cuff in my right shoulder that would require surgery. I strategically scheduled the surgery for January 3, 2017. With an April 10 retirement date looming a few months after I went under the knife, it appeared I would finish my career recovering from surgery and end with a short stint on light duty. January 1 looked to be the final day I would suit up and hit the street.

Always a reflective and introspective person, those qualities kicked into overdrive as I neared the end of my police career. I was proud of my career. I certainly made mistakes and there were definitely officers who were better than me. Still, I believe I served with professionalism and dedication. I was reliable and someone my co-workers could depend on. The opinions of the guys I worked with were the only ones I cared about. I didn't care what the administration thought about me. Only the real cops.

I was past feeling that the retirement I was so eager and desperate to achieve would never arrive. There were still tasks to perform and dangers to face, but I now knew the light at the end of the tunnel was not an oncoming train. This really was going to happen. While I was introspective, I was not overly sentimental during my last weeks on the street. I merely wanted to make sure I properly dotted all of the i's and crossed all of the t's without any snags.

Financially, I was in good shape though far from wealthy. However, I had remained fiscally conservative throughout my life so was debt free. I had sold my house in suburban Grand Rapids a few years earlier in preparation for retirement but had kept my cabin. I was preparing to make the final modifications to my cabin to make it a comfortable, full-time home once I retired. Barring runaway inflation or legislative theft of my pension, my monthly stipend should be enough to keep my modest lifestyle well into old age. I hope an investment nest egg will pick up any shortfall down the road when inflation begins to devalue my pension. Due to disciplined financial planning, I was entering retirement without an immediate need to find another job to make ends meet.

Each day was a finale of sorts. There was the last Thanksgiving I would work, the final long weekend. There was my last Christmas on duty, etc. I finally reached December 26, 2016.

The day after Christmas is typically a laidback kind of day. It's usually busier than Christmas Day itself, but not like a normal patrol shift. Traffic is lighter than a usual work day with the exception of thoroughfares around the malls and big box stores where shoppers are eager to make their Christmas gift returns. There are fewer family gatherings, which typically means fewer domestic conflicts as when Christmas Day glee turns sour. That was the backdrop for my little holiday farewell tour.

December 26, 2016, was a fairly uneventful, if unseasonably cold, day. In fact, I only remember one call from my shift. In the afternoon, I was sent to the eastern edge of my patrol district on the Leonard Street overpass over I-96. While far from rural, this is a somewhat open, windswept area without a lot of houses—typical of an area near a freeway overpass at the edge of the city limits.

I was dispatched to a simple motorist-assist on the overpass; a stalled vehicle was blocking the traffic lane. It's not the kind of call that typically provides closure for unresolved questions that had been festering in the subconscious for nearly two decades. However, this one did. I rolled up on scene and found an occupied car blocking one of the eastbound lanes. I remember noticing that the car appeared new and how unusual this was for a newer vehicle to break down in the middle of the road. As is standard procedure, I placed my cruiser behind the disabled vehicle and activated my lightbar. I could see that the vehicle was occupied, so I exited my cruiser to make contact with the people in the car.

As I glanced in the driver's window, I was met with what seemed like a ghost from the past. I immediately recognized Josiah Ward! I had not seen Ward since that fateful day back in 1998 when his girlfriend was killed. My last memory of him was when Chad Kooyer and I placed him in the back of our patrol car in the minutes after that tragic death. The moment that cruiser door slammed was the last second of freedom Josiah Ward would see for a very long time.

The sight of Ward hit me like a bolt of lightning. I was shocked! I had no idea he was out of prison. There had been a lot of what I had termed "frequent flyers" in my police career—people I had dealt with over and over again. However, Ward was someone I never thought I would see again in a million years.

I was struck by how much he looked the same. He remained very thin, almost gaunt. He still had a youthful appearance despite now being well into his thirties. However, any similarities to that Ward and the tragic 1998 night ended when he began to speak. Gone was the ghetto gangster twang and slang. Josiah instead spoke in a soft and respectful—albeit cautious—manner. I could tell that after many years in prison, he had an elevated level of anxiety regarding contact with the police. He nervously explained that his car had stopped running without warning. He advised me he had already called for a tow truck to take it to a local dealer for repair and was just waiting for it to arrive.

I, in turn, informed him I would keep my patrol car situated behind his to reroute traffic until the wrecker arrived.

I noted that Ward was dressed modestly, with none of the previous rapper bling or flashy attire. Also present in the passenger seat was an attractive, pleasant, and well-spoken young woman, who I assumed to be Josiah's girlfriend. I returned to my cruiser to wait while Ward remained in his car. I could tell he did not recognize me, which was understandable. It had been a long time since he last saw me and the years had not been as kind to my appearance as they had been to his.

Once back in my patrol vehicle, I took care of a few perfunctory investigative and reporting tasks such as running the vehicle's plate and entering needed information into the brief report I would need to file. I was distracted and preoccupied the entire time, however, by the stunned feeling that overcame me after seeing Josiah Ward again after nearly nineteen years. A plethora of emotions flooded me. This had been one of the few cases I investigated in which I had lingering doubts. What really happened that night back in 1998? Why did things escalate to that extreme? Probably most significantly, I always wondered what had become of Ward. It was such a sad case in which one young life was tragically extinguished and the other one would never be the same. The case stuck with me because of this, as well as the coming of age it represented for me at that point in my career.

After a couple of minutes reflecting on what was happening and pondering these questions, I was quickly brought back to reality. I suddenly realized I had not offered Ward and his passenger the opportunity to get out of the harsh elements. It was now bitter cold and the brisk wind on this open section of roadway made the chill feel that much greater. I exited my cruiser and returned to the driver's window of his car. I told Ward that he and his passenger were welcome to wait in my car to stay warm until the tow truck arrived. With his apprehension toward the police still obvious, he politely declined my offer.

Suddenly, without consciously planning to, I blurted out, "I was there that night." I was aware of his female passenger, so I did not get more specific. I did not know how much he had told her, and I did not want this simple motorist-assist escalating into a domestic argument when the woman found out her boyfriend was a convicted murderer.

I then said, "I was the first officer on scene." I followed up by asking, "When did you get out?" I tried to speak in a disarming, almost casual way. I did not want to appear confrontational or judgmental. I was speaking to Ward now as a fellow human being, not as a stern authority figure.

Josiah was obviously startled by the revelation I had just thrust upon him. He briefly fumbled with what to say and then said softly, "I did the whole fifteen years." Slowly he let his guard down. He became more at ease as we spoke briefly about that night. The conversation remained on the periphery of the incident, without either of us delving into the gritty details. After a couple minutes of conversation and the tow truck still not on scene, I returned to my patrol car.

A few minutes later, I saw Ward waving his arm out the car window trying to get my attention. He apparently did not feel he could exit his car without my permission, so this was his way of letting me know he wanted to speak to me. I returned to his car and he informed me that, with no tow truck in sight, he had changed his mind and he and his passenger requested they be allowed to wait in my cruiser to stay warm. I said that would be fine.

Since I was already at his driver's side window, I made room for him to exit his vehicle and led him back to my police car. I opened the back door and let his female passenger in first. She slid over and then Josiah entered the back seat. I closed the door, which locked both of them in the back of my cruiser. I then said to Ward, "I can't believe you fell for that twice!" For a fleeting second, Josiah had a panicked, deer-in-the-headlights look in his eyes as he remembered what had happened the last time I placed him in the back of a police car and locked the door. He then realized this was my attempt at ice-breaking humor, and he burst out laughing. We both got a good chuckle out of the joke, which accomplished my goal of making him feel at ease. That was it. Ward completely warmed up after that and we now had a solid rapport. Once trust was established, Josiah became downright friendly.

We waited another ten minutes for the wrecker to arrive. During that time, Josiah spoke about his time in prison. He was completely at ease. He mentioned how he had a job as a prisoner washing patrol cars for a Michigan State Police post near the prison. He spoke of the relationship he had developed with the post commander and what a positive effect it had on him. He spoke of his reverence for his family and informed me he had just left a Christmas gathering at his grandfather's house when his car broke down. Ironically, his grandfather still lived across the street from his old house where the homicide had occurred.

Ward now spoke with complete humility. There were no airs about him at all. The rebellious kid who had cultivated the image of thug life was now humble and speaking of his dedication to his family. He talked about completely changing his life around. He had moved hundreds of miles away to a small town in northern Michigan to get away from the element he used to associate with as a teenager in the inner city of Grand Rapids. He appeared completely genuine and sincere.

For those ten minutes, it was just Dave talking to Josiah. I was not speaking to him as if he was a convicted murderer, and he was not speaking to me as the cop who took away his freedom for the better part of his youth. He seemed to be gleaning every bit as much as I was from the conversation. We spoke to each other at the most earnest and human level, as kindred spirits. It was an almost soothing dialogue.

In the end, I did not have my question answered about what exactly happened during that 1998 night so long ago. I decided not to ask that question of Ward. I figured he had paid his debt to society and some things are better left in the past. Even without my question answered, the conversation moved me and put my mind completely at ease. He really appeared to be a changed man. The lingering questions I previously had now seemed irrelevant. I felt it better to no longer dwell on that tragic night, but to instead revel in the prospect of the new life Josiah appeared to be building.

The tow truck finally arrived, apparently delayed by having only a skeleton holiday crew on duty this day after Christmas. I let Josiah and his girlfriend out of the cruiser, again joking that this was a lot sooner than the last time we met. He shook my hand with a smile on his face and a look of relieved gratitude in his eyes. He then left to make arrangements for his vehicle with the wrecker driver. Before they drove away, Ward came back to my cruiser. He again thanked me. I could tell he was thanking me for much more than my limited help with his disabled car. He even asked to have his picture taken with me, which I gladly obliged. Josiah Ward and the tow truck then drove off into the cold December afternoon.

There have been few occasions where I felt the palpable hand of God's grace directly intervening in my life. I'm not typically a person with that kind of spiritual perception and intuition. This encounter, however, was one of the moments I did. I left the contact with Josiah Ward with a feeling that all was well. I believe Josiah did too. I felt for the first time something good had come out of deadly calamity. I felt I had witnessed a true example of redemption. As hokey as it may seem to some, I felt completely at peace. I felt divine grace.

Sense of closure

I believe God was helping me achieve spiritual closure as a police officer. He appeared to be giving me the opportunity to tie up the remaining loose ends in a long career—ending any lingering questions I had about my most nagging case and by allowing a moving example of redemption as a finish to my career. It seemed to be part of the process of one of life's doors closing before the next one opened.

It seemed that Josiah's chance encounter with me was part of a larger plan for him too. It was like he was making amends with the people he had aggrieved and I was another he could check off the list.

I, of course, cannot prove God had a hand in all of this. What I can offer is the extremely low probability of it being coincidence. After all, what were the odds that Josiah Ward's new car would break down in my patrol district on one of the last days of my career? What were the chances it would be me who responded? What is the likelihood we would cross paths on the only day of the year he was in Grand Rapids? The probability of this confluence of events happening at this crossroads in my life has to be astronomically low.

In a criminal justice system in which criminal recidivism and resulting police cynicism runs rampant, it was moving for me to see a young man who seemed to have matured and was on his way to being a good man. During that brief encounter, all of my career's trials and tribulations—from union conflicts to personal slights—seemed irrelevant. This was one of those moments that made the travails of a career spent on the front lines all worth it.

I wasn't born yesterday. Maybe the journey will still end poorly for Ward. I recognize that his seemingly heart-felt exchange with me could have all been BS; maybe prison had beaten him into submission. I don't think so, though. I think my innate ability to correctly assess and evaluate an individual had served me well one last time in this encounter, and I believe I had witnessed a genuine conversion in him.

Everything after the Josiah Ward call seemed anti-climactic. I worked another day or two before preparing for my shoulder surgery. The surgery went off without a hitch and I began a rigorous physical therapy regimen that started the day after the operation. I progressed so well that the surgeon allowed me to return to light duty after just three weeks.

I was assigned to follow-up investigations on domestic assault cases in the Family Services Unit of the Detective Bureau. For the only time in my career, I did not wear a uniform. I worked with a great group of detectives who were extremely adept at what they did. They took care of me, remaining patient as I stumbled through an aspect of police work that was completely foreign to me.

My physical therapy continued to progress ahead of schedule. Just six weeks after my surgery, the surgeon gave me permission to return to full-duty status. This meant I could finish my career on patrol. This was important to me. Many people told me I was stupid to return to the street with only a few weeks left before my retirement. They said I should remain inside and essentially run out the clock. Why take a risk this close to the end?

I didn't expect people to understand. After 27 years of being a first responder, it didn't feel right going out sitting behind a desk. I wasn't wired that way. I wasn't trying to prove how tough I was. I just didn't want to feel like a boxer going out sitting on his stool. I wanted to go out doing a brief victory lap in the arena. I wanted to end it all with the guys I had always worked with.

I remained low profile once back on the street. I didn't duck my responsibilities, but I shied away from high-risk, pro-active stuff that could get dicey or result in court subpoenas months after I had retired. If the reader will permit me one more sports metaphor, I was trying to do a few "quarterback kneel downs" and call it a career.

I did have one more foot pursuit, however. A shoplifter stole several electronic items from a Meijer store and fled from store security when confronted. Knowing the lay of the land, I correctly guessed the perpetrator's probable flight direction. I spotted him in the nearby Kent Career Technical Center parking lot. The culprit took off once he spotted me, and when I ran out of parking lot, he forced me to exit my cruiser and pursue him on foot. After a couple hundred yards, I caught him. I wish I could tell you that I caught him due to "the superior conditioning of a veteran officer still dedicated to his craft." The truth is that the bad guy, a pathetically out-of-shape drug addict, gave up and stopped running, allowing me to catch him. Oh, well. It wasn't pretty, but justice was still served.

I was also on the scene of my friend Tim Orent's officer-involved shooting. This was just a few days before my retirement. It was sobering when I thought about how different the end of my career could have been had the perpetrator run my way instead of Tim's. As if I needed any more reminders, it was another example of how cruel the streets really are. Threats are ever present right up until the end.

Last days

My last full day of work was March 30, 2017. I had by now completed all of the administrative tasks associated with pending retirement. I had signed my retirement papers, met with insurance services, and spoken to the chief's office. The last thing I wanted to do was say a heartfelt goodbye to the unsung people who had made my career easier over the years. I stopped by the fire stations I had frequented and bid farewell to my firefighter friends. There were several employees at our credit union who had treated me well over the years and I thanked all of them.

Mostly, I wanted to thank the employees and regulars at my break and lunch spots. For many years, employees of the Eastown Jimmy John's restaurant had cheerfully made my No. 4 turkey sub sandwich. Many days they would have it waiting for me on the counter when I walked in. I greatly appreciated the warm service they had given me and the friendships made with these young people. That little respite from the harshness of the streets provided by the Jimmy John's crew during my lunch break came to mean a lot to me over the years. After I took my final lunch there, I left a $100 bill in the tip jar. It was a small token of my appreciation.

I slept surprisingly well on the eve of my final day. Technically, I was scheduled to work the full twelve-hour shift. However, it had become customary at GRPD to work an abbreviated day on one's final shift. Most guys, in fact, left shortly after line-up. I arrived at my normal time, checking out my cruiser and logging into the in-car computer as I always had.

My last line-up was uneventful with our Watch Commander, Lt. Pat Merrill, acknowledging my last day and asking if I had any words of wisdom. I advised him I did not, but that I did have an outstanding piece of equipment I needed to return. Back in the mid-1990s, Chad Kooyer had loaned me his spare 4-cell Maglight flashlight when mine burned out. I carried it for many years without returning it. I presented the long-forgotten flashlight to him in front of everyone and reminded him it still had his name and badge number engraved on it. I joked that the fact that his name was still on it was the only reason I didn't lift it permanently.

I was intent on going out without fanfare. I declined a "retirement coffee" that the department offered and even skipped having the traditional cake at line-up. Instead, I asked Chad to snap a quick cell phone picture of me in the motor pool as I prepared to go on patrol for the final time. I then checked my cell phone countdown-to-retirement app and reveled in the fact that it was flashing all 0000s.

I hit the street for what was primarily a ceremonial tour. I was scheduled to turn in all remaining equipment, including the uniform I was wearing, at 11:00 AM. That would in reality end my day, as I no longer would have the means to perform my duties. One of my coworkers and long-time friend, Tim Johnston, requested to meet up with me. Well aware of my affinity for Detroit Tigers baseball, he presented me with a Tigers ballcap as a parting gift. He had written on the bill of the cap, "Dave, much respect for a guy who stayed on the field!—Tim."

My last call was a simple parking complaint. I then went into headquarters for a brief meeting with Chief David Rahinsky, at which time he presented me with my retirement badge and watch. I returned to patrol and spent the final few minutes sitting car to car with Chad at the Leonard/Plymouth fire station in our service area. Shortly before 11 AM, dispatch called me out of service for the last time with an over-the-air tribute. It was a nice gesture given to all retiring officers, but it mostly embarrassed me. I was unsuccessful in my earlier efforts to get dispatch to call it off. I then drove into the motor pool, parked my car, and prepared to turn in my gear.

Turning in 26 years worth of equipment was a brief trip down memory lane. I was struck by some of the old equipment and directives I still had tucked away in the nooks and crannies of my locker. It reminded me of the way the profession had evolved over the previous quarter century. I recalled how my first duty weapon was a Smith & Wesson .38 caliber revolver. I was now turning in my third generation of semi-auto pistol—a 9 mm Glock. As I cleared out my locker, there was a smattering of congratulatory well-wishers who stopped by and chatted. The department was kind enough to allow me to keep my uniform badge. I had worn the same badge on my uniform shirt for the entire 26 years, never needing a replacement in all that time. It was the only department-issued item that had any sentimental value to me.

Finally, it was time to fulfill my last obligation. The last thing a retiring Grand Rapids police officer does is turn in his parking card at the Watch Commander's office. Watch Commander Lt. Pat Merrill had been great to me. He had been a huge help during my last few months, helping me with scheduling conflicts related to my surgery and light duty, among other tasks. I entered Lt. Merrill's office and informed him that all my equipment had been turned in to property management, per procedure. I gave him my city parking card and he in turn gave me a parking pass to get out of the parking ramp. For the first time in 26 years, I would be leaving the parking ramp as a civilian. I then shook his hand and thanked him for all he had done for me. Pat seemed emotional and a bit uncomfortable and he looked away.

I've heard it said that there is nothing more sad or more glorious than the sight of generations changing hands. From a practical sense, this was evident to me by the fact that I needed help from a college intern with the electronic swipe cards controlling the exits to even leave the office. I no longer had one. I left GRPD headquarters through the Fulton Street entrance. From the moment I stepped outside into the cold, gray March day, I have not set foot again inside the Grand Rapids Police Department.

After more than 27 years and after responding to an estimated 32,000-plus calls for service, I was no longer a police officer. The moment seemed surreal. I had waited for this moment for so long that it just didn't seem real. Things almost appeared to be moving out of synch—not quite in slow motion, but not in regular time either. I remembered once watching an interview with 1980 U.S. Olympic hockey team member Dave Silk. He recalled not being able to feel his skates on the ice in the intensity of the opening period in the game against the Soviet Union. I felt similarly as I walked to my truck to go home.

I felt the full gambit of emotions. There was tremendous relief; there was happiness. I felt pride; I felt blessed; I felt a tinge of sadness. There was a sentimental dynamic present as well. I had fleeting thoughts about the people I had worked with. I remembered Stinky's last shift, and I wished he was still around to see mine. I thought about Bob Kozminski and all the other officers killed in the line of duty before they could ever see retirement. I thought of the people I would likely never see again.

I thought about my regrets. I felt bad about the times I was short with citizens when I was a young and impatient officer. There were other times when I was tired or close to the end of my shift and looked the other way instead of helping someone in need. I remembered that little girl who died in my arms at that horrific Christmas car crash and hoped I might see her someday in heaven to apologize for not starting CPR sooner. It's hard to describe the full range of emotions that envelopes a person when such a sought-after moment finally arrives. Great happiness melds into sorrow and then back to happiness, with all of the other emotions in between.

After leaving headquarters, I drove directly home to my cabin. The irony wasn't lost on me when the classic rock station I was listening to played one of my favorite 1980s songs, Motley Crue's *Home Sweet Home,* just as I pulled into my long, winding driveway.

I remained reflective. I had a ton of chores to do in the coming days to prepare for my upcoming pole barn project. Today, however, was going to be a relieved, pensive celebration. I stoked the fire in my woodstove, kicked my feet up, and proceeded to indulge in copious amounts of cheap beer.

I planned to formally celebrate my retirement with family and friends a week later. A buddy of mine, Jim Curran, had numerous political connections and secured a luxury suite at Comerica Park for an upcoming Detroit Tigers game, plus got a discounted rate for rooms at a downtown hotel. This seemed like the dream scenario for a retirement party. I got to celebrate retirement doing one of the things I enjoyed most: watching Tiger baseball with my best friends. A retirement party at a hall is fine, but this was something special and unique.

Thirty-five people made the 150-mile trek from Grand Rapids to Detroit for my get-together. I was touched by the great turnout and sincere well wishes. They even had a congratulatory message put on the scoreboard of Comerica Park! Several Grand Rapids officers rented a limo that they took to the game. About a dozen of us got hotel rooms and stayed overnight. It was a special gathering. I couldn't think of a better way to have celebrated my retirement. While a tremendously happy event, it was not lost on me that I might not see some of these people again as my guests filed out of the suite after the game.

I returned home the next day. That was it. It was all over.

I stayed busy over the next few weeks. I cut down thirty-one trees that dotted the site where my pole barn was to be built. There were also numerous calls to contractors and excavators. Things remained hectic.

I was still riddled by that sort of surreal feeling. I did not feel normal mentally. I was glad I was done with police work and I felt extremely fortunate, but I also felt out of whack. However, I was still looking forward to retirement. I was relieved to be out of the pressure cooker, grateful to be slipping the surly bonds that come from being under the thumb of an employer. I thought everything would be much easier from here on out.

Think again.

13

Aftermath

Service to others is the rent you pay for your room here on Earth
—Muhammed Ali

<u>March 31, 2017:</u> 4 AM alarm clock…drive…information overload…
workplace banter…emergency responses…IT…breaks…equipment
checks…jail…police radio…lights and siren…stress…ambient noise…
traffic…long-time friends…uniforms…citizen contacts…directives…
lineups…traffic…firestations…exhaustion…cynicism…peacekeeping..
bulletproof vests…reports…court…duty weapons…in-car computers…
ringing cell phone…text messages…

<u>April 1, 2017:</u> Silence.

The dramatic and abrupt change in lifestyle that came with
retirement—even a long-awaited one—was a huge jolt to me. I must
admit I did not expect it. I went from the constant bustle of being a
first responder to a feeling of retired uneasiness. I almost felt like I had
been plucked out of one world and placed in a completely foreign one.
For 27 years I had lived with constant external stimuli and with clear
purpose. Now everything was different. The silence was deafening.

I had a difficult time turning off the cop part of me. It took a while
to realize I was now a civilian. In early May, a couple lady friends

207

who couldn't make my retirement party took me out for drinks at a downtown bar as a belated retirement celebration. While walking down Ionia Avenue, I observed a familiar homeless person with mental problems who was panhandling. I witnessed him kick a passerby's car door causing a dent. He then spat on the car window after the driver of the car refused to give him money. This nutcase was no joke. We had fought with him on numerous occasions.

Without even thinking, I started to intervene. I was about to grab the psycho homeless panhandler, who towered over me and who was armed with a large walking stick he regularly used to cajole and threaten. I had no gun, no radio, and no handcuffs. I had to catch myself and remember that this part of my life was now over. I instead gave the victim the suspect's name. I informed him how to file a police report at headquarters and advised him he could put me down as a witness.

It wasn't necessarily bad being a civilian again, but my world had been completely turned upside down. I initially was not alarmed by the uneasy feelings I was still experiencing. I felt there would naturally be a period of adjustment after a sweeping life change like retirement. I stayed busy with builders working on my pole barn, and had finally cut up all the branches and tree trunks from the thirty-one trees I needed to remove from the building site. Always the conservationist, I cut up the hardwoods for firewood, while the pine trees I used to make brush piles for rabbits.

After a few weeks, however, I began feeling worse. I couldn't understand it. I had been sick of my job, so it was not as if I still wanted to be a police officer. I no longer liked the police culture or the cop mentality. It was not a case of regretting that I had retired. I was still very grateful to be out of it. Why was I feeling so bad?

Losing a sense of purpose

Suddenly, I was hit with a depression more severe than I had ever felt before. While I no longer wanted to be a cop, I felt I had lost my identity at the same time—more specifically my sense of purpose. I found this surprising because I was never one of those cops with a swagger. I didn't have my badge number tattooed on my body and I never wore any of the aftermarket police-related T-shirts or carried that kind of gear. I always rolled my eyes at those guys who did. I always believed being a police officer was what I did, not who I was. But now I felt completely unimportant. I was no longer the protector or the peacekeeper. I felt useless and unproductive; I felt like an old man with no function in society, that my best years were long behind me and all I had to look forward to was irrelevancy and a slow, steady decline.

Beginning at 16 years old, I had always had a job. Now I felt like a welfare recipient. At the same time, the last thing I wanted to do was go out and get another job. I needed to decompress from the last one. I had also never been the type who derived contentment from a job title, so I felt that getting another job just for the sake of having one would be putting a bandage on a larger problem that I needed to diagnose and mend.

There were also feelings of guilt that swept over me. I felt like I didn't deserve my pension and retirement; that there were many others in society more deserving. It was almost like I was doing something wrong by not working when I was still capable of doing so—but at the same time I didn't want to do it anymore. This created an intense inner conflict. I've heard these feelings described as "survivor's guilt." That might be what I was experiencing, but I'm not sure if it was exactly correct in my case.

I got mad at myself. Early retirement had been my life's dream since I was a young man. I had sacrificed long and hard with little margin for error to achieve it. I knew there is no perfect panacea in life, but I shouldn't be feeling like this. I had the world by the tail. What the hell was wrong with me?

I continued to soldier on, as I had always done before, putting on a brave face for family and friends. I did sub-contracting work on my pole barn, and made plans for putting on an addition to my cabin now that it was my full-time home. I tried to avoid the pitfalls of major depression, such as alcohol abuse—although I wasn't always successful. I was tempted to find temporary comfort in the booze-and-party crowd, but I resisted the false promise of partaking of that poisonous chalice. I maintained a regimented lifestyle, continuing to go to bed early and awakening early. I needed that order to keep from falling into a complete mental abyss.

Despite these efforts, I fell into the throes of the deepest depression I had ever experienced. I called a woman I had once dated who worked as a mental health therapist. She explained that my feelings were common among police officers and firefighters when they retired. I also read about depression being prevalent among athletes when they retired. Anyone in a career where personal identity is associated with a demanding job suffers this type of depression at a higher rate than the general population.

I'm sure this was partially true in my case. However, there seemed to be more to it, something deeper and multi-faceted. This was more than just garden-variety depression resulting from change in career status. I felt as if there was something else present. I don't think I had PTSD. I didn't have nightmares but I regularly dreamt about work.

During the height of it, I had a hard time concentrating on anything. I had a persistent, elevated sense of anxiety and a tendency to dwell on the perceived causes of my sadness—running them over and over again in my mind. It was kind of like when a computer program locks up and that little circle keeps spinning around endlessly on the screen.

As part of a little retirement gift to myself, I had subscribed to the MLB Extra Innings TV package so I could enjoy watching all available baseball games. I remember at my lowest point in the summer of 2017 staring at the TV for long periods of time with a game on and not even knowing the score or who was playing. My mind was racing fast and I was always preoccupied. It was reminiscent of the scene in *American Sniper* when Chris Kyle stares at the blank TV screen. I would try reading to take my mind off things, but I couldn't concentrate on or retain anything I read.

My condition seemed exacerbated by my lifestyle. I was single with no significant other. I lived in the woods. My family lived a long way away. I had several close friends, but they lived in Grand Rapids. I didn't take part in any social media, such as Facebook. I lived alone with my dog. I had very little in the way of support apparatus in place.

This had never bothered me in the past because I usually didn't need one. After all, I was a fiercely independent loner, a rugged individualist.

By now, all but a couple of work friends had faded away. I had expected that. At GRPD, there was an old saying that "no one remembers you three weeks after you leave," so I knew that would be the case. However, the loss of daily interaction with co-workers was a further reduction to an already fragile support network.

When I tried to reach out to friends, they had difficulty understanding. Without actually saying it, I could almost hear them thinking to themselves, "What do you have to be sad about?! You are fifty years old and retired!"

A long-time friend of mine also had the rare opportunity to retire early. While he didn't go through exactly what I was going through, he understood it. He told me he discovered that once he retired early, he was never allowed to have a bad day again in the eyes of others. It was as if negative life experiences could never again exist. I also found that attitude in those I interacted with.

I have always been extremely goal-oriented. I often felt that this was one of my mind's subconscious defense mechanisms to combat chronic depression. I constantly had my eyes on a bigger prize out in the future. This provided me with hope that the future would be better, as I rarely felt joy in the present. This focus on lofty, future goals may have kept me from stopping to smell the roses in the present, but it also kept me from falling into destructive instant-gratification behaviors as well. The loftiest goal of all was achieving retirement. I knew it wouldn't be the great elixir that would provide instant happiness. However, when this biggest of goals was achieved, I felt I had nothing else to work toward. This contributed greatly to my feeling of having no purpose.

I was extremely depressed, but not suicidal. My deep Catholic faith would not permit me to even consider suicide. I still clung to my belief that God never gives us more than we can handle, but I must admit that I had a strong feeling of hopelessness. For the first time in my life I could relate to the Andy Kilvinski character, played by George C. Scott, after he retires in *The New Centurions*. I certainly had no love of life during this time. I used this analogy to describe my feelings to a friend: "If I found myself submerged underwater and drowning, I would hardly give a kick to try to reach the surface."

My battles were no longer on the streets, but in my mind. There was the constant conflict between what I *knew* and what I *felt*. I *knew* that I was blessed and had a ton to live for, but I *felt* that everything was hopeless.

People who have never experienced major depression are often unaware of just how debilitating it can be. At its lowest point, there is an unrelenting feeling that you will never experience joy again. It can bring even the toughest people to their knees. If depression can lead Junior Seau—one of the toughest football players to ever play the game—to commit suicide, it's clearly a condition to be taken seriously. I read an excerpt from a book by a Catholic mental health therapist who wrote of a female patient afflicted by both depression and breast cancer during her life. In the book she stated that if given the choice, she would take cancer over depression. She felt cancer was the easier of the two awful conditions to overcome. Sadly, her situation ended in suicide.

Upon reflection, I believe my slide into major depression had been brewing for some time. I think retirement was a partial cause, but it served as more of a trigger than as the primary reason. I had felt an increase in my typical, low-grade dysthymic depression for about two years prior to retirement. I had begun withdrawing, socializing infrequently. When I did, I started to stray from some of the rules I had established for my well-being twenty years earlier. I began drinking more often. Despite my normal, fiscally conservative nature, I found myself impulse buying sports memorabilia and the like. None of it was extreme, but it was out of character; I appeared to be looking for any little glimmer of happiness I could find. Spiritually, I was not in a good place.

During that time, I recognized my personal and moral slippage. I noticed I was more depressed than usual; however, I attributed it to symptoms of job burnout. In my mind, I was merely trying to cope with the last couple years on the job. If that meant impulse buying an autographed baseball I didn't need or pulling a cork a little more often than normal, so be it. What was the harm? I kind of had a "smoke 'em if you got 'em" mentality. I rationalized, "Just do what you need to do to get through this." While my displeasure with the job was part of it, I believe now that these feelings were also warning signs of the major depression lurking ahead that I didn't recognize at the time.

Slowly, as the summer dragged on, I began coming out of my feelings of complete despair. I steadily improved in my mental, spiritual, physical, and social well-being. Instead of suffering deep depression every day, I began having good days and bad days. By late summer, there were more good days than bad. I was also old enough and wise enough to realize that our biggest dreams and our worst fears rarely come to pass. Things aren't as bad as they may appear. As hopeless as the bad days seemed, there were still many blessings to be counted.

I do not know precisely what caused this bout of major depression. I believe I identified the triggers, but the exact cause remains unknown. More than likely, there were a multitude of reasons ranging from existing genetic predisposition to biological to social and spiritual causes. I may never ascertain an exact cause.

Nonetheless, I remained dedicated to achieving the goals I had set forth at the commencement of my retirement. I was determined to not just curl up in a little ball. I reasoned that if I was going to feel like hell, I at least wanted to have something to show for the tumult. Rather than cursing the darkness, I lit a match. I pushed myself. I put my strong will to the test. The pole barn was mostly completed by the end of June. I put the final touches on it in September.

I spent much of July and August finishing off the interior of a three-season porch I had added to the front of my cabin. The hard work and satisfaction gleaned from each day's steady progress was very therapeutic for my troubled mind. The day-long rigors of carpentry work also left me physically tired at night and allowed me to sleep, instead of tossing and turning while constantly ruminating about my depressed state. Just as I had done when I was a kid, I often took solace in listening to radio broadcasts of Tiger baseball as I drifted off to sleep.

The mental and spiritual healing progressed slowly, but it was progressing. As jaded as a depressed mind's thought process can be, I did not give up hope. I knew that I would eventually come out of it. I viewed my condition as a sort of earthly purgatory—pain I needed to go through to come out a better person on the other side. The long process often involved me taking two steps forward and one step back. As hard as the ordeal was, I believe I came out of it stronger both psychologically and spiritually.

It would be easy for me to look at my depressive conditions as terrible and undeserved curses. As strange as this may sound, I do not. I instead view them as a blessing in many ways. When you come to the realization that you are incapable of sustained happiness, there comes with that an eventual acceptance. This in turn brings a kind of peace. It creates a humility and a grounding. I learned that nothing brings me long-term joy—no job, no love interest, no amount of money, no vice. While this on its face seems devastating, in reality this realization also allows me to avoid sinful worldly temptations that would otherwise derail my moral and mental well-being. There is a recognition that none of these temptations results in real happiness.

I remember Grand Rapids Police Chaplain Fr. Dennis Morrow once explaining to me that, "We don't get to choose the crosses we bear in life." I fully accept depression as one of the crosses I must bear. I view depression as a lot easier burden to endure than those of many of the people I have seen in my career and lifetime. I feel lucky to only have to bear depression, as odd as that may seem to others.

Back to "normal"

By autumn 2017, I was feeling mostly normal again—meaning I was back to my life-long, low-grade, dysthymic chronic depression. Things were manageable again. In September, I fulfilled a long-time dream of going to Boston to see the New England Patriots play their home opener at Gillette Stadium and raise their Super Bowl LI banner. I had become a huge Patriots fan after their magical 2001 season. The team's disciplined yet cerebral "Do Your Job" way of conducting business suited my personality and life's mantra perfectly. The next night I saw a Boston Red Sox game at historic Fenway Park. It was this sports fan's ultimate vacation.

I continued getting my modest little homestead the way I wanted it. When the carpentry work was completed, in October I hired an excavator to enlarge my pond. One of the few things I enjoyed in my summer of deep despair had been bass fishing in my pond. I bought a used paddle boat so I could drift around the pond as I cast along the shoreline. With the pond expanded to nearly two acres, I have that much more area to fish in the years to come—hopefully enhancing the enjoyment that much more.

October and November yielded some of the most enjoyable deer hunting I ever had on my property. The hours in the tree stand also served as a great time to process all that had transpired in my life over the last year. I once saw a T-shirt with a picture of a bowhunter in a tree stand, the caption under it reading "Gone thinking." The tranquility of the forest coupled with hours of down time is perfect fodder for taking mental and spiritual inventory. It's almost like going on a daily retreat. Deer season culminated in the successful harvest of a nice eight-point buck on the opening morning of Michigan's firearm deer season.

I was finally starting to enjoy my new-found freedom. It was great being able to hunt any day I wanted without the constant hassle of work interrupting things. I was beginning to live a bit of that mountain man lifestyle I had always yearned for by living on my own terms. I embraced the daily rituals of battling the elements. I relished the challenges of cutting and stacking firewood for the upcoming winter. I began to smell the roses (or pine trees) as best I could.

As the fall turned into winter, I had a chance to better assess my police career from the more objective vantage point that only comes with time. I concluded I had few regrets. I'm not sure I would have changed much. Sure, there are times when I look at the financial advantages a promotion would have provided. It would've been an easier life, with better hours and working conditions mostly out of harm's way. However, I've concluded that for a guy with my values, that extra money in my pension would almost feel like blood money.

I now often look at the administration with pity. I don't have animosity nor bitterness toward them. I feel bad that they don't know that man-made titles such as "chief" or "captain" mean so little in the larger scheme of things. I feel sorry that they don't get what police work is all about. All the wrangling, scheming, and jockeying for position in a sordid den of paper tigers has to be so unfulfilling in their career's final assessment—kind of like the subjects of T.S. Elliot's poem, *The Hollow Men*.

I've often pondered over what suffices for a feeling of accomplishment to a police climber. In a career of schmoozing, angling, giant egos, and palace intrigue, what does the pretend cop count as a source of pride when the realization finally hits that his title really meant nothing in life's big picture?

There is a famous line in the opening monologue of the movie *Patton*, where George C. Scott as Patton informs the men in his command, "Someday, when you are sitting by your fireside, with your grandson on your knee and he asks you, 'What did you do in the great World War II?' You won't have to say to him, 'Well, I shoveled shit in Louisiana.'" The police command person spends his entire career shoveling that shit. How sad; how unrewarding. I'd have left my career feeling as dirty as a whore had I done that. Imagine having to tell your grandchildren not about accomplishments measured in lives saved or dangerous criminals removed from society, but in terms of how many times you acquiesced to public pressure, or in terms of bureaucratic policy debacles. Bragging rights for command people must be something like, "Well, Sonny, there was this time when I filled out a great federal grant application..."

I've gotten to the point where I am over myself. I do not look at *my* wants as paramount. Money and material things are secondary, money only important in that I have a profound sense of personal responsibility. I view money as important in that I need enough to ensure that I am never a burden to society or to my family. If I knew how much that was going to be, I would probably give the remainder away. I don't understand active or retired cops who seem to never have enough. I see some of these guys still scratching for every dime they can make even though they don't have a financial worry in the world—and despite the fact that their remaining life expectancy is down to being measured in single digits.

I feel fortunate to have not lost my humility or my human heart. Amid all the tragedy, chaos, political double-crosses, confrontations, and conflict, I still can empathize and sympathize with others. I do not look down on those less fortunate, but instead remain grateful that I was born to the parents I was and into the situation I was placed. There are still remnants of a healthy cop cynicism and suspiciousness of others, but no self-righteousness. There are people from the profession that I do not like, but I have no hate in my heart for them. It troubles me when I see sheltered suburbanites with no concern for the downtrodden or for those with little opportunity, and insist that to get out of their desperate situations they simply need to "work harder."

If given the choice, I'd rather associate with down-to-earth working people than the rich or supposed powerful. I've found it's the common man who is the most decent. The higher I scaled the political ladder and the more "important" people I met, the more deceit, selfishness, and disloyalty I saw. My interpretation of the Bible verse "The meek shall inherit the earth" is that in the end it will be honest, unheralded, common people—regular people who don't cheat to get ahead or don't live through selfish ambition—who will be rewarded. I take up ranks with these regular folks, even if it costs me in lost material goods or privileged status in this life.

I'm still troubled and conflicted in many ways. I do not want to leave the impression that I have been saved from all darkness and have found the light. There has been no life-changing epiphany. I continue to struggle with life's next mission. I worry that I am wasting some of the talents God has given me, but at the same time I have no idea how he wants me to use them. I try to step outside my comfort zone— ever so slightly—from time to time in hopes that it may lead to some discoveries. However, I recognize that finding God's mission for me may be like my version of a *Moby Dick* white whale that I may never capture. I may never get it.

In the meantime, I try to improve on my status as a "B-" human, while still trying to enjoy the fruits of my hard labor. I am at a stage in my life where I know I am closer to the end than the beginning. This has led me to look at my actions and how they will impact the final judgment in the next life more than how these actions may benefit me in this one. However, I am still flawed enough where I don't always make the right decision.

The former street cop is ever present. I instinctively look at every license plate in front of me to see if the plate is expired. When I stop at an intersection, I continue to leave space between my vehicle and the car in front in case I need to get around it to respond to an emergency. When I go to a restaurant, I sit with my back to the wall and where I can see the entrance to see who is coming and going. However, the part of my psyche that associates police work with my identity is waning, as I willingly settle into civilian life.

My former coworkers are always on my mind. I still get angry when I see a news story unfairly depicting police officers, or when a pretend cop posing as a chief sells out the working cops in his charge. I often know the local guys affected. At the same time, I'm regularly struck by how many officers I don't recognize whenever GRPD is featured in the news. Time marches on. Young officers almost look like boys to me, which further drives home the point that I'm getting old. But no matter how old I get or how far removed I become from the job, there will always be part of me that remains a cop.

Life's meaning

So, what did it all mean? What did my police career accomplish? The answer is that I have no idea. At minimum, I attained personal goals. I secured my status as a self-reliant member of society. I achieved my boyhood dream of retiring relatively young and living a life where I control much of my destiny. I proved to myself through my union actions that I could be a good leader. Probably most noteworthy is that I did it all on my own terms. There are people who know me who have strong and perhaps differing opinions about Dave Leonard. The one thing they will all agree on, however, is that I never kissed anyone's ass. I never compromised my principles and I always had the courage to stand up for them. In a world with more than its share of selfish cowards, sellouts, and backstabbers, that was no small accomplishment. I served honorably and with integrity. I held the line.

The fact that I did the entire 27 years on the street remains a source of great pride. There aren't a lot of officers in the modern era of policing who have the mental fortitude or makeup to do that anymore. I'm like one of the last Mohicans.

As far as broader impact on society, I don't think I had any at all. I am acutely aware that I was a single spoke in a very large wheel. I do hope, however, that there were small, subtle victories—like the person who left a contact with me feeling good about the police. Or maybe the person who wasn't victimized because of a bad guy I caught earlier. There could be victims who found closure when justice was served in a case I investigated. Perhaps there are a few other Josiah Wards out there I helped and never realized it.

Over the years, I had many supportive citizens approach me and thank me for my service. I was always grateful for the gesture. Despite the recent bad press, citizens overwhelmingly still support the police.

It is disconcerting, though, that other jobs get so little public gratitude but are doing more for people than I ever did. The real heroes are those who work for little pay in homeless shelters or soup kitchens. The unknown workers caring for the elderly in nursing homes or hospice positions do more for others than I did—and they do it for much less pay and with few public accolades. Catholic clergymen and nuns devote their lives to service and yet often struggle in abject poverty in their elder years. Most paramedics deal with every bit as harrowing situations as I did but do it for nominal money and no pension. Perhaps this is why I felt guilt when I retired and saw these folks still toiling away. In many ways, they are far better than me. Certainly, it was a calling that led me into law enforcement. But I'm not sure the calling would've lasted an entire career had I not received a fair wage for a fair day's work—or as Stinky used to joke, "I'm no do-gooder. I'm only in it for the money!"

Some may view my story as a dark or sad one: a career spent navigating human tragedy and a good portion of a personal life battling inner demons. But my life is only dark in that there are certain aspects of being a career street cop that have a bleak reality associated with them. I hope my personal life will be seen as an example of a common man's indomitable spirit to overcome the trials that all of us face, and not as a sad story.

I feel genuinely blessed. I'm an incredibly fortunate man. I feel that the Lord has given me much more than I deserve. I look to the future with optimism, ambition, and determination. I love my life. With the possible exception of Tom Brady, there is no one else I would rather be. I also realize that for those to whom much is given, much is also expected. I'm eager to improve from that B- status to a point where I deserve the many graces I've been afforded. I'm grateful that I can pursue my next mission and self-improvement plan without being encumbered by such a demanding job.

For a man who always fashioned his Walter Mitty-style daydreams of personal triumph in the context of never-achieved athletic glory, it is befitting that I end with a quote from one of the greatest coaches and sports icons of all time. I think it best sums up my personal drive and inexorable determination amid recognition of my flawed humanity. Vince Lombardi is reported to have said the following words in a speech to his Green Bay Packers players:

> "Gentleman, we will chase perfection, and we will chase it relentlessly, knowing full well we will not catch it, because nothing is perfect. But we will relentlessly chase it, because in the process we will catch excellence."

There is still hope for a former real cop.

Afterword

As the dust settles after an epic 2017, I look forward with anticipation to life after law enforcement. This work is an important first step. As I write this, I have no idea whether this book will ever be published—much less how it will be received. Regardless, the hundreds of hours it took to write it was a significant step outside my comfort zone. It was also something I could not have done while working full time on the street. There were just too many distractions and obligations.

The pursuit of this work to its yet-undetermined conclusion has given me a major goal to work toward in 2018 and beyond. To have an unattained objective gives me focus again, even if this book remains tucked away on my hard drive and never sees the light of day. When it comes to writing and the publishing industry, I'm that slick-sleeved recruit again. I have a steep learning curve to attempt to overcome.

I began writing this book a month or so after I retired. I felt it was important to start writing while the emotions and incidents were fresh in my mind. I'm glad I did. Upon reviewing many of the incidents recorded in the early pages of the book, I noticed where I had forgotten many of the details. Had I waited another year or two, I'm not sure I would have captured things with the same vividness or from the perspective of a cop just home from the wars.

One of the biggest challenges was winnowing the thousands of incidents I responded to in more than 27 years into a succinct list of recollections relevant for providing background or examples of the topic addressed in each chapter. There were countless other incidents I responded to that I obviously did not include, but that were still a major part of my career. These included high-speed car chases, homicide investigations, friendships, and touching citizen contacts. However, my objective was to write a book that highlighted some of my many patrol experiences without digressing into a rambling, scatter-shot journal of war stories. I hope I accomplished this.

I continue to decompress from my time as a police officer and continue to work toward healing from the major depression I suffered in the months after I called out of service for the last time. I learned from that trying time about some of the warning signs before a major depression. I have now endured three bouts of major depression over the course of my life. Experts claim that a person who has suffered three or more incidents has a 90% chance of suffering another episode. This possibility leaves me much more aware of how delicately balanced my mental well-being is.

Day-to-day life remains regimented by choice. I try to keep things simple and disciplined, but usually busy. It's still very important to keep options open so I avoid feeling trapped in a situation. It's also nice not having to wake up to an alarm clock at 4:06 AM any longer.

With most of the major construction and carpentry completed, I set a goal of a more structured and regular physical fitness regimen. I try to walk three miles a day, five days a week. I sometimes up this to six miles in good weather. I don snowshoes when the northern Michigan winter kicks into full force.

I also do weight training three times a week, although the heavy weights of my youth are no longer part of the routine to give my half-century old joints a break. Physical fitness helps immensely with managing depression. I feel better when my body is running on all cylinders. I have held off seeking other employment to this point. I would like to see this book project to its conclusion—boom or bust— and then look at my options. That independent streak has always made it difficult to find fulfillment punching a clock and working for someone else. I'm better suited for some kind of freelance or volunteer work when the time comes.

I stay in contact with some of my closest friends from GRPD. I interact with the rest of my former coworkers on my own terms—remaining discriminating about which police-related events I attend. I was sincere when I divulged that I no longer want to be part of the police subculture, so I have limited interest in engaging in it as a retiree. I also do not want to be that guy who lives in the past—constantly trying to relive past glories. It's healthier to live life looking forward, rather than in the rearview mirror.

I remain a fierce advocate for the labor movement. I find it troubling that so many young officers are apathetic and unwilling to help the cause of protecting their benefits and bargaining rights. When I began as a union steward, there were numerous contested steward elections and heated but healthy debates. Now I see many young people with little interest despite their futures in a precarious state.

I fear what the future has in store for the police profession in general. I do not believe it is as good a career choice now as it was when I started; benefits, pensions, and compensation have been greatly reduced. This is complicated by the enormous scrutiny police are subject to today. I can't imagine having to do the job for 25 or 30 years in today's environment. I worry that police work will no longer remain a profession, but will be relegated to "starter job" status. Society will suffer greatly if this occurs. Whatever the future holds for the police profession, I know that being a street cop defined me and was one of the biggest honors of my life.

About the Author

David Leonard is the author of *Real Cop, A Memoir of a Career Street Officer.* Leonard served as a police officer for over 27 years. He spent most of his career in Grand Rapids, Michigan, a Midwestern city of 200,000 people.

A Grand Rapids native, Leonard graduated with a Bachelor of Science degree in Criminal Justice from Grand Valley State University in 1989. He began his career in law enforcement as a deputy sheriff in Michigan's Montcalm County, before returning to Grand Rapids. Leonard served the Grand Rapids Police Department from 1991-2017.

Active in the police labor movement for most of his career, Leonard was instrumental in establishing an independent union at GRPD in 2007, The Grand Rapids Police Officers Association (GRPOA). He was the GRPOA's first president. David was also active in establishing the union's political action committee. Additionally, Leonard sat on the boards of the Michigan Association of Police Organizations (MAPO) and Grand Rapids' Friends of Labor.

Now retired from law enforcement, Leonard lives in northern Michigan, where he is an avid outdoorsman.